Leading from the Periphery and Network Collective Action

Political revolutions, economic meltdowns, mass ideological conversions and collective innovation adoptions occur *often*; nevertheless, when they happen, they tend to be the *least* expected. Based on the paradigm of *"leading from the periphery"*, this groundbreaking analysis offers an explanation for such spontaneity and apparent lack of leadership in contentious collective action. Contrary to existing theories, the author argues that network effects in collective action originating from marginal leaders can benefit from a total lack of communication. Such network effects persist in isolated islands of contention instead of overarching action cascades, and are shown to escalate in globally dispersed, but locally concentrated networks of contention. This is a trait that can empower marginal leaders and set forth social dynamics distinct from those originating in the limelight. *Leading from the Periphery and Network Collective Action* provides evidence from two Middle Eastern uprisings, as well as behavioral experiments of collective risk taking in social networks.

Navid Hassanpour is an associate professor of political science at the Higher School of Economics in Moscow. Previously he taught at Columbia University and was a Niehaus Fellow in Regional Political Economy at Woodrow Wilson School of Public and International Affairs at Princeton. He studies politics in hybrid regimes: collective action and elections under authoritarianism leading to social revolutions or stable electoral institutions. His ongoing research in Tehran, Moscow, Beijing, and Istanbul examines the inception of electoral institutions past the era of constitutional revolutions and the logic of their pursuing transformations.

Structural Analysis in the Social Sciences

Mark Granovetter, editor

The series *Structural Analysis* in the Social Sciences presents studies that analyze social behavior and institutions by reference to relations among such concrete social entities as persons, organizations, and nations. Relational analysis contrasts on the one hand with reductionist methodological individualism and on the other with macro-level determinism, whether based on technology, material conditions, economic conflict, adaptive evolution, or functional imperatives. In this more intellectually flexible structural middle ground, analysts situate actors and their relations in a variety of contexts. Since the series began in 1987, its authors have variously focused on small groups, history, culture, politics, kinship, aesthetics, economics, and complex organizations, creatively theorizing how these shape and in turn are shaped by social relations. Their style and methods have ranged widely, from intense, long-term ethnographic observation to highly abstract mathematical models. Their disciplinary affiliations have included history, anthropology, sociology, political science, business, economics, mathematics, and computer science. Some have made explicit use of social network analysis, including many of the cutting-edge and standard works of that approach, whereas others have kept formal analysis in the background and used "networks" as a fruitful orienting metaphor. All have in common a sophisticated and revealing approach that forcefully illuminates our complex social world.

Recent Books in the Series

Philippe Bourgois, *In Search of Respect: Selling Crack in El Barrio* (Second Edition)
Nan Lin, *Social Capital: A Theory of Social Structure and Action*
Robert Franzosi, *From Words to Numbers*
Sean O'Riain, *The Politics of High-Tech Growth*
James Lincoln and Michael Gerlach, *Japan's Network Economy*
Patrick Doreian, Vladimir Batagelj, and Anujka Ferligoj, *Generalized Blockmodeling*
Eiko Ikegami, *Bonds of Civility: Aesthetic Networks and Political Origins of Japanese Culture*
Wouter de Nooy, Andrej Mrvar, and Vladimir Batagelj, *Exploratory Social Network Analysis with Pajek*
Peter Carrington, John Scott, and Stanley Wasserman, *Models and Methods in Social Network Analysis*
Robert C. Feenstra and Gary G. Hamilton, *Emergent Economies, Divergent Paths*
Martin Kilduff and David Krackhardt, *Interpersonal Networks in Organizations*
Ari Adut, *On Scandal: Moral Disturbances in Society, Politics, and Art*
Zeev Maoz, *The Networks of Nations: The Evolution and Structure of International Networks, 1815–2002*
Noah E. Friedkin and Eugene C. Johnsen, *Social Influence Network Theory*
Sean F. Everton, *Disrupting Dark Networks*
Dean Lusher, Johan Koskinen, and Garry Robins, eds, *Exponential Random Graph Models for Social Networks: Theory, Methods, and Applications*
Silvia Domínguez and Betina Hollstein, eds., *Mixed Methods in Studying Social Networks*
Benjamin Cornwell, *Social Sequence Analysis*
Luke M. Gerdes, ed., *Illuminating Dark Networks*
Mariela Szwarcberg, *Mobilizing Poor Voters*
Isabella Alcañiz, *Environmental and Nuclear Networks in the Global South*
Cheol-Sung Lee, *When Solidarity Works*

Leading from the Periphery and Network Collective Action

NAVID HASSANPOUR
Higher School of Economics, Moscow

CAMBRIDGE
UNIVERSITY PRESS

University Printing House, Cambridge CB2 8BS, United Kingdom

One Liberty Plaza, 20th Floor, New York, NY 10006, USA

477 Williamstown Road, Port Melbourne, VIC 3207, Australia

4843/24, 2nd Floor, Ansari Road, Daryaganj, Delhi – 110002, India

79 Anson Road, #06-04/06, Singapore 079906

Cambridge University Press is part of the University of Cambridge.

It furthers the University's mission by disseminating knowledge in the pursuit of education, learning and research at the highest international levels of excellence.

www.cambridge.org
Information on this title: www.cambridge.org/9781107141193

© Navid Hassanpour 2016

This publication is in copyright. Subject to statutory exception and to the provisions of relevant collective licensing agreements, no reproduction of any part may take place without the written permission of Cambridge University Press.

First published 2016

Printed in the United States of America by Sheridan Books, Inc.

A catalog record for this publication is available from the British Library

ISBN 978-1-107-14119-3 Hardback
ISBN 978-1-316-50645-5 Paperback

Cambridge University Press has no responsibility for the persistence or accuracy of URLs for external or third-party internet websites referred to in this publication, and does not guarantee that any content on such websites is, or will remain, accurate or appropriate.

Contents

List of Figures		*page* vi
List of Tables		ix
Acknowledgments		xi
1	Mobilization from the Margins	1
2	Decentralization of Revolutionary Unrest: *Dispersion Hypothesis*	27
3	Vanguards at the Periphery: A Network Formulation	69
4	Civil War and Contagion in *Small Worlds*	103
5	Peripheral Influence: Experimentations in Collective Risk Taking	140
6	Decentralization and Power: Novel Modes of Social Organization	163
7	Appendix	171
Bibliography		196
Index		206

Figures

1.1	Participation levels in 2011 Egyptian Revolution among survey respondents	page 21
1.2	Size of *minimal core* as a function of *radius of connectivity*	23
1.3	Daily dispersion of conflict in Damascus and its suburbs	24
1.4	Sum action rates in cascade sessions of the network experiment	25
2.1	Rumors as instigation during the Russian Revolution of February 1917	29
2.2	Email sent out by the April 6 Youth Movement calling for protests on January 25	39
2.3	Protest dispersion and internet traffic, 2011 Egyptian Revolution	43
2.4	Fully connected → Local sparse graphs	44
2.5	Participation levels among all survey respondents and the vanguard, 2011 Egyptian Revolution	60
3.1	Centralized sources of information and individual consumers	76
3.2	Topology of dispersed clusters of contention shaping in the absence of centralized media	77
3.3	Connectivity is not always helpful to collective action, an example	78
3.4	Equilibria of a homogeneous network game	80
3.5	Equilibria of a heterogeneous network game	80

3.6	Equilibria of a network game with the vanguard at the periphery	81
3.7	Increasing size of the minimal core with higher connectivity	88
3.8	Size of the minimal core for two-dimensional grids	89
3.9	*Radius of diffusion*, regular ring network	91
3.10	A ring network with bridges	92
3.11	Suppression of the public signal in a four-member signal space	98
3.12	A *small world network* with random bridges	100
3.13	Decentralization and localization processes after media disruption	100
4.1	Conflictual incidents in 1 square mile cells, 2012, Damascus and suburbs	114
4.2	Communication disruptions during the Syrian Civil War	116
4.3	Dispersion of conflictual incidents in Damascus, 2012	118
4.4	Population and elevation patterns, Damascus and suburbs	125
4.5	Damascus, neighborhood delineations superimposed	126
4.6	Histogram of distances from the nearest incident in space and time, Damascus, 2012	127
4.7	Average distance from nearest neighboring incident, Damascus, 2012	128
4.8	OLS coefficients, distance from nearest incident regressed over indices for coordination, orientation, communication disruption	131
4.9	Coefficients from Poisson regressions in Table (4.9)	136
4.10	Odds of violent incident based on previous violent incidents in the spatio-temporal vicinity	137
5.1	Two realizations of the Erdös-Rényi graphs used in the network experiments	147
5.2	Rounds 1, 8 and 15 for peripheral, random and central assignments	149
5.3	Proportion of sessions in *action* cascade status for each treatment in the network experiment	151
5.4	Sum of action rates in all sessions in cascade status	153

5.5	Kaplan–Meier survival analysis for each of the three network treatments	156
5.6	Temporal evolution of risk taking for peripheral action cascades	158
6.1	Romanian Revolution and the denial of emblem, December 1989	168
7.1	Demands of the protesters in the announcement sent on January 22, 2011 Egyptian Revolution	173
7.2	Groups' assignment to each six locations in Cairo on January 25, 2011 Egyptian Revolution	174
7.3	Preparations: distribution of pamphlets before January 25	175
7.4	Preparations: 15,000 pamphlets were distributed before January 25 in Cairo, 15,000 more in other cities	175
7.5	Distributing mobile numbers of the "control room" members on the 25th	176
7.6	Disruption of *control room*'s communications	176
7.7	*Control room*'s reaction to disruption of communication	176
7.8	Call to protests on January 28, 2011, "Friday of Rage", in all major Egyptian cities	177
7.9	4 p.m. update	178
7.10	5 p.m. updates	178
7.11	6 p.m. updates	179
7.12	7 p.m. updates	179
7.13	Cairo neighborhood where face-to-face interviews were conducted	186
7.14	A scan of sample filled questionnaire, Cairo protest survey	190
7.15	Media usage levels for the vanguard and nonparticipants	192
7.16	Distribution of *first incidents*, Damascus, late 2012	193
7.17	A snapshot of subject instructions for the second phase of the network experiments	195

Tables

2.1	Communication disruptions, 2011 Egyptian Revolution	page 38
2.2	Main protest locations in Cairo, January 25–February 11	42
2.3	Components of protest dispersion in Cairo, OLS regression	45
2.4	Components of protest participation on January 28, logistic regressions	63
2.5	Protest participation on January 25–27, media consumption components, logistic regression	64
2.6	Components of participation in protests in Tahrir on January 25, logistic regression	65
2.7	Components of participation in protests in Tahrir on January 28, logistic regression	65
2.8	Media consumption patterns and subjective reaction to media disruption, logistic regression	66
4.1	Four possibilities of coordination and orientation and their effect on clustering of conflict	108
4.2	Dispersion level at time t: three definitions, OLS regressions	119
4.3	Major neighborhoods in Damascus and suburbs	121
4.4	Components of number of violent incidents in each spatial cell, Poisson count regression	124
4.5	Components of distance from the nearest incident, OLS regression	130
4.6	Components of distance from the nearest incident, disruption index included, OLS regression	130

4.7	The relation between orientation and coordination indices, OLS regression	131
4.8	Four possibilities of coordination and orientation and their effect on clustering of conflict	132
4.9	Components of the existence of conflict in each cell-day, Poisson count regressions	134
4.10	Interaction of media disruption and contagion during the Syrian Civil War, Poisson count regressions	138
5.1	Summary statistics of collective risk taking in the network experiment	150
5.2	OLS regression, average centrality of risk taking in the first round on action cascade status by treatment	155
5.3	Logistic regression, subject-level components of collective risk taking in the network experiment	160
7.1	The distribution of participation in the four phases of the 2011 Egyptian uprising	191
7.2	Number of violent incidents in each spatial cell, Syrian Civil War, Poisson count regression	194

Acknowledgments

The initial idea of this project occurred to me early during my stay at Yale. At a seminar James Scott pondered if the French Revolution was called a "revolution" in 1789 and if not, he asked when and how that event came to be known as a revolution to its instigators as well as the global audience. That curious point led me into a phase of archival research on revolutions and similar historical turning points. During my time in the archives I noticed how much the narrative of the momentous events I was studying had been transformed in the prism of time, and felt motivated to pursue a more careful exploration of their origins. As I was researching the candid media reflections of the Iranian and Russian Revolutions I became aware of occasional gaps in media activity during the events, an observation that later, combined with the predictions of a number of network stylizations I was simultaneously developing in Fall 2010, became the starting point and a major building block of this book. The protest wave of 2011 unfolded right in time, providing an opportunity to see similar historical processes as they happened in real time. Hence, my research strategy shifted from exploring the archives to surveying live processes of collective contestation, mainly taking place in the theaters of Middle Eastern capitals, and later led into a final phase of controlled experimentation with the dynamics of collective risk taking in a laboratory setting.

During the five years I spent observing and formulating the paradigm of *leading from the periphery*, I was fortunate to benefit from working with a group of remarkable collaborators. In particular, I would like to mention, in temporal order, the research assistance of Ji Liu with model building,

Sergio Peçanha and Miral Brinjy with my examination of the Egyptian Revolution and the Cairo Survey, Stacey Maples and Joseph Holliday with the geolocated study of conflict in Damascus, and Dominik Duell and Mark McKnight with the network experiments of collective risk taking. The contributions of anonymous respondents to several surveys in Cairo and Damascus were also instrumental.

During my time at Yale and Princeton I benefited from countless deliberations with the faculty and graduate students at both institutions over the topic of this monograph and will remain indebted. I would like to thank Yale Political Science Department, Yale Law School's Information Society Project, Yale Institute for Network Science and Princeton's Niehaus Center for Globalization and Governance for their indispensable financial support.

1

Mobilization from the Margins

Nobody is my name.   Odyssey 9.366

Collective acts of risk taking pose a puzzle to the social sciences. One minuscule contribution to a precarious collective endeavor does not improve its prospects, but it often puts the individual perpetrator at grave risk. So why do political revolutions, economic meltdowns, mass religious conversions, linguistic shifts and collective innovation adoptions happen often, and when they do occur, why are they the most unexpected? One could argue that given the scale of these social reversals, the premonitions should be clear enough. Then why do movements encompassing absolute majorities arrive as surprises to the illuminati and the powerful, not as mere predictable, perhaps governable outcomes?[1] I provide an answer in this book based on the idea of *leading from the periphery*. I argue that marginal leaders set into motion collective cascades of risk taking that are distinct from centrally generated coordinated campaigns. Keys to "surprising" and "rapid" elements of social and political uprisings are to be sought not at the centers of social attention, but in the margins, where switching to the far fetched and dangerous is more likely and less costly.

The existing solutions to the *collective action problem* stress economizing means for creating unity among the masses: central and focal forces of ideologies, repertoires of action, carefully designated incentives rewarding individual acts, as well as centers of social life, structural or ideational,

---

[1] See Kuran (1991).

all help to generate action in concert.[2] In their emphasis on central and visible themes, the more recent solutions to the collective action problem follow the early modern writings on crowds, in their interpretation of collective action as monolithic and unified. Only that now we have a more sophisticated way of discussing crowds in unison: more reasonable and verifiable than the holistic and anthropomorphic idea of crowds as the representation of some "primitive state of human mind".[3] Nevertheless, the thrust of the argument has not shifted much, still that unity, that simplifying holistic idea of the collective action in concert is central to the existing explanations. There is also a clue to the same line of reasoning in one of the folk pillars of collective action theory, which is the division between socially *central* vanguards, and following masses. The division between the vanguard and the population, has been key to theories advancing a more heterogeneous outlook of collective action among the crowds.[4] In political communication studies, interestingly enough, the same elitist trait lives on, *opinion leaders* are the dominant gate keepers of the public opinion.[5] All these theories share one common trait: the leaders are *central*. They start at the *center* of social, political and economic life. The actions of the vanguard in those positions strengthen the unity of masses after the preordained leaders' cause. Early theorists of collective

---

[2] A pioneering formulation of collective action as a problem of coordination over public goods can be found in Olson (1971). Olson (1971) and Lichbach (1995) proposed a solution based on *selective incentives*, rewards for participation that can override the risks of collective action on the individual level. Hardin (1995) outlined *ideology* as a solution to the collective action problem, an economizing means of unification. Tilly (1978) introduced *repertoires of action*, routine and practiced acts of contention, such as strikes, sit ins, demonstrations, as likely vehicles of collective acts of contention despite the inherent dangers. Along the same lines, Schelling (1978) saw *focality* as the answer to the problem of coordination among many. Focal points, a central square, a canonical time or place, similar to *repertoires*, again economize on coordination. The role of public information in coordination, normalization and establishment of the status quo is also discussed in Chwe (2001).

[3] See Le Bon [1895] (1960) for the origins of a holistic view of crowds as a special, singular social force, categorically apart from the combination of its individual components. In my characterization, crowds are not prior to individuals, but mass mobilization is a product of individual decisions, whose origins, unlike the existing formulations, can be the most remote and the least connected.

[4] Marx's early formulations of the division between *the vanguard* and the followers (Marx and Engels [1848] 1978, p. 484), gave way to many similar divisions in the following formulations, including the oft cited party-based mobilization tactics Lenin [1902] (1975).

[5] The division between the masses and the opinion leaders is deemed to be the main feature of the modern public sphere Habermas (1991), the two-stage model of political information propagation, from opinion leaders to the masses, is one of the starting points of contemporary political communication theory. See Zaller (1992).

action, Marx included, put the well positioned vanguard at the top of a hierarchical network of influence and communication. They are to incite rebellion among clueless and unsuspecting masses. To reiterate, the separation between the two categories, in theory, still persists: central opinion leaders are the source of social information. The alternative I propose in the book prioritizes leading not from the center, but from the margins. If no conclusive clue can be found where it is expected, one has to look elsewhere. I implement a pedestrian fix to the longstanding conundrum of collective action. Simply put, dynamics of mobilization originating from marginal leaders are different from those emanating from centrally established, well connected instigators.

Mass mobilization, in contrast to institutional politics, has been the realm of a stark division between the individuality of the leaders and the malleable uniformity of the marginal masses. Instead of individuals in reified bureaucracies, unpredictable crowds, their politics ambivalent and inefficient, are one part of a dichotomy that separates well studied elite coordination from the poorly understood politics of the margins. *Leading from the periphery*, is a mobilization paradigm that has been largely ignored since the beginning of the systemic study of mass mobilization. The best known schemes of collective action situate the informed, well connected and harmonious vanguard in front of the rest. Such theories see mass uprisings as surprises,[6] mass social conversions as haphazard, innovation adoptions as flukes.

Describing and decoding such surprises requires a formulation for leadership structure that accommodates peripheral vanguards, away from the gaze of the status quo, in addition to better known central schemes. I explore the very same possibility in order to detect dynamics that are different in their pace and reach from those originating from central, visible and seasoned leaders. The theoretical expositions and empirical evidence I outline in the following chapters portray processes that are characteristically outside the organizational narrative of the existing theories of collective action. As importantly, the idea of peripheral instigation is at odds with faceless theorizations in the form of mere power of numbers. In a network formulation it is possible to differentiate marginal actors, expect leaders in the margins and generate theoretical predictions that are now verifiable given the introduction of personalized media. The process clarifies the less explored logic of the transition phase between seemingly amorphous agitation and institutionalized politics.

---

[6] Kuran (1989).

It detects familiar political patterns in unexpected places, among those actors who, unassumingly, play a crucial and defining, at times temporary, role toward historical transformations.

This is by no means a new question. Pondering the very same puzzle, was none other than Leon Trotsky, who residing in New York City at the time of the February 1917 revolt in Petrograd, the one preceding the October takeover, inquired about the leaders of the rebellion: "who led the [February] revolution? Who raised the workers to their feet? Who brought the soldiers into the streets?" His answer, expectedly, but hardly supported by much evidence, was "the Party".[7] That illusive division between the spontaneous outpouring of grievance in February 1917, and the organized politics of summer and fall 1917 is a showcase of a similar contrast between two modes of collective action. One is characterized with spontaneity and speed, the other with organization and ostensibly rational calculations. Institutions, ideology, information and centralization provide one resolution for the collective action problem, but do not fully answer the recurrent historical question posed above: who led the surprising waves of communal risk taking so frequent in the historical context? Rational individuals should know better.

The answer I propose is the theory and empirics of action originating from the margins. The periphery in the following chapters is not that *everything other than* the *opinion leaders*. It *is* the source of action in concert, via leadership that takes hold in small and dispersed circles of radicalism, peripheral collective action that emanates to centers of the society via a steady, at times fast strides. The key to the formulation is assuming that effective vanguardism can take hold far from the most connected, visible and "informed" areas of the social network. It is not clear if the dynamics of collective action from the margins are different from those of centralized agitations. The theory and empirics in the following chapters anticipate the effects, and are distinct from the logic of coordinated action from a central command. The contrasts between the centralized, hierarchical and well rehearsed narrative of the post-World War II social movements and the amorphous dynamics of recent uprisings all motivate similar questions. The collective memory of robust action during the Civil Rights Movement, for example, is regularly invoked in

---

7 See Trotsky (1937, ch. 8).

contrast to the amorphous leadership and decentralized organization of more recent global waves of unrest in 1989 and 2011.[8]

Mapping and decoding the dynamics of collective acts of the abrupt and decentralized kind also paves the way for harnessing their potential. The most adroit revolutionary leaders, knowingly or unwittingly, are experts in such methods. *Influence maximization* in social networks, using new technological means for advertising and information propagation is, in fact, a move in the same direction; however, there are few signs that those planning such programs think outside the conventional focus on the *center*. To influence voters, or buyers, they pay online *luminaries*, the most central and visible opinion leaders, to promote an innovation, be it political, social or technological.[9] The idea of actualizing a network of innovation from the periphery is not as frequently tried. For doing so, one needs a total map of the social network, a technological feat that has become feasible after advances in personalized virtual networks. If we know the map of contentious social network in Paris in 1789 or in Petrograd in 1917, or an approximation of their topology, a temporal progression of transactions could reveal the direction and trajectory of mass mobilization. In the absence of personal and immediate means of recoding, it would be a futile attempt to map the footprints of the process. The same lack of empirics encourages more emphasis on highly visible leaders instead of ephemeral processes that would immediately become difficult to discern after their meteoric occurrence.

FIVE MAJOR DIFFERENCES BETWEEN CENTRALIZED COLLECTIVE ACTION AND LEADING FROM THE PERIPHERY

In the next five chapters I combine a series of theoretical demonstrations and empirical evidence to examine collective action processes that involve peripheral mobilization.

I use network parameters, including proxies for the spread and diffusion of collective action in the context of the 2011 Egyptian Revolution, the Civil War in Damascus in 2012 and a network experiment

---

[8] For the former see McAdam (1982), an account of more recent "connective action" is included in Bennett and Segerberg (2013).
[9] The theoretical foundations of influence maximization literature equate influence with centrality in the process of its formulations (Kempe et al. 2003); empirical studies of influence in virtual networks depict a more heterogeneous picture (Bakshy et al. 2011).

in collective risk taking, inter alia. The results provide evidence for the predictions of network models I develop in conjunction with the data. The idea of instigation from the periphery has significant implications in at least five distinct, but interconnected domains. First, a revision of the role of information in collective action–more communication does not always help collective action, it can at times impede it; second, it is important to study theoretical requirements for a sustainable concentration of radicalism in the social periphery on par with required conditions for generating a *critical mass*;[10] third, decentralization and contagious spread of violence, in locally concentrated and globally dispersed cells, are as important for the study of civil conflict as the role of selective incentives and coordination in orchestrating collective contention, from the type traditionally assumed in studying such phenomena; fourth, the extremes of collective action cascades and total apathy are more frequent when the vanguard are set at the periphery; fifth and finally, the recognition of the existence of such network interactions leads to acknowledging action that is at times inspired by doubt instead of conviction, driven by lack of information instead of abundance of it and benefits from decentralization, not hierarchy.

To see the intuition behind the five aforementioned items note the following.

1. When the line of command is from the most connected to the rest, lack of communication disassembles the schemes of mobilization, but when severing lines of information generate circles of leadership in the periphery, empowering local leaders, then at times reducing the levels of information transactions can help to sustain growing clusters of contention. For example, adding indiscriminate communication links in a heterogeneous network, on average, only helps to reinforce the conservatism of the majority.
2. Sudden disruptions of communication media provide a testing ground for the effects of such communication links on the levels of the *dispersion* of contention. In particular, if after controlling for confounding and contributing parameters, one finds that the absence of communication caused escalation of a conflict, not the opposite, then there should exist processes other than pure

[10] The idea of *critical mass* is for formulating a fully encompassing movement, in contrast, the focus of a decentralized analysis is on minimal conditions for sustenance of risk taking in small cliques in the network periphery.

coordination that abet a contentious escalation. According to the traditional collective action theory, lack of communication should suppress coordinated contention, not the opposite. In the following chapters, I have employed two stark examples of blanket communication blackout in two Middle Eastern capitals for testing the *Dispersion Hypothesis*, that disruption of media connections decentralizes coordinated conflict on the collective level, and that this decentralization exacerbates revolutionary action, not the opposite.

3. Furthermore, if the peripheral clusters of contention are capable of initiating global cascades of collective action, then the conditions under which they endure and sustain themselves become a pressing theoretical question. I formulate and examine this mathematical question, finding the minimal requirement for sustenance of collective action in dispersed decentralized cells in some basic configurations, and pose the general mathematical puzzle to be explored.

4. Next, to detect *contagion*, and to formulate its relation to lack of communication, I parse the urban conflict in Damascus in space and time. Speaking about dynamics necessitates an analysis that takes both space and time into account. In particular, I will demonstrate contrasts between the dynamics of *contagion* and *coordination* in the context of an urban conflict. The results hint at the importance of decentralized, but highly concentrated islands of contention in the urban environment, a characteristic of *small world networks*.

5. Finally using controlled experiments, I demonstrate a first step into learning about the dynamics of leading contention from the periphery of the social network. The results of the behavioral experiments show that the extremes of total action and apathy are more frequent when the vanguard are positioned in the periphery of experimental networks. In contrast, the central risk-takers are more likely to be influenced by the risk aversion of the majority.

The mere possibility of such processes hints at organization from the type that, in its emphasis on early marginal adopters and its reliance, at times, on lack of information instead of abundance of it, is distinct from formulations built on coordination and global unity. It can provide explanations for phenomena which are difficult to account for with hierarchy and coordination.

Clearly, the processes I propose do not rule out the possibility of collective cascades through strong and hierarchical binds, but my emphasis in this book is on establishing the existence of alternative modes introduced above, an introduction of *network collective action*.

In contrast, the existing theories of collective action start from the economy of coordination, they emphasize central, public, accurate and focal elements versus decentrality, local, inaccurate and peripheral. In social revolutions, innovation adoptions and financial meltdowns, the individual choice is between a safe status quo and a precarious yet appealing option that becomes increasingly agreeable on the individual level when more of the others take the same risky leap of faith.[11] The dynamics of such collective processes were known to the early modern writers, including Montesquieu and Locke.[12] Despite allusions to its political importance, a careful study of collective behavior, particularly in the context of crowd behavior and crowd psychology, faced empirical difficulties in the absence of a network-based theory which could dissect the crowd into its moving parts.

Despite the increasing capacity for recording and sifting through decentralized data, the modern treatment of collective action is preoccupied with its traditional emphasis on the *center, central leaders, focal points*, well known *repertoires of action* and mass *coordination* based on centralized communication or mutually held *identities*.[13] In contrast, *spontaneity*, *local* action and *surprise*[14] are given a secondary position. To see how recasting revolutions and bank runs in the regulated and familiar imagery of centralized power of numbers could be counterproductive, in the following, I review a number of existing explanations for risky collective behavior; mainly to show that what they have in common is an emphasis on the *central, public, focal* social and structural elements, while the effects of decentralization, local action and *inaccurate* information[15] in the context of collective action are left unexplored. The move can be described as economizing both in theory and empirics. Focal point explanations simplify the theory, and provide explicit empirical evidence.

---

[11] In Schelling's (1978) formulation this means there are *positive externalities*.
[12] See Locke [1689] (1980, ch. 19) and Montesquieu [1721] (2008) for examples.
[13] Each of these represent one of the existing explanation, for the emergence of collective action from inaction.
[14] See Tilly (1978) for a pioneering introduction of *time* into the study of collective contentious behavior.
[15] Inaccurate according to the centralized narrative. This is what Foucault calls *misinformation*, see Afary and Anderson (2005).

Before tending to the peripheral theory and empirics, a summary of existing theories is apropos.

FOCAL POINT EXPLANATIONS: CENTRAL COMMAND, REPERTOIRES OF ACTION, COMMON IDENTITIES, PUBLIC INFORMATION

The existing explanations for acting in concert take centralization and coordination to exist prior to the escalation of collective action. However, collective action can emerge and surge without them. Centralization, before escalation, is procedural, spatiotemporal, conventional and ideational. Coordinating on a plan of action, alignment of actors in space and time and mainstream rituals are essential to collective action's taking hold; sharing a common identity brings about acting in concert.

Collective action via coordination is the first formulation. Mancur Olson introduced an explanations for collective action based on coordinating *selective incentives*: if the benefits from joining exceed its costs, then individuals can overcome their individual risk aversion and shift from the status quo to acting for the collective cause, which is risky by nature, but provides benefits if it is successful.[16] If group action is possible at all, it should happen through providing incentives to the individuals involved, and administering such provisions becomes increasingly difficult as the size of the group grows; on the other hand, the costs of acting in small groups are too high to induce action, because the costs are divided among too few, so the conclusion is that mid-sized groups are the most likely to sustain collective action based on selective incentives. The issue of coordination is key, because in Olson's framework, given the actions of all the others each individual is better off free-riding. In a group of thousands the absence of one would not count. If the others are incurring the cost, and the attainment of the collective benefit does not rely on one's own action, then why should the individual pay the costs? Coordinating actions and policing benefits ensure that cascades of free-riding do not occur, simply because there will be no action once every individual decides to free-ride.[17] Nevertheless, group behavior and action in concert are recurring phenomena, even in the absence of visible coordination.

[16] See Olson (1971).
[17] The situation is similar to an n-person Prisoners' Dilemma.

During catastrophic episodes of communal violence, of the type seen during civil conflicts fought in close quarters, *contagion* of action in social networks operates more effectively than *coordination*. Later in the book, using a geolocated daily record of conflict locations in Damascus, I argue that progression of conflict in the city shows significant signs of spatiotemporal *contagion*, a process which operates differently from *coordination*. Given the consequences of coordinated contention in Damascus and the inherent risks of being found out, the possibility of spillovers of behavior in space and time effectively operated in parallel with better known processes of coordination.

The puzzle of action en masse in the face of individual free-riding has induced a variety of scholarly solutions, a majority of which rely on the importance of unified goals, centralized information sharing and focal actors and places already known to the actors. Thomas Schelling's notion of *focal points* is one representative solution: two individuals have to meet in New York City and have forgotten to coordinate over the location and time of their meeting on a given day. They are the most likely to converge on Grand Central Terminal at noon. *Grand Central Terminal at noon* is the focal spatiotemporal point of convergence.[18] In the absence of any other information collective action shapes around the most likely hub. However, in the course of the book I argue that if the New York social network is of a specific type, talking to one's neighbors about the rendezvous can at times be as effective. The alternative solution would be to produce a meeting place and time, pass it on to a number of one's social ties (perhaps on one's social networking platform) and ask them to pass it on. Contingent on the topology of the social network, the missing friend should be contacted in a reasonable number of steps. Note the different logic: one of network-based propagation of ideas and action as opposed to the one that assumes focal points.

According to the logic of centrality and visibility, central squares become major theaters of contention in the city. This is an important point.[19] Later, using a live account of events in Cairo recorded in emails and online announcements, I discuss the protests' gradual convergence on Tahrir Square in the afternoon of the first day of the protests. What I show is that planned protest locations did *not* include Tahrir at all

---

[18] See Schelling (1960).
[19] I will discuss the 2011 Egyptian Revolution in Cairo, during which Tahrir, the main square in downtown Cairo, became a focal point for contention toward the end of an 18-day standoff between protesters and Hosni Mubarak's security apparatus.

during the first day (January 25, 2011) and that Tahrir was the *least* focal during the *most* defining day of the contentions (January 28, 2011). The convergence mechanisms on the 25th, and decentralization processes on the 28th open windows into the importance of dispersed action *prior* to convergence. Furthermore, using survey data I find the vanguard of the 2011 Egyptian revolt, those who protested on the first defining day on January 25, to be as dispersed on January 25, as the overall average protester on the turning point of the Egyptian Revolution on January 28. In other words, the vanguard, in contrast to the average protester, were spread out across the urban sprawl of Cairo during the first day of the protests.

Charles Tilly introduced *repertoires of action* as rehearsed practices of contention as a solution to the dilemma of participation: street marches, sit ins and strikes become *conventions*, vehicles for action. Through their universal recognition among contentious crowds such de facto rituals can streamline resistance against authority.[20] The dynamics of protest *conventions* as such, are known to everybody, and everybody also knows that all others know about the technicalities of the concerted action.[21] The only problem with this reasoning is that once a repertoire is expected, its antidote also becomes routine. Disrupting an expected act of protest is easier than facing a collective surprise act.

In addition to procedural, spatiotemporal and conventional focality, *ideational* focal points are also proposed as a solution to the coordination problem. Ideologies often turn to the rallying cry of a movement. Russell Hardin outlined the importance of a common *identity* in organizing action in concert in the absence of coordination mechanisms.[22] Ideologies too, shape common identities, and in forging new alliances ease coordination between disparate elements of a collective.

All three of these explanations, focal locations, focal routines, and focal identities, implementing public spaces, conventions and ideologies, stress the importance of centralization, either in structural or in cultural domains. The importance of mutual information in organization in such context is clear. They economize on mutual information necessary for coordinating the ways to act, places to go, and times to convene. In contrast, later I argue that the very lack of centralized beacons of

---

[20] For example, see Tilly's (1978) history of *strike*, its evolution to a well rehearsed, *focal* practice in *Mobilization to Revolution*. After regularization and streamlining, the *strike* convention effectively contributed to robust protest movements across Europe.
[21] Convention as defined by Lewis (2002).
[22] Hardin (1995).

information at times can put decentralized processes of risk taking into motion. These processes are much harder to control than a predictable, centralized movement that is fully visible to the authorities from the start.

There are reasons to go beyond focal point explanations, be it ideational, spatial, conventional or coordinative. They simplify too much. They facilitate a first order understanding of action in concert and point in the direction of the most easily available empirics, but that is not enough. There are at least four considerations that demonstrate the necessity for moving beyond centrist explanations of collective action. These observations, outlined in the forthcoming chapters, cannot be explained solely based on existing formulations. Instead, they hint at processes that originate in heterogeneous social networks, and operate based on contagious processes of implicit and explicit leadership from the margins.

ACCURATE INFORMATION IS NOT ALWAYS CONDUCIVE TO COLLECTIVE ACTION

Information facilitates coordination. Free flow of information promotes coordinated contentious action, the cognizance of that fact is one of the cornerstones of existing collective action theories. The revelation of *accurate* information about the *real* level of unrest, the *total* degree of dissatisfaction in the society and rates of conversion to contention among the population are among explanations provided for the emergence of collective action on a massive scale.[23] However, in addition to globally accessible information, such as the size of protests in the main square of Cairo or Leipzig, the information or misinformation available to members of local circles of information sharing, either face to face or virtual, is as important. In local circles, there is more flexibility in terms of the usage of information for inciting action: the members' universe of available facts is smaller, and rumors can take hold more easily. Under severe control of the public sphere the horizon of visibility is limited. When the access to information is limited, local patterns of interpersonal communication become paramount. Individuals have to rely on each other to gain news and information. Not only does the existence of alternative islands of contention become a possibility, a decentralization of these heterogeneous cells transforms the dynamics of collective action on the local level.

[23] Kuran (1989, 1995); Lohmann (1994).

Rumors in local circles, are often cited as the sources of mobilization, in the information blackouts, either intended or unintended, during bouts of contention.[24]

Note the difference between the role of accurate information for the authorities and among the population. Unlike the concrete logic of strategic transactions, *accurate* information about the status of the regime does not fully capture the balance of power between the state and a dissatisfied population. Political legitimacy, or durability of it, for that matter, is not always a result of accurate information about the material situation of the state, but at times it is the product of perceptions not fully matched to material indices. These perceptions among individuals can perfectly be a local affair, instead of a globally shared sentiment. Rumors can simmer in the margins, incite resurrections that would be out of question had an accurate state of affair, news loyal to *reality* or the *real* dangers of rebellion, been communicated to all. The state threats and perception of power are more likely to be effective when *accurate* information is available to all.

The antidote of local information propagation processes operates on the level of the hierarchical state: accurate information about the extent and nature of contention is central to the durability of the state in the face of opposition, it is an indispensable part of prediction and maintenance of the status quo. In the following chapters, I show that the prevalence of local information is key to the transition of collective action to alternative dynamics.

POLITICAL MOBILIZATION TAKES HOLD IN CLOSE QUARTERS OF *SMALL WORLD NETWORKS*

Learning about the events from the social neighborhood instead of the centralized outlets, in addition to changing the perception of and propensity toward risk, irrevocably links the dynamics of contention to the structural elements of its theater. Urban environments, in particular, because of the variety and effectiveness of their landscape can induce a specific flow on the events. The advent of the Paris Commune is said to have been shaped fatefully by the Haussmannization of Paris between 1848 and 1871. While the rebellion in 1848 was based on socioeconomic divisions, the one in 1871 was influenced by the demarcations of new neighborhoods, the geography of the novel urbanization of the

---

[24] I will review some historical and recent examples in the next chapter.

previous few decades.[25] In the following chapters I argue that dense and interconnected neighborhoods[26] are susceptible to shaping *small world networks*, a web of locally dense, but globally separate, clusters of social interconnections that, as I will show with theory first, and empirics later in the book, become more susceptible to collective action in the absence of *public information*.

In a contextualized theory of collective action, local leaders, in regimes of limited information, are constricted by the nature of their access to the local population. Rumors are more likely to shape in small circles, and as the flow of information and social interactions are mostly local, contagion of contentious activity is more likely to be an effective conveyor of collective risk taking from one circle to another.[27]

Locally clustered and globally dispersed social fabric act as the promoter of the dynamics of action from the periphery. In two chapters on civil conflict in Damascus and behavioral network experiments on collective risk taking, I argue that cascades are facilitated by such conditions, and conditioned upon occurrence, the speed of their proliferation from one locality to the neighboring areas can overwhelm the social network. The centralized dynamic cannot function well in societies that are organized among many dispersed interactive hubs. When the reinforcing power of centralized media and connective communication do not exist, local interactions are expected to activate and aggravate the contagious progression of collective contentious action. I will show that the same happened during a recent episode of the Syrian Civil War.

MARGINALS ARE MORE LIKELY TO BE EARLY ADOPTERS OF RISK

When local mobilization, as a process, is taken into consideration, the position of the vanguard in the social network becomes a part of a scientific study of revolution or any other major and rapid social transformation. The limiting assumptions of the existing theoretical formulations can be relaxed, the vanguard can be in positions other

---

[25] See Gould (1995) for a detailed description.
[26] Particularly those common in the Middle Eastern traditional city centers.
[27] See Chapter (4). Note that theories of civil conflict with an emphasis on rural contention emphasize social networks of different structure. In the urban environment, the shape of landscaping can become a proxy of control Scott (1998).

than the most visible platforms.[28] Marginal movers are less restricted in terms of their ability to convert their small social circle. Centrally located vanguards, on the other hand, are more constrained by the myriad sociopolitical connections that constitute their power, and cannot be as dynamic as the marginal ones.

In a celebrated work on the diffusion of innovations, Rogers attributes the effectiveness of marginal innovators to their ability to "under conform".[29] Unlike centrally located and well connected leaders, they are influenced by few social connections, and tend to adopt social innovations free from the conformity inducing pressure that comes with a large following. In introducing "weak ties" as social instruments that can result in notable macrolevel social behavior, Granovetter cites Rogers' example as evidence, and notes that weak ties of marginal leaders can transmit innovations more effectively than strong and cliquish ties, because those connected via strong social bonds are likely to already share similar traits.[30] Viral cascades of social conversion and commotion, on the other hand, are more likely to travel via loose social links in the boundaries among dissimilar social circles. Similar dynamics are discernible in the results of the network experiments I present later. The cascades, either of collective risk taking or full apathy, are more frequent when the risk-takers are in touch with fewer, not more neighbors. Midway outcomes are more common when risk-seekers are central to the experimental social network.

Influence is often equated with centrality in networks.[31] Get Out The Vote (GOTV) campaigns, as well as marketing operations on social media outlets seek central figures for the sake of promoting a political or technological novelty.[32] If decentralization, weak ties and marginal leaders can generate effective collective dynamics that are different from centrally initiated waves of collective conversion, then there exist methods for promoting ideas and social practices other than central operations. The first step is to confirm the existence of such processes in observational and experimental data.

---

[28] For examples of central positioning of the instigators see Gould (1993), Centola and Macy (2007) and Siegel's (2009) formulations in three independent contexts.
[29] Rogers (2003).
[30] Granovetter (1973).
[31] See Banerjee et al. (2015) for a recent example from influentials in the field of influence maximization.
[32] For example, tweeters with the highest number of followers.

REVISITING COLLECTIVE ACTION: DECENTRALIZATION, CONTAGION AND SPONTANEITY AS KEYS TO MOBILIZATION WHEN HIERARCHY AND COORDINATION FAIL

Hierarchy, predictability and coordination underlie the institution of politics. Facing an organized suppression mechanism, a weaker collective movement is unlikely to succeed if it fully mirrors the superior streamlined structure of the state. In Tilly's words, after formulating collective action as a social process, i.e. importing a temporal element into the picture, *spontaneity* and *contagion* emerge as two components of collective action worthy of a careful examination.[33] Massive uprisings serve as showcases of *the hidden transcript*,[34] the aggregate language of the seemingly weak, the marginals. If the authorities were aware of these processes, they would disrupt them. The narrative of *public transcript*, the language of the powerful, on the other hand, offers an incomplete reconstruction of subversive and decentralized collective action: there are processes which surge with decentralization, lack of information, prevalence of rumors, contagion in place of coordination, when the regular and routine ways of collective contention fail.

Now, based on the imports of temporal progression, and differentiation among the agitators in terms of their location in the network, one could turn the question on its head, and ask if leadership, that starting point of power hierarchy, in the least visible and most peripheral places, induces effects that are different from the traditional formulations. Obviously, differentiation among the agents of change, radicals or the vanguard and the masses, as well as the existence of temporal dynamics, are staples of classical collective action theory. The most crucial contribution of this manuscript is allowing peripheral vanguardism. The network formulation is susceptible to a theory of decentralized contention. And the basic mathematical and empirical tools give way to fundamental questions, to some of which I have responded in the following, the remaining is future work. Unification and central coordination are replaced by dispersion and contagion. Instead of a centrally located vanguard, I have assumed peripheral leadership. The spatiotemporal data on mass collective action, from the current format, are unprecedented. Former studies had to rely on simplifying explanations.

The most defining of the revolutionary movements came as surprises to the outside world, because if they were well known and advertised

---

[33] *From Mobilization to Revolution* (Tilly 1978).
[34] See Scott (1990).

from the beginning, they could not have existed. Their separation from the conventional sources of information dissemination was a defining part of their ascendancy. That surprise is not inherent in the movement itself, but is an indicator of the nature of *knowledge* the way it is defined and obtained in centers of power and influence, away from the margins. The acts of the marginal vanguard are individually important in the initial seeding of social change, although centralization and solidification of social hierarchies that ensue from such massive acts of social reversal may have little to do with each of these peripheral leaders. Imagining contentious collective action similar to patterns of elite institutions with strong ties and hierarchical and static organization structure does not capture the dynamics of *leading from the periphery*.[35]

There is an empirical reason for choosing the dynamics of the ephemeral over average effects. In the following chapters, I will demonstrate that the majority of the effects of interest in the data are invisible in *average*, but become evident when events are studied in their path dependent and limited spatiotemporal context.[36] This is no coincidence, the deviations in the margins are indecipherable in average; it is common wisdom that they do not count.[37] The underlying forces would work the same way irrespective of seemingly random affairs. During the early modernist period, this assumption was necessary for the existence of an emerging breed of reified governance and a matching science of society. To build a framework for inquiry on par with those of natural sciences it was necessary to search for simplifying rules in historical data. In the eyes of Hobbes and Montesquieu, contemporary with the initiators of modern natural sciences, this was a rational route to take. Only

---

[35] This change of framework also represents a departure from the two-tier classification of opinion leaders and followers in the classics of political communication Katz and Lazarsfeld (2006); Zaller (1992). I will discuss the deviation from this dichotomy in the argument over the experiments in Chapter (5).

[36] Multiple examples exist in the following chapters. For example, the spillover of violence between spatiotemporal neighborhoods in the Syria study in Chapter (4) disappears once one moves to a complete temporal average of occurrences in each spatial neighborhood. A similar averaging effect, but in a different context is evident in Chapter (5).

[37] The importance of minutiae in historical processes, small deviations with significant eventual results, has been a matter of long-lasting debates. In *The Pensées* Blaise Pascal [1670] (1995) lamented that the fate of the Roman Empire hung on the size of Cleopatra's nose. Montesquieu, a modernist pioneer, later pondered the very same question in *Considerations on the Causes of the Greatness of the Romans and Their Decline*, Montesquieu [1735] (1999), but reached a different conclusion. For him, the Romans were destined for destruction, regardless of Mark Antony's infatuation with Cleopatra and his ruinous rivalry with Julius Caesar; rationalizable undercurrents of history, not details, including Cleopatra's appearance, directed the Roman trajectory.

recently have we devised efficient tools to scientifically study the details in order "to identify the accidents, the minute deviations, the errors, the false appraisals, and the faulty calculations that gave birth to these things that continue to exist and have value for us".[38] Now we have the data to detect such aberrations: peripheral network effects are not necessarily lost in the economizing narratives of grand histories. An approach that is obsessed with static institutionalized data is incapable of capturing ephemeral dynamics, hence the detailed microlevel methods implemented in the following chapters. On the methodological level, the network dynamics of politics on the large scale becomes significant when small entities grow in importance and cascade effects and collective behavior are taken out of the closet of "irrational", "contingent" and "epiphenomenal". What was disparaged as base, primitive and uncouth is now scrutable, giving political voice to elements outside the realm of the self-aggrandizing manipulating elite. Similarly, clues to the origins of a sudden disruption of the status quo are unlikely to be found in the mainstream and closely edited narrative of *the public transcript*, hence the frequent commentary on its surprising and contingent elements. The roots of rupture are recorded as *transgressions* of the editorial, not dissimilar to the remnants of a clandestine mischief captured in the background of a scenic image. The focus on the microlevel details of interactions, conflictual events and experimental dynamics ensures that averaging mechanism of summarizing narratives does not hide crucial details. The naiveté of uncouth data is necessary.[39]

Now that there exist network data apt for testing theories of decentralized collective action, one could go beyond the more expected and the most visible. The project in the following chapters is built around the same idea. On multiple occasions I show that the effects of interest, are not discernible in average, but are the most clear in *instances* of the data, for example invisible in the temporal average, but existent in the day to day dynamics (Chapter (4)), or absent in cross-sectional averages, but visible in the disaggregate data based on each singular occurrence of the experimental session (Chapter (5)).

My emphasis on decentralization, contagion and periphery does not mean that collective action cannot be orchestrated from the center. However, the dynamics would be different, and that difference has

---

[38] Michel Foucault (1984, p. 81).
[39] Nevertheless, while both institution and economy are fixed in the duration of rapid history, they influence the *onset* of rebellion.

not been discerned and singled out in the existing scholarship. In the following, I propose the possibility, formulate a few models for the logic of *leading from the periphery* and put the implications to the test using empirics from collective contention, in the form of urban protests, civil wars and laboratory experiments of collective risk taking. Confirming the existence of such processes, particularly in localized *small world networks*, hints at new possibilities of social organization, ones that we have been impervious to, because the easiest solutions to the conundrum of governance favor the most visible and the most powerful.[40]

OUTLINE OF THE BOOK: DESIGN AND MAIN FINDINGS

The book presents theory and evidence on the dynamics of mobilization that originates from the margins, not the center. Such *network collective action* spreads in ways distinct from centralized coordinated collective action. An array of empirical evidence and a parsimonious theoretical formulation establish the existence and import of *leading from the periphery*.

The inquiry starts from a curiosity: during the 2011 Egyptian Revolution, the data on the location of major collective action incidents through the 18 days of contention point at the highest geographical spread of conflict in Cairo during a complete blackout of communications. In Chapter (2), I present the detailed account of mobilization on January 25, 2011 in Cairo, according to a series of emails sent out to multiple hundreds by the leadership of the April 6 Youth Movement. These emails, some just minutes apart, portray the microlevel convergence of contentious flows from many corners of Cairo into its focal theater, Tahrir on the 25th. The defining question for the study, and the book, is the importance of the centralization of contention for the eventual

[40] One could interpret the findings in different dimensions. From the network science perspective, centrality is not necessarily equivalent to influence. From the social psychology perspective, crowd behavior is not necessarily uncouth and unrefined. From the collective action theory perspective, coordination is not all that there is to mobilization, contagion and diffusion are also of utmost importance. From the political communication perspective, the distinction between opinion leaders and the periphery, and the two-level structure of influence are not always plausible. From the mechanism design perspective, influence can be applied from the margins, not necessarily from the center. From the spatial analysis and urban design perspective, decentralization and the spatial composition of the actors are important. From the media theory perspective, at times lack of information is as important for incitement to action as the abundance of it.

success of the movement. Descriptive evidence points at an increase in the dispersion, i.e. geographical distribution of the contention, simultaneous with a complete blackout, put in place by the government with major unintended consequences. If coordination would have been the sole process in place, a media blackout should have stifled the opposition, as the regime intended. The results were the opposite. Mapping the dynamics of the protest became possible after fielding a survey of more than 700 Cairo residents. The respondents were asked if they participated in protests in distinct phases of the 18-day rebellion, and if they did, they were asked about their going to Tahrir. The results provided a dynamic picture of centralization of protesters in Tahrir. There are two noteworthy results, both reflected in Figure (1.1): first, as implied by the descriptive data, protesters reported the smallest rates of participation in Tahrir during the media blackout. This is an effect, which I argue, cannot be solely attributed to the actions of the government. The second piece of corroborating evidence is revealing of distinctive, and overlooked, dynamics of *leading from the periphery*: the *vanguard*, those who protested during the first phase of the protests, before the 28th, were more dispersed than the typical protester, most importantly during the first phase of the protests, as well as during the blackout. In other words, the vanguard of the Egyptian Revolution were more likely *not* to be in Tahrir on the first days of protests. That high dispersion, compared to the average protester who naturally was conditioned to converge on Tahrir, was instrumental to the success of the rebellion. The same decentralization during the blackout on the 28th exacerbated the revolutionary unrest.

An online appendix includes the reproductions of more than 60 hourly emails sent by the April 6 Youth Movement leadership during the early days of the 2011 Egyptian Revolution. The survey dataset and the full text of respondents' remarks on the effects of the blackout, as well as the scans of more than 500 print surveys conducted in Cairo, are also included in the online appendix.

Chapter (3) embarks at formulating a theoretical foundation for *leading from the periphery* and a network collective action theory which can describe the emanation of collective action from leaders situated at the periphery of the social network. Central to the possibility of *leading from the periphery*, are the conditions under which cells of contention take hold and persist in the margins. Instead of *critical mass*, for generating an all encompassing wave of contention, I explore the conditions for sustenance of sleeper cells, which can persist under threshold dynamics of collective

Outline of the Book

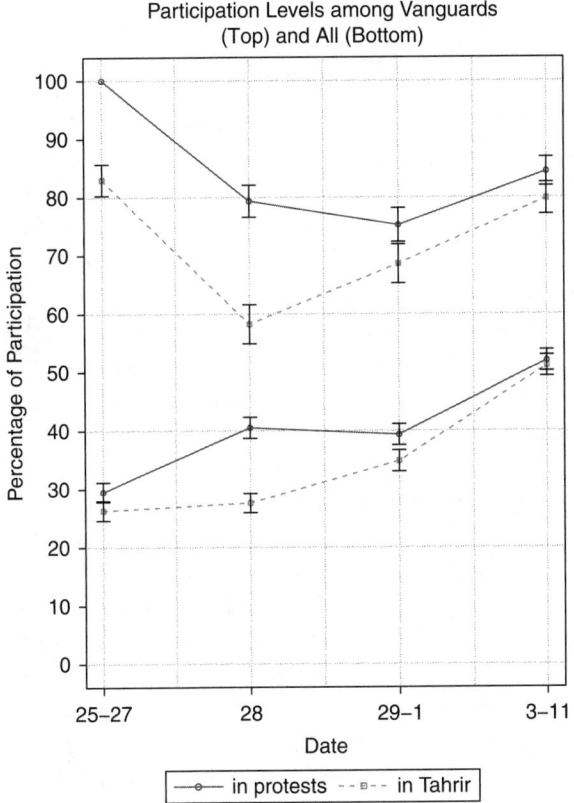

FIGURE 1.1. Participation levels among all survey respondents, $N = 740$, bottom figure, and among the vanguard, $N = 218$, defined as those participating in the first phase of the protests. Note two main points: first, the protesters are away from Tahrir in the largest proportions on the most defining day of the protests, January 28. More importantly, the vanguard reported dispersed protest activity, away from Tahrir during the first phase of the protests, on par with their dispersion on the 28th.

action. For any given graph of connections, this puzzle translates to a fundamental mathematical question itself.[41] I will show that under some conditions, the existence of such cells is connected to the smallest subset of a network in which all members have more neighbors inside the subset as

---

[41] Related to a group of fundamental mathematical puzzles called *isoperimetric* problems.

opposed to outside of it. I call this smallest set a *minimal core*. Clandestine collective action in the periphery is the most likely to persist in such cells.

The importance of these marginal pockets of risk taking at the margins of the society lies in their singular response to modes of communication in a world of dispersed contention. I will show that, with threshold dynamics of collective action and a minimally demanding learning dynamics, these networks become more sustainable in the absence of communication, not its abundance. For example, in Figure (1.2), the size of the *minimal core* increases when the reach of communication is increased. In other words, for sustaining islands of action among a majority of risk averse individuals, curtailing communication is beneficial. Increasing connectivity can diminish network collective action, and islands of action in the social networks wither away when connectivity increases.

In Chapter (3) I also outline a model of network collective action based on public–private signaling. The signaling model shows that the value of *public* information lies in the structure of the relevant social network, and that removal of public signal, depending on the network structure, can be beneficial to collective action in specific network configurations, an important example of which is the *small world network*. The value of social information depends on the structure of the underlying social network. This fact, and the role of *small world networks* in *leading from the periphery* becomes clear after a detailed study of an urban conflict in Chapter (4).

Chapter (4) contains further evidence on the importance of contagion during blackout and escalation via decentralization of conflict in the absence of communication media. In this chapter, I present a GIS (Geographic Information System) analysis of the Syrian Civil War in Damascus using a detailed daily dataset of conflict locations in the city of Damascus proper. Similar to the Egyptian case, I show that the dispersion of the urban conflict increased during the blackout. Figure (1.3) shows a daily profile of the normalized dispersion of the conflict, defined as the sum of pairwise distances between each possible pair of conflict locations, divided by the total number of the incidents. The dispersion parameter peaks during the blackout, and the findings are robust to a number of dispersion parameter definitions. Using a number of control variables, I argue that this effect cannot be attributed solely to the regime's activities. In the search for an explanation, I define and measure *contagion* processes in Damascus in the last nine months of year 2012, and show that contagion was effectively activated during the blackout. The spatial

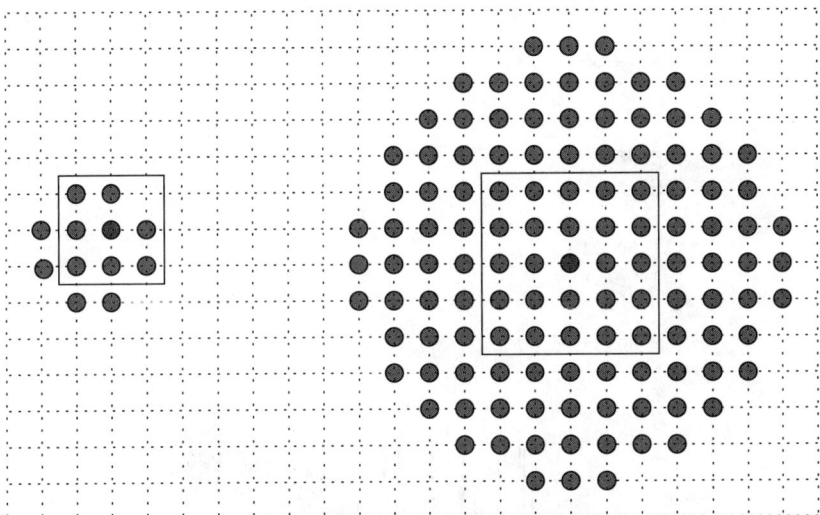

FIGURE 1.2. A comparison between the size of *minimal core* for $m = 2$ dimensional grids, radius of connectivity $n = 1$ (left), and $n = 2$ (right). The nodes reachable from a given central node are demarcated with an overlay box. Increasing radius of connectivity by one unit increases the size of *minimal core* to 121.

and temporal profile of the conflict in Damascus portrays locally dense, but globally dispersed clusters of violence. This topology, interestingly enough, is the structure of a *small world network*. In Chapter (3) I showed that the *absence* of public signals in such network structures escalates the contentious process, it does not impede it. The blackout itself, exacerbates the localization process, producing a positive feedback channel, fanning the flames of localized and contagious collective action in the absence of communication media. It is a self-reinforcing cycle of decentralization and escalation, set into motion by a complete communication blackout.

The online appendix for Chapter (4) contains the comprehensive GIS dataset itself.

Two elements of mass collective action – the rapid spread of risk taking and the "surprise element" inherent in their appearance-require explanation, particularly because both are key to a successful movement, as they are the mirror opposite of the state's controlling structure. Furthermore, conscious emulating of a centralized hierarchy does not

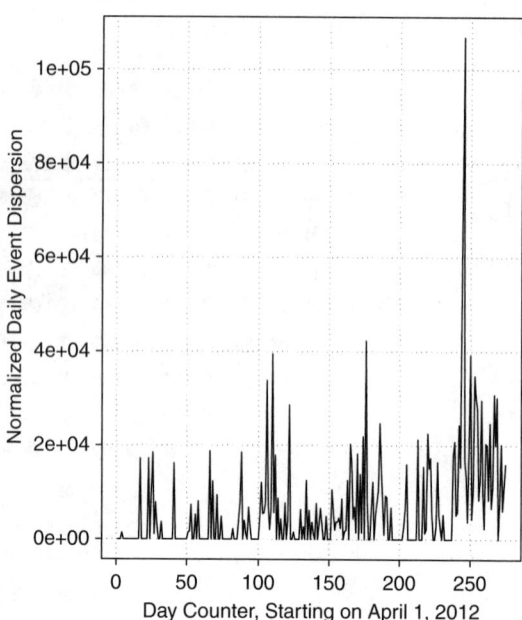

FIGURE 1.3. Normalized dispersion of conflict based on the sum of pairwise distances between all conflictual incidents per day in Damascus and its suburbs. The visible peak corresponds to the duration of the two-day blackout.

assist mobilization from the periphery. To examine the dynamics of collective action from the periphery, Chapter (5) outlines the results of a series of network experiments in which the vanguard, i.e. those more prone to adopt risk taking before the others, are deliberately installed in different locations of experimental social networks. The subjects engage in a game of collective risk taking, which is a lottery that, similar to a revolution, rewards when a majority of the social network take part in taking risk, and punishes when they fail to do so. The status quo is always the safe, but hardly rewarding choice. The results of three network treatments, outlined in Chapter (5), show that collective waves of risk taking or, in contrast, complete apathy, are more frequent when the vanguard are located in the periphery, as opposed to the center, and when the cascades do happen, they happen more quickly. Central leaders are swamped by the risk aversion of the majority, to many of whom they are linked. Peripheral instigators, on the other hand, do not bear the pressure of a large following, and their influence is amplified in small circles, before spreading to more central locations in the network.

Outline of the Book

Figure (1.4) depicts the dynamics of risk taking in experimental sessions resulting in *cascades*. The sum rates of risk taking, and apathy, in the peripheral assignment, i.e. the extremes, are more likely to happen when leaders are positioned in the periphery of the social network.[42]

This is a result that would be invisible if the simple total average levels of risk taking were compared between peripheral and central assignments of the vanguard. However, the disaggregate results reveal the often ignored dynamics of *leading from the periphery*. The details of

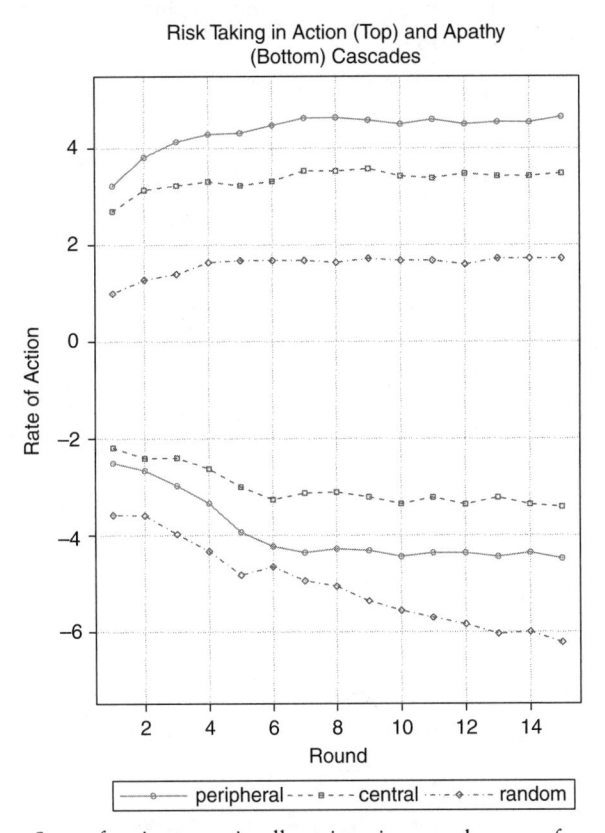

FIGURE 1.4. Sum of action rates in all sessions in cascade status for action (top) and apathy (bottom) cascades. Note that peripheral assignment generates higher rates of action and apathy in cascades. The results are more extreme when the vanguard are assigned to the periphery. Total number of subjects in the experiment $N = 720$.

---

[42] A random positioning of the vanguard would cause the smallest rates of collective action.

the experimental results, along with illustration of the collective action dynamics in an experimental setup are included in Chapter (5).

Finally, Chapter (6) examines the implications of the findings. If the peripheral vanguard are capable of embarking on singular cascades of collective action, then that possibility can redefine the way political power is imagined. Hierarchy, control and predictability are the heart of the modernist state and society, and the application of power relies on a centralized institutional structure. The results of the distinct processes I outline, on the other hand, give a glimpse of alternative modes of social organization, whose potential is not as directly governable as the traditional modes of mobilization.[43]

---

[43] The online appendix includes the pointers to the Cairo survey dataset at https://goo.gl/S9Jm3e, Damascus GIS dataset at https://goo.gl/ZCjY9b, network experiments of collective action dataset at https://goo.gl/FQ6PEo, as well as scans of mobilizational emails during the 2011 Egyptian Revolution at https://goo.gl/EERpPC, scans of hundreds of survey interviews in Cairo at https://goo.gl/7keQ9O, and network visualizations pertaining to all experimental sessions at https://goo.gl/Dr7mW6. The author maintains the online appendix on his personal webpage at https://navidhassanpour.com/.

2

Decentralization of Revolutionary Unrest
Dispersion Hypothesis

> ... *too many protests in too many places.*
> Peter Bouckaert, emergencies director of Human Rights Watch, Cairo, January 28, 2011

Following three days of unrest and to counter the growing urban protests across Egypt, in the early hours of January 28 Mubarak's regime shut down the Internet and cell phone networks across the country. The surprising events of the next day suggest the incumbent's tactics were misguided. The protests in Cairo which were contained in Tahrir Square and surroundings up to that day, proliferated across the city and flared in every corner of Cairo. By 6 p.m. on January 28, the police forces were overwhelmed, and the military was called in to replace the police.[1] In the following days a practically neutral military played a major role in the political developments of the country resulting in the ousting of Mubarak on February 11. The expansion of the protests on the 28th questions common wisdom on the role of social media in civil unrest, and the traditional logic of collective action. If an unlimited flow of information were to be indispensable to the escalation, then the disruption of the media across Egypt in the early morning hours of January 28th, should not have proliferated the unrest and exacerbated the decentralized nature of revolutionary contention.

In the following, using tens of mobilizational emails sent prior to the first day of unrest, I focus on the minute by minute developments on January 25, and contrast the dynamics of collective action on that day

---

[1] *Al-Masry Al-Youm* (2011); El-Ghobashy (2011).

with those on the 28th. I argue that disrupting social and mobile media, contrary to Mubarak's intent, fostered more contention of a decentralized nature. An analysis of the singular dynamics of collective action in urban environments during blackouts reveals the distinct characteristics of *leading from the periphery*. It is as if in the absence of centralizing powers of far reaching communication, clandestine components of decentralized contention come to the fore.

Interestingly enough, disrupting media is a common characteristic of many revolutionary situations. Sometimes it is a byproduct of the paralyzing unrest; often it is the result of a governmental crackdown. In both cases, I will argue that the disruption acts as a catalyst of the revolutionary process and hastens the disintegration of the status quo. The recent Egyptian uprising provided a unique opportunity to put such a hypothesis to the test. The findings in this chapter, combined with theoretical formulation in the next chapter, and the following empirics in the rest of the book, formulate an explanation for escalation and decentralization. These processes are often ignored in favor of more visible tactics of centrally coordinated leadership.

MICHEL FOUCAULT IN TEHRAN

The disruption of media prior to major revolutionary upheavals is not limited to the case of the stillborn Egyptian Revolution of the 2011, only that the evidence is not as clear-cut. On November 6, 1978, in solidarity with the other factions of the Iranian society and in opposition to the Shah's newly appointed military government, Iranian journalists and newspaper staffers announced an indefinite strike plunging the country into an information blackout for two months till the reopening of the press on January 5, 1979. Few of them might have known they were contributing to the collapse of the Shah as much as their partners on strike in the oil industry. The largest demonstration of the Iranian Revolution of 1979 took place during this news industry hiatus between November 6, 1978 and January 5, 1979.[2] The information vacuum was filled with audio cassettes, pamphlets and other decentralized means of face to face communication. Not surprisingly, during Tehran's post-election protests of 2009, the authorities repeatedly disrupted mobile communications and Internet-based social media, but never imposed a universal blackout.

---

[2] See Kurzman (2004).

Michel Foucault who was reporting from Tehran for the Italian daily, *Corriere della Sera*, noted the importance of the blackout: "It is said that De Gaulle was able to resist the Algiers putsch, thanks to the transistor. If the Shah is about to fall, it will be due largely to the cassette tape, it is the tool *par excellence* of counterinformation."[3]

Similarly on February 25, 1917, in the midst of an urban revolt, Petrograd newspapers ceased publication just a few days before the Duma's dissolution. They resumed circulation on March 1, after which the Duma acted quickly to limit and control the actions of the press, see Figure (2.1).[4] The proliferation of protests happened on the 26th immediately after the disruption of normal communications across the city on the 25th. The violent response to the unrest on the 26th culminated in an army rebellion and the take over of the Duma on the 27th.[5] The decree issued by the Russian provisional government shows they were fully aware of the importance of "fantastic rumors", and to return to the normal state of affairs, they saw it necessary to control the flow of information in one location.[6]

> "A general meeting of the association of Russian editors has decided against a renewal of the newspapers, with the view of preventing the spreading of fantastic rumors which might harm the common cause. Therefore only one newspaper is to be issued twice a day. It is to be distributed free and edited by a committee of Petrograd journalists, whose rooms are in the Duma building.

FIGURE 2.1. The Russian Revolution of February 1917. Rumors were recognized as instigation, *New York Times*, March 17, 1917.

---

[3] A recent translation of the reports can be found in Afary and Anderson (2005, p. 219).
[4] "Guard regiments started uprising", from Historical New York Times (March 17, 1917).
[5] Hasegawa (1981); Wade (2005).
[6] Moreover, Wade (2005), singling out one unidentified individual, notes the common presence of the same local and anonymous vanguards in several photos remaining from late February 1917. See Wade (2005, p. 41, plate 3).

MEDIA DISRUPTION AND THE REVEALING OF PERIPHERAL PROCESSES

The utility of a complete information blackout is its revealing function. In the absence of communication media, local processes of social behavior become more pronounced. Now, such a decentralization of information media need not result in an escalation and proliferation of collective action. In the following, I show that the occurrence of a highly destabilizing combination of localization and proliferation is contingent upon two side effects of an information vacuum: the shaping of local circles of contact and communication replacing prior media channels, and the dynamics of influence emanating from the *peripheral* vanguard who operate more effectively in the absence of routine social connections.

For detecting the level of decentralization in this chapter (and later in Chapter (4)), I have employed measures of dispersion based on counts, and distances among major instances of contentious collective action. After detecting changes in levels of decentralization, I have explored the underlying localization processes to show that the social dynamics were transformed in a way that helped the mobilization: peripheral leaders come to the fore when the informative means of centralized information propagation are not in place.

In the absence of that unified narrative,[7] the dynamics of collective risk taking against the status quo can generate a window to the alternative dynamics of political activism in a society. Collective action based on a logic of coordination should be diminished in the absence of much needed communication. In contrast, the logic of *leading from the periphery*, i.e. decentralized contention, predicts emergent nuclei of collective action in the margins, and a pursuant increase in the *dispersion* of popular contention. I call this the *Dispersion Hypothesis* and put it to the test using data from two major instances of urban contention in Middle Eastern capitals. These cities are the most likely candidates for simulating the conditions of a *small world network*. The logic of network collective action I outline in Chapter (3) demonstrates how a removal of public information in *small world networks* can, counterintuitively, result in an increase in levels of collective action.

---

[7] In James Scott's (1990) terminology, *the public transcript* is in contrast and at times in opposition to *the hidden transcript*. A similar concept is *mass self-communication* in the terminology of Castells (2009a).

DISSENT AND THE MEDIA

The debate on the role of the media in social unrest was revitalized during the Arab Spring and in the ensuing conflicts. In the past two decades, the rise of the Internet and decentralized online communication coincided with numerous instances of mass uprisings across the world. Many analysts have taken the social media to be an indispensable part of the mobilization process in mass protests in places as diverse as Ukraine, Iran, Moldova, Thailand and Egypt. Various arguments have been put forward: some suggest that the new technology makes coordination easier, while others highlight the role the media play in broadcasting scenes of confrontation to the outside world, thereby encouraging the aggrieved population. Monitoring communication in the context of the social media also seems to be more difficult.

The proponents of such arguments overlook several facts. Social media can act against grass roots mobilization. They discourage face to face communication and mass presence in the streets. Similar to more traditional and highly visible media, they create greater awareness of risks involved in protests, which in turn can discourage people from taking part in demonstrations. In the following, I will argue that lack of credible information at times benefits cascades of contention.[8] Similar processes are outlined as an explanation for why watching West German television broadcasts might have discouraged East Germans from applying for visas to travel to the West: once they saw it on television, they were less likely to embark on a personal exploration to see the unknown.[9] Similarly knowing about the situation on Facebook and Twitter and having access to news propagation sources may make personal moves and physical presence unnecessary.

The lack of the intermediary sources of communication between the state and the people fosters local news production and propagation on the individual level, deprives the state of a normalizing apparatus and sets the stage for cascades of collective action. I would like to argue that the paralyzing mass demonstrations and widespread antagonistic uprisings in question would not have happened if the media had continued channeling their supervised, censored and perhaps realistic narration of the events.

In the absence of the mass media, information is communicated locally. Without state intervention, crowds shape an idea of risk that

---

[8] In fact a number of mass uprisings in the Eastern Bloc were initiated by rumors.
[9] Kern and Hainmueller (2009).

is independent from the state, testing their perceptions by staging demonstrations. The government's response to the acts of public defiance signals either weakness or strength on the side of the state.[10] If the demonstrators' speculations about the weakness of the incumbent regime turn out to be correct as they did in Tehran in December 1978 or Leipzig in 1989–1990,[11] the cascade of events can grow to unanticipated dimensions.[12]

REVOLUTIONS AND COUNTERINFORMATION

The Weberian definition of the state[13] anticipates destabilizing moments of information vacuum. The state is defined as the monopoly over physical force and bureaucracy. In addition to the military and police, the press act as a proxy for the state's control bureaucracy, hence any interruption of the culture industry would alter the functionality of the state. Weber's definition is also in line with the transformation of the press after the French Revolution. While decentralized pamphleteering was a common practice among the revolutionaries, the state they created moved to standardize and regulate the process.

According to Schumpeter these notions extend to democracies and dictatorships alike.[14] In a well functioning democracy the media are used to shape electoral opinion.[15] Likewise in Gramsci's depiction of

---

[10] Chwe (2001); Kuran (1991).
[11] Lohmann (1994).
[12] On the difference between revolutions and riots: in this study revolution is defined as a mass violent act targeted at the governing body, intended to topple the incumbent regime. Mass uprisings under the title *revolutions* show distinctive common traits: they are large in scale (thousands involved if not millions); their major aim is to dismantle the political status quo and the ruling apparatus; the new rulers (in the case of successful execution) would be the prior underclass; the ruling elite would be confiscated from their political and economic power; and finally successful revolutions bring vast and far reaching changes in legal and judicial practice. Defined as such, revolutions are rare events. They are different from riots in several aspects. First, they affect lives of a sizable population inside the domestic polity, second the stakes are higher. Participants face higher risks, their ultimate goal being a standoff against the ancien régime. Both of these characteristics are in contrast with the defining factors of riots Wilkinson (2009) as smaller gatherings, which although can be violent, are not of the magnitude of revolutionary movements and are not directed toward the demise of the principal political hegemony.
[13] Weber [1919] (1958a).
[14] Schumpeter (1950).
[15] Media often reflect the wants of the political elite Bennett (1990). They are used as a means of framing sensitive topics for political purposes Entman (2004). The networks of communication constitute the streamlined power of the state Castells (2009a).

totalitarianism,[16] the media impose an aura of normalcy and oppressive calm under the cultural hegemony of the state. What is left out from Schumpeter and Gramsci's accounts are the brief moments where the outreach of the media does not exist or is interrupted. When the normalizing force of the media collapses, production of opinion outside the reach of the incumbent regime can force the polity to change course under the pressure of an opposing public sphere.

In a society on the verge of political unrest, the state's control over news media prevents widespread dissatisfaction from turning into a united opposition. Media outlets are highly visible and not hard to control. The population that relies on media for estimating the political atmosphere is provided with a view that is supervised by the ruling power. The elite use their influence to pacify the population or discourage sedition. Nevertheless, the widely acknowledged view of the role of the media in revolutions points to the opposite direction. Many have noted the positive impacts of the free media on bringing about revolutions.[17] Print and virtual media disseminate knowledge and awareness, the constituents are informed about political possibilities and grievances; therefore they are more inclined to engage in a resurrection against oppression and incompetence. This argument is misguided on two grounds, first it overlooks the fact that most seditious communication is invisible to the ruling elite. If they were aware of it, they would disrupt it. The centralized media, including semi-autonomous dailies, are too exposed to foster revolutionary contention. Second, those who engage in radical acts of dissidence usually are not primed by potential free discussions in the press. The free media excites the intelligentsia and is more likely to result in a political transition of more usual types. What incites mass revolts is "counterinformation" properly defined.

Consider the case of the Czech Velvet Revolution. According to recent accounts, the movement was ignited by false rumors of the brutal death of a 19-year-old university student.[18] At times of civil unrest, exaggeration tactics are known to be highly effective. In a similar manner, the fall of the Berlin Wall started with a false and ambiguous statement at a news conference.[19] A vaguely communicated decision on Eastern German television prompted protesters to demand free passage to the Western side of Berlin.

[16] Gramsci [1926] (1971).
[17] Popkin (1995) among others.
[18] Bilefski (2009).
[19] Sarotte (2009).

To confirm such hypotheses and to add to the descriptive and speculative statements on the role of alternative processes in mass protests, one needs to find situations in which media coverage changes sharply, then gauge the impact of such a change on the level of unrest. In fact authoritarian regimes repeatedly provide such a scenario: in the course of street protests, mobile communications are often disrupted and Internet access is restricted. However, ideally the disruption should be ubiquitous and universal, and the level of confounding factors kept to the minimum for the conclusions to be meaningful. In the following, I outline the Egyptian case in the first step, and later present a detailed daily description of violent incidents in Damascus during the last nine months of 2012 to further test the predictions of a network logic of collective action based on leadership from the social periphery.

EMPIRICS AND THE PARADIGM OF *LEADING FROM THE PERIPHERY*

In the above I argued that a complete disruption of communication transforms mobilization in two consecutive and consequential ways: first, it decentralizes contention; one can measure this increase in dispersion. Second, and as importantly, it promotes activists who are more likely to build new social links relevant to the revolt, in smaller and more local spheres of rebellion. In other words, a disruptive action meant to stop the rebellion turns into a catalyst for it. Now, this localization of the vanguard, as the second component of the theory, can be measured and verified either positively, or negatively. Finally, if the vanguard do happen to be local or localized, the dynamics of collective action cascade they put into motion will be different from those led from the center of the social network. These are the three components of a verifiable hypothesis system I will put to the test in this chapter, and the rest of the book. The 2011 Egyptian Revolution is a testing ground for the first and second components. After gaining insights in this chapter, I present a basic network formulation in the next chapter, and then in Chapter (4) employ the dynamics of the Syrian Civil War to check the recurrence of some of the effects seen in the Egyptian case. Finally, in Chapter (5) I present an experimental study of network collective action, as the first step to study the dynamics of collective risk taking in a controlled setup. In other words, three components of an empirical appraisal of *leading from the periphery*—decentralization in the absence of communication, the existence of peripheral vanguard per se and the singular dynamics of *leading from the periphery*—are covered.

FROM PAMPHLETS TO CENTRALIZED MEDIA

One of the more interesting facts about the French Revolution is the prevalence of pamphleteering immediately before the revolution.[20] While the established periodicals of the time, e.g. *Gazette de France* and *Gazette de Leyde*, mostly ignored the rebellion during the summer of 1789, many of the leaders of the Third Estate (and later revolutionary leaders during the struggle of summer 1789) published pamphlets to disseminate news and make their own take on the situation known to the public. At the beginning of the summer of 1789, Louis XVI tried his best to block the growth of pamphleteering,[21] but did not succeed. Later pamphleteers such as Mirabeau and Abbe Sieyès led the revolution. After victory, the revolution redefined the relation between the state and media; pamphleteering was discouraged. Instead the printed press with wider circulation replaced grass roots means of written communication and reporting. Compared to modern mobilization, honed by centralized media, it is likely that modes of collective action had been very different at times of decentralized communication of the pamphleteering type.[22] The very same speculations can be put to the test using observational and experimental empirics.

Prior to the culmination of the February 1917 unrest in Petrograd, the city's newspapers stopped circulation immediately before the Duma's dissolution on the 27th. They resumed on March 1. Afterwards the Duma tried to maintain a monopoly on the press.[23] It is believed the confusion caused by the absence of printed media might have hastened the collapse of the ancien régime.[24]

Similarly during the Iranian Revolution of 1978–1979, the printed press stopped circulation on November 6, 1978 and did not return to normal till two months later.[25] The largest protests of the Iranian Revolution happened during the very same period when media coverage

---

[20] Popkin (1990).
[21] Ibid.
[22] See Habermas (1991).
[23] Hasegawa (1981); Historical New York Times (1917); Wade (2005).
[24] See Wade (2005) for a note on the role of blackout in the collapse of the status quo. It is necessary to mention that literacy rates among the urban Russian population around 1917 were around 70 percent Mironov (1991), i.e. the printed press as the sole formal news propagation mechanism (prior to television and radio broadcast) played a major role in everyday news learning. Their absence acted as a catalyst for the revolutionary unrest in Petrograd.
[25] *Kayhan* (1978–1979), Michel Foucault's report for Corriere Della Sera, *The Revolt in Iran Spreads on Cassette Tapes*, November 19, 1979, included in Afary and Anderson (2005), p. 216, as well as *Kayhan*, January 6, 1979.

was at minimal levels and the scant broadcast of the state media was widely disregarded in favor of pamphlets, audio cassettes and foreign radio stations.[26] Again in this case the spread of grass roots rumors had a major impact on the success of revolutionary mobilization. Instead of the state setting the general political agenda across the society, the opposition encouraged repetitive cycles of rebellion.

In both of the above cases it is difficult to estimate the impact of the absence of media because of confounding factors. The evidence we have is not accurate enough to test the *Dispersion Hypothesis* – especially because the treatment (disruption of the media and cutting down venues for communication) was not always complete, i.e. did not include all means of news propagation. In more traditional societies constituents relied on a wide array of traditional communication processes, hence stopping a number of state controlled channels, e.g. newspapers might not have had the same impact as cutting all mobile and Internet communications overnight. That is exactly what Mubarak's regime did in the early hours of January 28, 2011.

THE CENTER AND THE PERIPHERY IN THE EGYPTIAN REVOLUTION

In response to the opposition staging demonstrations for three consecutive days in Tahrir Square and promising a yet larger one on a Friday of Rage, Mubarak's regime shut down the Internet and cell phone coverage across the country in the early hours of January 28, 2011. Instead of stalling demonstration in Tahrir, the consequences caught the regime by surprise. Protests flared across Cairo, Alexandria and Suez.[27] The protests were unusually diffuse and overwhelmed Mubarak's security forces.[28] Around 7 p.m. on January 28, the military was brought to the scene to replace the dysfunctional police force.[29] After deployment of the military, the dynamics of the interaction among the political players, i.e. the incumbent, the military and the opposition, changed. The military's inaction, accompanied with the unexpected implications of the regime's bold experimentation with the mass media in the following days, put an end to Mubarak's 30-year rule. At the turning point of January 28, lack of cell phone coverage and Internet connection forced

---

[26] Ibid.
[27] El-Ghobashy (2011).
[28] Mackey (2011).
[29] *Al-Masry Al-Youm* (2011); El-Ghobashy (2011).

the population to find other means of communication, encouraging local mobilization. Meanwhile, the apolitical strata of the Egyptian society, aggrieved by the ventures of a dysfunctional state, were pushed into joining the confrontation. Instead of protests converging on Tahrir Square in Cairo, during the blackout sizable demonstrations appeared in numerous locations in the city.[30]

The Egyptian uprising was the result of a longstanding contentious process fueled by economic hurdles and flagrant abuses of individual freedoms.[31] The online mobilization campaign was the final trigger.[32] Meanwhile, January 28 is seen as a "tipping point".[33] The diffusion of the protests is cited as a major contributor to the opposition's victory.[34] The case offers a unique opportunity to test the plausibility of the *Dispersion Hypothesis* in a context similar to a quasi-experiment (alas run by Mubarak's regime). The disruption was abrupt, and its timing (around 1:30 a.m. on January 28) ruled out any preparation for countering the blackout on the previous day. Between 10 p.m. and 2 a.m., SMS and Internet communications were shut down; more importantly, cell phone communications were interrupted and remained dysfunctional during the 28th. For a detailed time line of disruptions, see Table (2.1).[35] While the regime had experimented with selectively disrupting network coverage and websites such as Twitter and Facebook, and had tampered with disabling activists' mobile phones, it was the first time a *universal* communication blackout was imposed on the nation.

Dismantling regular venues for communication incited Egyptians to find new ways of staying online or forgoing online communication altogether. On the first day of immense protests, January 25, the presence of social media and mobile communications had helped the protesters to converge on Tahrir Square. Later, after an appraisal of the spatial dynamics of the protests, I parse a collection of mobilizational emails sent from a central *operations room* to a select list of activists on the 25th. Figure (2.2), for example, shows an email sent out by the April 6 Youth Movement for mass mobilization. In contrast to January 25, the lack of communication on the fly on January 28 stalled global

---

[30] Shehata et al. (2011).
[31] The "durable authoritarianism" Masoud (2011) of the Egyptian polity enacted a state of emergency since 1981.
[32] El-Ghobashy (2011).
[33] Beinin (2011).
[34] El-Ghobashy (2011).
[35] Sources: Cowie (2011), Raoof (2011), Dunn (2011); the Lede blog and Renesys.com.

TABLE 2.1. *Communication disruptions, 2011 Egyptian Revolution*

Date	Type of Disruption or Restoration
January 25	Twitter blocked
	Live video streaming services blocked at 2 p.m.
	Activists' mobile lines shut down
	Network coverage shut down in Tahrir
January 26	Facebook blocked
	Blackberry services shut down 7 p.m.
January 27	SMS shut down 10 p.m.
January 28	Internet shut down – except one ISP, 1:30 a.m.
	Mobile phone calls shut down for one day
	Landlines shut down in some areas
January 30	Al Jazeera Cairo bureau shut down
January 31	Last ISP shut down
February 1	State media campaign against protesters (text messages)
February 2	Internet service restored 12:30 p.m.
February 5	SMS restored 12:35 a.m.

convergence on Tahrir. Many local focal points instead absorbed the crowds who did not know about the developments around Tahrir. During the social media hiatus, older mobilization tactics were used in conjunction with new means of mass communication. For example, after the 28th, satellite television stations such as Al Jazeera broadcast the news that was communicated to them via landline phones.[36] In addition to these spontaneous innovations, the protests proliferated through much more mundane means. On the 28th, those worried about their friends and family members participating in protests could not reach them via cell phones, and had to join the crowds in the streets to find out about their acquaintances.[37] In the hazardous conditions of the ongoing standoff across the city, focal points on the local level became gathering locations. Many congregated in local squares, strategic buildings and mosques instead of trying to reach Tahrir.[38] Radicals became more effective on the local level, because they could directly contact more people on the

---

[36] See Shehata et al. (2011). Al-Arabiya also started broadcasting informative tweets on the radio. At the same time, tweeting over the phone became a possibility using Google's Speak2Tweet Dunn (2011).
[37] Shehata et al. (2011).
[38] Mackey (2011).

إعلان: اماكن التظاهرات ونقاط التحرك ليوم 25 يناير بالقاهرة والمحافظات :Fwd

---------- Forwarded message ----------
From: **April 6 Youth** <media@6april.org>
Date: 2011/1/22
Subject: إعلان: اماكن التظاهرات ونقاط التحرك ليوم 25 يناير بالقاهرة والمحافظات
To:

أعلنت حركة شباب 6 ابريل الأماكن والنقاط التي من المفترض بدأ مظاهرات 25 يناير منها بعد التنسيق مع المجموعات الشبابية داخل مصر وخارجها.

ومن المفترض أن تبدأ التظاهرات في القاهرة والمحافظات في تمام الساعة 2 ظهرا

ومن المفترض أن يشارك بجوار القوى الشبابية المصرية والحشد من المواطنين المصريين، كل من الألتراس الأهلاوي والألتراس الزملكاوي وطلاب من جامعات مصرية خاصة، وعمال مصنع الغزل والنسيج بالمحلة وموظفي مراكز المعلومات "حسب الإعلان حتى الأن"

كذلك سوف تنطلق تحركات أخرى لكل من الأطباء والمحامين والمهندسين وأساتذه الجامعات والمعلمين

أماكن التجمعات في القاهرة :
* (شارع جامعة الدول العربية (المهندسين
* دوران شبرا
* ميدان المطرية
* جامعة القاهرة

أما المحافظات المشاركة
1- القهليه "المنصوره"
2- الاسكندريه
3- الغربيه في المحله الكبير
4- السويس
5- الاسماعيليه
6- كفر الشيخ
7- اسيوط
8- بورسعيد
9- دمياط

ومن المفترض أن ينضم المتظاهرون من الشرقية والقليوبية والمنوفية إلى المتظاهرين في القاهرة وكذلك سينضم المتظاهرين في قنا وسوهاج والمنيا إلى المتظاهرين في أسيوط

ومن المفترض أن يكون هناك تحرك واسع من أهالي سيناء للمشاركة في يوم 25 يناير بشكل واسع.

المطالبة والشعارات الخاصة بيوم 25 يناير:
1- حد أدنى للأجور 1200 جنية
2- ربط الأجور بالأسعار
3- إلغاء حالة الط ا

FIGURE 2.2. A snapshot of the email sent out by the April 6 Youth Movement calling for protests on January 25. As for the initial protest locations, there are only four listed destinations in Cairo: Mohandeseen; Shubra; Matariya Square; University of Cairo. Eventually all converged on Tahrir Square. These locations match the description of protest locations on the 25th from other sources, including El-Ghobashy (2011).

ground. Moreover, the networks underlying collective action and news propagation became smaller and more diffuse, making it more difficult for the regime to contain the protests.[39]

To summarize, the disruption of cell phone coverage and Internet on the 28th exacerbated the unrest in at least three major ways: it implicated many apolitical citizens unaware of or uninterested in the unrest; it forced more face to face communication, i.e. more physical presence in streets; it effectively decentralized the rebellion on the 28th through new hybrid communication tactics, producing a quagmire much harder to control and repress than one massive gathering in Tahrir.[40]

BLACKOUT AND MEASURES OF PROTEST DISPERSION IN CAIRO

If coordination on universal themes of space, time and action were to be the only significant component of collective action, then a complete disruption of communications should severely debilitate any major act of collective risk taking. If that is not the case, then a logic of leadership, other than uniting themes, could be the process in action. To test the possibility of such decentralized network collective action, I measure a proxy of dispersion, i.e. geographical spread of major mass conflicts, during a prolonged event, the 2011 Egyptian Revolution here, and later in Chapter (4) during the Syrian Civil War.

A first order study of protest locations in and around Cairo shows that while on January 25, the first day of the protests, the eventual destination was Tahrir, in the following days, a good number of other local focal points—squares, mosques, major streets—became gathering points and turned into the foci of large scale demonstrations. For example, on the 28th, I will show that eight locations, not one, were reported to have seen large scale demonstrations. The effect tapered off as the communication blackout was lifted. Interestingly enough, the results of a face to face and online survey on protests participation in Cairo confirms this increase in dispersion, and gives clues on how it may have operated in the aftermath of the information vacuum.

---

[39] Hassanpour (2014).
[40] Even in Tahrir there was no single leadership Shehata et al. (2011): "Nobody was in charge of Tahrir" and "a lot of those who joined the protests on January 25th in Tahrir were not aware of the Facebook campaign, they had heard about it from the protesters in the square and surrounding streets". According to Mourtada and Salem (2011), a majority of respondents to an online survey on the role of media disruption on the protests, run shortly after the end of the 18-day uprising, believed it had a positive effect on the demonstrations.

The details of protest locations are included in Table (2.2). Based on contemporaneous media reports,[41] I have constructed a dynamic profile of the protest locations in Cairo during the 18 days of uninhibited collective action in Cairo's public spaces. Later I corroborate the main findings using a survey. For now, these descriptive results portray the first dynamic picture needed.[42]

In the summing of the number of protest locations in Table (2.2),[43] I paid attention to spatial proximity of the locations listed in the reports. For example I coded National Democratic Party (NDP) headquarters, Egyptian National Museum and Tahrir Square as one location, as the crowds in these places were often contiguous. Protest dispersion can be defined as the number of locations in Cairo where protests were happening each day. Maximum dispersion from the reports is eight major locations, while sometimes the only major gathering was reported from Tahrir.

The proliferation of protests on January 28 was simultaneous with an abrupt and ubiquitous disruption of all communication in Cairo and other parts of Egypt. A log of state interruptions of media and cell coverage is included in Table (2.1).[44] It is important to note that while the regime was experimenting with cursory blockages of social media

---

[41] In the reconstruction of the events, and for identifying the location of the protests, I used graphic designs from the *New York Times* in addition to the accounts from the Lede blog. These designs facilitate a dynamic view of protest proliferation through the 18 days of the unrest, in the first order of precision.

[42] Protests, as massive contentious events, are often diffuse and ephemeral. Neither a single observer, nor a team of a handful of reporters can capture the whole picture in every corner of a city. In such a situation, a steady reporting style and a fixed number of reporters in Cairo ensures a uniform *sampling* of the unrest across the city. Because the parameter of interest is the increase or decrease in the dispersion of protests and the absolute value of dispersion is not central to the analysis, as long as the number of reporters and their distribution across the unit of study, i.e. the city of Cairo, is constant and uniform during the course of the unrest, the differences in dispersion are efficiently captured using the reports from the same team. However, it is plausible to assume that the numbers and the distribution of reporters are correlated with the level of unrest; more coverage is expected when the protests endure and spread. Nevertheless, Friday the 28th was the beginning of the universal unrest in Egypt El-Ghobashy (2011); Shehata et al. (2011), three days after the mere beginning of the movement. Hence it is unlikely for the mechanism for reporting on the dispersion measure on the 28th to be drastically different from the days immediately before or after the 28th.

[43] Source: Bloch et al. (2011) and Mackey (2011).

[44] For reconstructing different stages of media disruption I have used online information from Egyptian bloggers (sources are Ramy Raoof, Egyptian Activist and blogger, Alix Dunn, blogger and Renesys.com) and coded the data after cross-checks with Al Jazeera reports.

TABLE 2.2. *Main protest locations in Cairo, January 25–February 11*

Date	Dispersion: Protest Locations
January 25	1: Tahrir
January 26	1: Tahrir
January 27	1: Tahrir
January 28 Friday	8: Tahrir–NDP headquarters-Egyptian National Museum/Kasr al-Nil bridge/6 October bridge/TV headquarters/Al Azhar Mosque/Mohandeseen/Mustafa Mahmoud Mosque/l–Istiqama Mosque
January 29	4: Tahrir–NDP headquarters-Egyptian National Museum/Interior Ministry/Corniche al-Nil/Abu Zaabal
January 30	3: Tahrir/Heliopolis/Abu Zaabal
January 31	3: Tahrir/Mohandeseen/Arkadia Shopping Center
February 1	2: Tahrir/Kasr al-Nil bridge
February 2	3: Tahrir–Egyptian National Museum/Mohandeseen/Corniche al-Nil
February 3	1: Tahrir–Egyptian National Museum
February 4 Friday	1: Tahrir–Egyptian National Museum
February 5	1: Tahrir–Egyptian National Museum
February 6	1: Tahrir–Egyptian National Museum
February 7	1: Tahrir–Mugamma
February 8	2: Tahrir/Egyptian Parliament
February 9	4: Tahrir/Zamalek/Ministry of Health–Egyptian Parliament/Dokki (organized labor protests)
February 10	4: Tahrir/TV headquarters/Egyptian Parliament/Abdin Palace
February 11 Friday	5: Tahrir/TV headquarters/Presidential Palace/Mustafa Mahmoud Mosque/Egyptian Parliament

websites, the major and far reaching disruptions in the SMS system, the Internet and mobile communications did not happen till the late hours of January 27 and early on January 28. The most acute phase of operations was less than fourteen hours, from 10 p.m. on January 27 to 1:30 p.m. local time on January 28.

In Figure (2.3) the disruption of the Internet is depicted vis a vis the dispersion of the protests. The dispersion rates were clearly high when the disruption was effective between early January 28 and midday February 2.

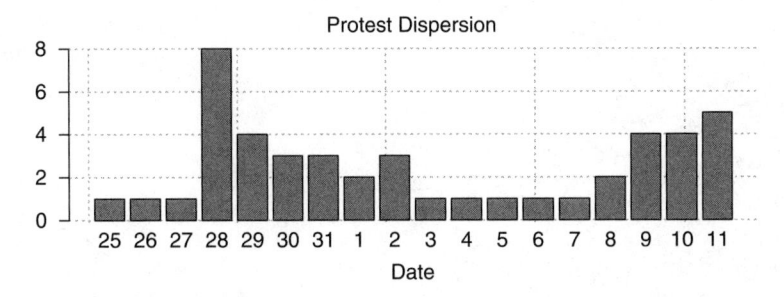

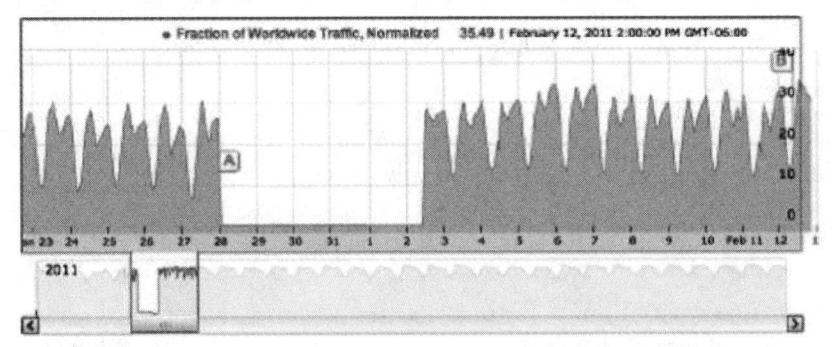

FIGURE 2.3. Top: protest dispersion (number of distinct protest locations according to Table 2.2). Bottom: all Google products, Egypt traffic, from http://bit.ly/h3Q1FZ.

Later I will argue, in detail, that this increase in the dispersion of protests in Cairo cannot be solely attributed to government operations, blockades around Tahrir or to Friday prayers around the city. I call the proposition the *Dispersion Hypothesis*: that a sudden shutdown of all communications decentralizes collective risk taking in a spatial domain.[45] Furthermore, later in this chapter I show that the clear decentralization of protests is confirmed in the results of a survey conducted with hundreds of Cairo respondents. The dynamics of protests extracted from the survey, point to a clear process of decentralization driven by the need to gain information from the closest in one's social network. Many of the active protesters reported turning to friends and family to gain news in the

---

[45] If the dynamics of collective action cascades from the periphery is different from one originating from the center, then the differences between the end result of the two contentious processes, in this specific case study, can open a pathway into studying mobilization processes away from the center.

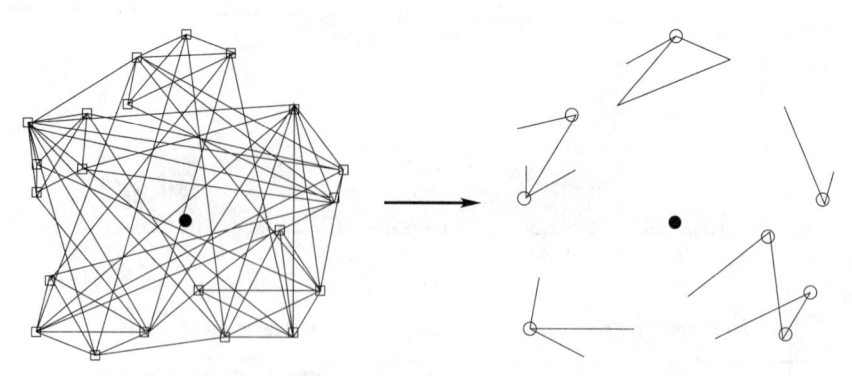

FIGURE 2.4. Fully connected → Local sparse graphs.

absence of regular outlets. Figure (2.4) shows the typography of the decentralization process. Many locally centered networks of exchange were shaped, in which a new peripheral vanguard rose to prominence. The result was a dynamic process very different from the regularly connected situation.

It is necessary to note the convergence processes that worked on the first day of the protests on January 25 and were absent on the 28th. Later, I detail a sequence of mass emails, sent by the April 6 Youth Movement, which shaped and reported on these processes on the first day of the unrest.

A simple test using an Ordinary Least Squares (OLS) regression further demonstrates the effect of the disruption, and the insignificance of "the Friday holiday", as well as motivational announcements from centralized media. Consider the following linear model.

The regression model in equation (2.1) gauges the effect of media disruption, on daily differences in protest dispersion in Cairo,

$$\Delta \text{Dispersion}(t) = \text{Dispersion}(t) - \text{Dispersion}(t-1),$$

controlling for Fridays and major media announcements, inter alia. The dependent variable's being a daily difference in dispersion helps mitigating the influence of background conditions that are fixed during the events.

$$\Delta \text{Dispersion}(t) = a + b_0 \Delta \text{Dispersion}(t-1) + b_1 \text{Disruption1}(t)$$
$$+ b_2 \text{Friday}(t) + b_3 \text{Announcement}(t) + \epsilon \quad (2.1)$$

This model accounts for the effect of disruption, coded as one dummy on the 28th, and zero elsewhere. January 28 was the first day of blanket disruption and the only day in which cell phone communications, Internet

TABLE 2.3. *Protest dispersion in Cairo, OLS of ΔDispersion over ΔDispersion on the previous day, treatment (disruption dummy on January 28 and zero otherwise), controlling for Fridays, and announcements*

	Estimate	Std. Error	t value	Pr(> |t|)
(Intercept)	−0.08333	0.37411	−0.223	0.82719
ΔDispersion($t-1$)	−0.31250	0.16199	−1.929	0.07584*
Disruption1	6.85417	1.85882	3.687	0.00274**
Friday	0.22917	1.27896	0.179	0.86056
Announcement	0.04167	0.89708	0.046	0.96366

Signif. codes: 0 *** 0.001 ** 0.01 * 0.05 . 0.1   1
Residual standard error: 1.296 on 13 degrees of freedom
Multiple R-squared: 0.7187, Adjusted R-squared: 0.6321
F-statistic: 8.303 on 4 and 13 DF, p-value: 0.001491

services, SMS and occasionally landlines were unavailable, see Table (2.1). Lack of cell phone coverage is more far reaching among the population than the absence of the Internet. In January 2011, there were 23.51 million Internet users compared to 71.46 million mobile subscribers.[46] Hence compared to Internet outage, any disruption in mobile communications directly implicates a much larger portion of the Egyptian population. Also mobile phones are a more effective means of communication on the fly during protests in the streets. On the other hand, Internet disruption complicates longer term planning and organization. Cutting cell coverage had an immediate impact on personal communication in the streets. Considering these issues and the fact that dismantling the Egyptian online network came as a surprise during the very first day of the outage, I code the treatment (Disruption1) as a dummy, 1 on the 28th and 0 otherwise.

To account for the correlation between successive time units in the time series analysis,[47] I include the dispersion differences at the previous time, i.e. ΔDispersion($t-1$), as an independent variable. The results are included in Table (2.3).

The effect of the change in dispersion in the previous day, ΔDispersion($t-1$), is small and is not statistically significant.[48] On

[46] There were 23.51 million Internet users (30 percent penetration), 71.46 million mobile subscribers (90 percent penetration) in January 2011. Source: the report by Egypt's Ministry of Communications and Information Technology at http://slidesha.re/mtrPuM.
[47] Douglas A. Hibbs (1974).
[48] As a robustness check, similar results are obtained when ΔDispersion($t-2$) and ΔDispersion($t-3$) are included alongside with ΔDispersion($t-1$).

the other hand, the coefficients show that based on the model the disruption on the 28th had a highly significant influence on the change in dispersion levels. None of the controls are either comparable or statistically significant. Controls include a dummy for Fridays (January 28, February 4, 11). Controlling for Fridays is necessary because Friday is the Muslim weekly holiday, in which more people have the time and latitude for demonstration. Friday prayers can also act as focal events. The second parameter is a tally of national announcements. Announcements are included as a control for the influence of mainstream media. Whenever there is a national address by the heads of the Egyptian state or the opposition, the control dummy is coded as one. The list of major developments during the 18-day Egyptian Revolution of 2011, and a list of major state announcements are included in the appendix.

I also consider an extended version of the disruption variable, where disruption is coded over the five-day span of January 28–February 1, and the dependent variable is dispersion itself. The results are similar, and point to the influence of the blackout on the decentralization of the protests.[49]

The results provide a first order demonstration of the decentralization effect that the *Dispersion Hypothesis* predicts. Now, if a massive social network is re-seeded with smaller and more peripheral rebellious cells, the dynamics of collective risk taking in the society changes.

---

[49] Implementing variations of the model above yields similar results. Consider the following simpler linear model

$$\Delta \text{Dispersion}(t) = a + b_1 \text{Disruption1}(t) + b_2 \text{Friday}(t) + b_3 \text{Announcement}(t) + \epsilon \quad (2.2)$$

Results are included below. Disruption had a significant influence on the change in levels of dispersion, having Fridays and announcements included.

	Estimate	Std. Error	t value	Pr(> |t|)
(Intercept)	−0.08333	0.40886	−0.204	0.84143
Disruption1	5.91667	1.96080	3.017	0.00923**
Friday	1.16667	1.29291	0.902	0.38213
Announcement	−0.58333	0.91423	−0.638	0.53373

Signif. codes: 0 *** 0.001 ** 0.01 * 0.05 . 0.1 1
Residual standard error: 1.416 on 14 degrees of freedom
Multiple R-squared: 0.6382, Adjusted R-squared: 0.5606
F-statistic: 8.23 on 3 and 14 DF, p-value: 0.002109

Protest Dispersion in Cairo, OLS of ΔDispersion over treatment (disruption dummy on 28th and zero otherwise), controlling for Fridays, and announcements.

WHAT ELSE COULD HAVE CAUSED THE DECENTRALIZATION? A DISCUSSION

A number of confounding factors could have simultaneously increased the dispersion of the protests on the 28th. Two of them are Friday prayers and police limitations on citizen movements. On that Friday, mosques acted as local gathering points. Nevertheless, without the population's *prior* decision to engage in protests and to congregate in their neighborhoods, Friday prayers could not account for participation levels and the dispersion seen on the 28th.[50] Protesters did not take part in public demonstrations simply because they were all outside for Friday prayers and then they decided to protest. They were attracted to local focal points including mosques *after* venturing into public places. On the 28th many were motivated by a heightened sense of urgency on that specific day, a similar increase in dispersion did not happen on the

> In addition to the regression results based on daily changes in protest dispersion, I also code the disruption across the five-day period of January 28 to February 1. Taking the comparative penetration of mobile devices and the Internet into account, I implement the treatment vector [3 1 1 1 1], based on the comparative levels of Internet and cell phone penetration in Egypt. Even with the new coding, the impact of the disruption on protest dispersion is large and statistically significant. In this case, the dependent variable is the dispersion itself, not the daily differences.
>
> $$\text{Dispersion}(t) = a + b_1 \text{Disruption2}(t) + b_2 \text{Friday}(t) + b_3 \text{Announcement}(t) + \epsilon \quad (2.3)$$
>
> The results are included below for comparison.
>
> | | Estimate | Std. Error | t value | Pr(> \|t\|) |
> |-------------|----------|------------|---------|-------------|
> | (Intercept) | 1.2845 | 0.3980 | 3.227 | 0.006083** |
> | Disruption2 | 1.8223 | 0.4328 | 4.210 | 0.000873*** |
> | Friday | 0.6526 | 0.9048 | 0.721 | 0.482635 |
> | Announcement| 1.3610 | 0.6818 | 1.996 | 0.065752* |
>
> Signif. codes: 0 *** 0.001 ** 0.01 * 0.05 . 0.1 1
> Residual standard error: 1.205 on 14 degrees of freedom
> Multiple R-squared: 0.6746, Adjusted R-squared: 0.6049
> F-statistic: 9.676 on 3 and 14 DF, p-value: 0.001025
>
> Protest Dispersion in Cairo, OLS of Dispersion over treatment (disruption dummies on 28th to 1st [3 1 1 1 1] and zero otherwise), controlling for Fridays, and announcements. The impact of social media and mobile communication disruption is positive and statistically significant.

[50] One of the interviewees noted that "many irreligious protesters were at mosques, because of the protests" *Cairo Protest Dataset* (2012).

following Fridays, February 4 and 11. The regression analysis above does not show any significance for the Friday temporal variable.

The police also tried to block the passages to Tahrir on adjacent bridges on the Nile. For example clashes on the Kasr al-Nil and 6 October bridges were well documented. However, even after accounting for police activities, i.e. taking the clashes on the aforementioned two bridges to be parts of an extended protest in Tahrir, similar results hold. Changing the dispersion on the 28th from eight to six does not drastically alter the regression results. It is important to note that on the 25th police operations to block the passage to Tahrir were similar to the 28th;[51] however, the end results of the convergence processes were centralized in one, and highly dispersed in the other.

Furthermore to show that the government disrupted the media in anticipation of a major increase in the size and dispersion of the protests,[52] or that the closing down of the media was simply a byproduct of the escalating unrest, one should demonstrate that if the increasing dispersion was a result of the deteriorating power of the incumbent, similar outcomes should have occurred in the days following the disruption when the incumbent was progressively becoming weaker, i.e. the proliferation process should have continued, because similar contextual conditions existed immediately after the 28th. However, such a sharp proliferation never happened again during the course of the protests, in spite of media restoration and the enduring contention in Tahrir, even when the numbers in Tahrir were unprecedented and upon the return of the Internet on February 2.

The regime did not disrupt the Internet and mobile communications in the anticipation of an increase in the *dispersion* of the protests. The size and dispersion of the protests are not directly correlated. As can be seen in the results of the survey presented below, the size of the protests grew as they became more concentrated in Tahrir Square. The Mubarak regime's response to the growing threat of protests was not directed at their *dispersion* per se.[53]

---

[51] The similarity was also reported in El-Ghobashy (2011).
[52] Namely, the endogeneity concern.
[53] During the unrest in Cairo disrupting the media charged the population and overwhelmed the authorities; however, there are conditions under which such disruptions may not be as mobilizing. There are multiple cases of failed rebellion during which access to the social media was highly restricted, e.g. the post-election unrest in Iran 2009. At the height of the protests in Tehran in June 2009, mobile communication was cut off and press reporters were banned. Opposition leaders' communication with the outside world was very limited. In spite of limited access to social media at the time of the unrest, there

There is one intriguing connection between the vague language of the mobilizational email sent for the "Friday of Rage" (February 28) protests, and the theory behind the dynamics of mobilization from the periphery. Some of the organizers, perhaps sensing the possibility of a preplanned governmental confrontation, had given up hopes for administering protests on that day. The mobilization email (see Figure (7.8)), sent a few hours before that defining day, reads: "We will come out [to the public space] from all alleys and streets and squares in all regions and governorates, for demanding our rights."

HOURLY UPDATES FROM THE "OPERATIONS ROOM"

Two defining days of the 2011 Egyptian Revolution, January 25 and 28 were starkly different in terms of mobilization dynamics. The first day of unrest was the culmination of an orchestrated campaign of online mobilization. Interestingly enough, the online logging of the events of the 25th continued throughout the day, a fact that I will use in the following to reconstructe the rapid convergence of the human flow in the Egyptian streets into main streets and squares, in particular the main square in the Egyptian capital, Tahrir. The same reporting and coordination processes were absent on the 28th. The vanguard who were well connected and highly informed about the process on the 25th, were left to their own wit. The social network was seeded differently, and the end result of the collective action process was different.

The climax of collective fervor on January 25, itself came after a long period of dormant grief and aspiration. In early 2011 a wave of political unrest swept Egypt. Riled by the torture and killing of *Khaled Said*, one victim among many others, and encouraged by the success of a recent uprising in Tunisia,[54] a number of Egyptian opposition groups seized on

---

was never a blanket interruption, but limitations were targeted, local and temporary. In such situations, a slow flow of supervised communication is allowed – as a shadow of the routine and the status quo; on the other hand, face to face means of mobilization are actively disrupted.

54 Compare to Tilly's (1978) idea of *opportunity structure*: the Tunisian uprising started after self-immolation of the Tunisian street vendor, Mohamed Bouazizi. In turn, the movement in Egypt became an inspiration for resurrections in Libya and Syria in the same geographical and social sphere. Elements of spatial diffusion between these Arab nations are clear. The proliferation is akin to the diffusion of "Nationalist mobilization" after the collapse of the Eastern Bloc Beissinger (2002).

the momentum and called for protests on January 25, ironically enough a national holiday to commemorate the Egyptian police forces.[55]

Using a unique trove of email communications on the approximate location of the protests during the 18 days of the protests, here I redraw the path of the Cairo demonstrations particularly on January 25 and 28. Outside observers are often squarely focused on the most central theater of the revolution;[56] however, Tahrir was hardly the only place where massive demonstrations of public defiance occurred in Cairo. The convergence of human flows on Tahrir and the emergence of a singular axis of collective action was not planned either.

In the anticipation of upcoming protests, the April 6 Youth Movement itself called for a protest, 10 days before the start of the main phase of the clashes, on January 15, in front of the Tunisian embassy in Cairo, to show solidarity with the Tunisian uprising.[57] During the days leading up to the defining moment of January 25, the group started an online campaign of mobilization to energize its activist base, and to coordinate with other groups for proposing a number of demands as a part of a universal call to protests.[58]

The locations set for the protests of the 25th in Cairo were "1. The Arab League Street 2. Shubra Square 3. Matarria Square 4. Cairo University." Nowhere was Tahrir mentioned as a destination for protesters, or the point of convergence of any kind. In the same announcement one can see that in addition to Cairo, protests were organized in the governorates of "1. al Mansurah 2. Alexandria 3. Suez 4. El Esmaila 5. Kafar Shaykh 6. Asyut 7. Port Said 8. Demiatte", see Figure (2.2).

---

[55] On that day, similar protests took place in other Egyptian cities including Alexandria and Port Said, as well as satellite urban sprawls of Cairo and Alexandria (in Mahallah). See the April 6 Youth Movement announcement email sent on January 22, 2011. The book's online appendix contains the snapshots of several emails at https://goo.gl/EERpPC.
[56] See Alexander (2011) portraying the Egyptian Revolution as a spectacle in Tahrir.
[57] *April 6th Youth Movement, Email Collection* (2012).
[58] The April 6 Movement's namesake was a major labor demonstration in Mahalla Kobra, a working class neighborhood in the Nile Delta, on April 6, 2008. In the initial call for protests on January 25 the group emphasized four demands: "1. raising the minimum wage to 1200 Egyptian Guinea (approximately $160 in January 2015) 2. Adjusting wages to prices 3. The abolition of the State of Emergency in the country (at the time in place continuously since 1981) 4. dismissal of Habib el-Adly (the Interior Minister at the time) and the trial of military officers who have committed crimes against the Egyptian people." For a snapshot of April 6's mobilization email, sent on January 22, 2011, see Figure (7.1) in the appendix.

Closer to the designated date, January 25, "the operations room" reported the assignment of organizing groups to each neighborhood in Cairo and other Egyptian governorates, see Figure (7.2). The point of congregation is reported to be Mustafa Mahmoud, not Tahrir. There is no mention of Tahrir in the pertinent email.[59]

Thousands of pamphlets were distributed in the days preceding the planned demonstrations. In the anticipation of sizable protests on January 25, April 6 activists distributed tens of thousands of pamphlets calling for protest on police day on the 25th. More than 10,000 of these pamphlets were distributed in Cairo, "thrown down from main bridges, distributed in crowded areas, and in front of universities and in cars and key public places". The activist group announced that it had succeeded in distributing 30,000 more pamphlets across the country, and 15,000 in the city of Cairo alone.[60]

The description of the operations room starts to emerge a day before the 25th. A number of designated phone numbers were distributed in mass emails. In other words, on the 25th, when operational, a central source of information, operations room, coordinated the available information, at least among the hundreds of core receivers of the email announcements. A few hours before the start of the protests, at 2 p.m., an announcement was sent out regarding phone numbers that would be emailed in order to *coordinate* the protests and to report any abuses by the security forces.[61]

---

[59] The locations and the assigned groups to each of these locations were as follows: 1. Arab League (April 6, El-Baradei campaign, Justice and Freedom, the El-Bradei Support Association, AlGad, AlKerama, the Front et al.); 2. Shubra (Hashad and Kefaya groups); 3. the High Court (People's Parliament) and Bar Association (lawyers), note the change from Matariya Sq., Doctors' Syndicate in Daar ul Hokama; and finally 4. Cairo University. There is also a mention of workers mobilizing in downtown Cairo, but the names of their groups are not divulged. Similarly, there is a list of locations in governorates of Al-Mansura, Alexandria, Asyut, Al Gharbiya, Al Ismailia and Al Fayum. See Figure (7.2) in the appendix. Other groups not mentioned in this email, but extracted from witness accounts, and interviews with protesters are: National Association for Change, Ultras (Ahlawy and Zamalek), Wafd, Muslim Brotherhood Youth (MB leadership did not take part), Mahalla textile workers and "We Are All Khaled Said".

[60] The email from January 21 reports on distributions in "Bulaq, Heram, Shubra, Ma'adi, Imbaba, Sayda Zeynab, Sayde Nafise, Ramsess Sq., Sayida Aisha among other places". There are mentions of help from El-Baradei campaign as well. Distribution also in universities in Cairo, Ain Shams and Al Azhar universities.
See Figures (7.3) and (7.4) in the appendix, for a snapshot of the email announcement.

[61] Figure (7.5), in the appendix, is a snapshot of an email coordinating the information regarding the operations room. Such sources of public information were severely limited three days later during the complete shutdown of communication media across Egypt.

The same operations room sent out updates via email on the 25th, starting from just before 2 p.m. on an hourly basis till 7 p.m. sending messages parsed with time tags. The audience of these emails were at least hundreds of activists directly receiving the emails from the central command in the operations room. The hourly updates show that on the 25th, the protesters, as planned, started congregating in central squares and major streets starting at about 2 p.m..

The emails depict a fast moving escalation between 2 and 4 p.m. from many neighborhoods of Cairo and other Egyptian cities. The police forces repeatedly tried to counter the movements of the protesters. Many times the governmental sieges were broken and the determined population continued toward their final destinations. Arrests, at times of the leaders of the crowds, were constant during this time period.

The organizers, and the members of the "operations room", informed the multiple hundreds of others on the mailing list, and those who could be reached via phone, about the convergence on Tahrir and other areas. By 4 p.m. when the extent of the protests and the severity of unrest became clear, the regime started manipulating the organizers' means of communication as well as citizen access to electricity and communication in certain areas. For example, at 5 p.m. it was reported that cell communication was disrupted and access to Twitter blocked in Tahrir. The activists found workarounds: instead of calling they promised emailing.[62]

Similar patterns of disorder continued till the 28th, when, in an utter shock to the population,[63] *all* connectivity in the country was disrupted in the early morning hours.

Soon after 2 p.m. on January 25, reports of fast spreading contention were being announced from the operations room. There were announcements of thousands of demonstrators amassing in Cairo and other Egyptian cities.[64] Tahrir starts to figure prominently in the reports after 3:45 p.m. For two hours, the hourly reports, parsed by time tags, at times just a few minutes apart, depict the fierce skirmish between security forces and thousands of demonstrators in and around the square and other public spaces in Cairo, Alexandria and Suez. From the reports, it is possible to discern the height of the clashes to be between 4 and 6 p.m.

---

[62] See Figures (7.6) and (7.7) in the appendix.
[63] I will include more on the population reactions to the blackout in the following description of the Cairo protest survey.
[64] Email reports included in the appendix.

The tug of war between large crowds and the police spread around Tahrir, targeting the headquarters of the state party NDP around the square. In addition to a physical standoff, several mass arrests were made.

Tahrir is mentioned once at the start of the communication chain, but gradually becomes a more frequent term in the emails. By 5 p.m. it was obvious that many in Cairo were attempting to reach Tahrir; a similar convergence mechanism via communication channels did not exist on the 28th. On the 25th, on the other hand, premeditation and targeted reporting among the vanguard was the norm. Images of minute by minute reports from Cairo and elsewhere on January 25 and transcripts of the emails are included in the appendix.[65]

The unprecedented and surprising dimensions of the unrest on the 25th encouraged further contention and a call for a "Friday of Rage" on the 28th across the country. The last call on the 27th asks the audience to come out in "all and each direction and corner of the country". There is no planned location or path, see Figure (7.8). The contrast between the barrage of the email updates on the protests on the 25th, and the radio silence on the 28th meant mobilization did not happen the same way in the two days. Nothing similar to the coordination mechanism during the first day existed on the 28th. In the absence of digital communications, decentralization became the theme of the Friday of Rage and its ubiquitous contentious process. Processes of convergence operated globally on the 25th, but locally on the 28th. On the 28th, all were left to their own pondering, erratic landlines and local connections – often face to face. In contrast, the demonstrations proliferated to every corner of Cairo when there existed no tools of fast communication, no email or social media tools for organization. Transient flows of contention congealed in local focal points. The details of such processes can be gleaned from the results of the survey I outline in the following.

LOCAL INFLUENCE AND COLLECTIVE ACTION: A SURVEY OF PROTEST PARTICIPATION IN CAIRO

In 1945, New York's newspaper industry, eight major dailies to be exact, ceased to operate, starting a strike stretching for two weeks. The psychological effects on the population were stark. Those interviewed

---

[65] See Figures (7.9) (4 p.m.), (7.10) (5 p.m.), (7.11) (6 p.m.), (7.12) (7 p.m.) in the appendix. On the 25th, the operations room sent out these emails on an hourly basis.

shortly after the event, expressed considerable grief and distress.[66] The daily function of news media, their ability to inform and sustain a flow of public information, on the psychological level, played an important stabilizing role. Interestingly enough, a similar study on the consequences of a 23-day hiatus in phone services in a 300 block area of Manhattan, following a fire in a switching center in 1975, shows similar levels of distress among the interviewees. The complaints are about psychological discomfort, losing the security of everyday control over one's means of news and arrangement.[67] The situation is not dissimilar to what occurred in Egypt in the early hours of January 28, 2011: the trauma of the situation, acts as a temporal placeholder, clearly delineating the different stage of the 18-day conflict for its main audience, the Egyptians, involved, drawn to or consciously withdrawn from the clashes happening in their country since three days before.

I used the same psychological placeholders in search for further evidence for the *Dispersion Hypothesis*. I administered a survey of a total of 908 subjects in face to face and online interviews, which used the stark changes in communication media as tools for separating four stages of the Egyptian Revolution in January 2011. A total of 523 respondents in 15 Cairo neighborhoods were asked about their protest activity during the 18-day conflict in early 2011 in personal interviews. After filtering the online responses from outside Cairo, I outline the results of 740 survey responses based on a convenience sample in the city. Answers on protest participation, in four distinct phases of the conflict, provide a *dynamic* of the Egyptian Revolution, in which I can see the ebbs and flows of the rates of participation. Furthermore, by distinguishing *participation in the protests*, from *going to Tahrir* I can measure a first order *dispersion* level for the protests in each of these four distinct periods of the protests. Given the focal status of Tahrir during the contention, if many participated in the protests, but few went to Tahrir, then the dispersion levels were high; if many participated and all went to Tahrir then the dispersion levels of the protests were low. The difference between levels of participation and presence in Tahrir gives a parameter for observing the levels of dispersion before, during and after the media blackout in Cairo.

I will demonstrate that there are two main findings: first, that in line with the descriptive evidence outlined above, the survey responses do

---

[66] See the pioneering study of Berelson (1949).
[67] See Wurtzel and Turner (1977). Also another use of information vacuum as a research tool in relation to local electoral politics is found in Mondak (1995).

show an increase in the dispersion of the protests during the information blackout. Furthermore, and more importantly, *the vanguard*, those who participated in the first phase of the revolution, reported dispersion levels that are on the same level before the blackout (during the first phase of the protests) as those during the blackout. This has significant implications for the *leading from the periphery* paradigm: in Cairo, the surprising dynamics of the 25th and 28th were partly driven by the vanguard who were more spread out in the city, than the average protester who, in contrast, was primarily attracted to Tahrir. The dynamics of such processes are different from the well studied dynamics of collective action led from the center.[68]

Along the same lines, a growing body of evidence shows that mass mobilization during short periods of urban unrest largely operate on the local level[69] instead of globally coordinated massive acts of contention. In the Cairo survey, too, an analysis of the dynamics of news communication in relation to protest activity provides evidence for the importance of local interactions for protest mobilization. The results emphasize the singular component of personalized communication: the possibility of interaction in real time with those who are physically present in a tangible act of protest, something that is impossible with centralized outlets, either because of latency, or physical distance. Communications on the fly provide a flexibility in action absent in centralized communication. News communication, on the other hand, informs about the global prospects of a movement and the overall condition of contention. Personal means of communication facilitate action in more transient and pedestrian settings: knowing of one's friends' location, or an attempt to find such information can be conducive to action on par with cognizance of the movement's ultimate goals.

In the absence of strong organization and control[70] from the type characteristic of protracted insurgency, local patterns of diffusion and organization become as important as the global prospects of success or failure. One's decision making in such situations is locally conditioned.

---

[68] Another recurrent observation in almost all of the regression models is a strong connection between protest activity and local news consumption. The blackout motivated face to face interactions. Those seeking news turned to their friends and family *Cairo Protest Dataset* (2012).

[69] See Beissinger (2013).

[70] Bennett and Segerberg (2013) outline a theory of collective action based on weak and decentralized connections, in contrast to theories of collective action in strongly connected networks. In their terms term these are "connective actions".

If, during the blackout, local interactions were central to mobilization during the Egyptian uprising, then gaining news from one's friends and acquaintances should be positively and significantly connected to participation in protests. If the local processes were not important, then one should not see a significant correlation between interactions with one's close circle of friends and family, and participation in protests. I will show that the data confirm the former: local news consumption was tied to high protest activity. Participants who received information from their friends and acquaintances were more likely to engage in the protests. The significance of local interactions in gaining information is in line with the high dispersion of the vanguard activity during the early phases of the rebellion, which is also reflected in the survey data.

I also find that among the subjects of the study, the *steadfast protesters*, i.e. those participating in all of the four stages of the 18-day protests, overwhelmingly described the complete communication shutdown of January 28 as a catalyst of rebellion. *Nonparticipants*, those who never ventured onto the streets, on the other hand, ascribed a negative effect to the blackout in relation to mobilization.[71] Removal of means of communication should have resulted in a deflation of contentious activity based on coordination – an aim of the regime to be exact – but those who most actively took part deny such a consequence, and report an opposite effect. It is likely that those who caused the blackout to diffuse the protests were of the same opinion as the *nonparticipants*.

> you ended up with a bunch of curious morons ... who don't give a damn about the cause, going down to the streets to see what was going on, and they just ended up being part of it, [the blackout] diluted the people who were actually dedicated to the cause, and turned this revolution into one big joke.
>
> Remarks by online survey respondent # 97[72]

The survey was conducted by a team of research assistants in Cairo and administered locally by a head research assistant. The subjects were asked about their protest activity the approximate location of their protest activity, and their methods for gaining news.[73]

---

[71] Finally, those who took the survey online were more likely than the face to face respondents to portray the disruption as a catalyst to rebellion. All these differences are statistically significant.

[72] *Cairo Protest Dataset* (2012), verbatim translation from Arabic by interviewers. See the online appendix for the scans of all printed survey responses.

[73] For each time period, respondents were asked to choose their news sources among state media, satellite and private television, e.g. Al Jazeera, newspapers, e.g. *Al Masry*

In addition to the interviews conducted across the Egyptian capital, an online version of the survey was advertised over Cairo-based mailing lists and social media websites. Face to face surveys were conducted in Arabic, while online questionnaires were both in English and Arabic. Between April and June 2012, a total of 908 subjects participated in the survey. In total, 523 respondents in 15 Cairo neighborhoods[74] took part in the survey in person; simultaneously 385 respondents took the survey online. The subjects were approached in public spaces, the questions were asked in person or the participants were given printed questionnaires to fillout. After filtering online respondents from outside Cairo, 740 responses were used in the analysis, including 523 in person interviews.[75]

Al Youm, and the Internet (when available), e.g. Facebook, Twitter, blogs and finally contacts with their friends and acquaintances, as well as alternative modes of communication not mentioned in the list. The name of Al Jazeera was explicitly included in the option on satellite and private television networks. Respondents could choose more than one source of information if necessary, and they were allowed to enter general remarks. The classification of news sources in the questionnaire was based on the nature of associated social networks underlying the news propagation. For example, local networks of friends and acquaintances are different from television networks – either state or private. Consider the utility of a highly visible Facebook page, such as "We Are All Khaled Said" which is different from email communications among a group of local friends. Both can be classified as "Internet", but the news communication networks they induce are different. Later I examine the significance of the interaction terms between several independent variables, e.g. *Internet usage* and *news communication among friends and acquaintances*. The statistical significance or insignificance of some of the interaction terms vis a vis the others provides a tool for process tracing (Kam and Franzese 2007).

[74] Nasr city, Heliopolis, Ain Shams University campus, Mohandeseen, Dokki, Zamalek, Agouza, Giza, October 6, Cairo University, Wrraq, Embaba, Sakkia, Sawy Cultural Wheel and the AUC campus. See Figure (7.13) in the appendix for a map of surveying locations.

[75] Our convenience sampling strategy lies between the static sampling of households, and surveying only among the protesters (in Tahrir and other main protest sites) (Beissinger et al. 2012; Tufekci and Wilson 2012). In between surveying the protesters in the focal scenes of contention, e.g. Tahrir and surroundings and randomized sampling, we opted for an intermediate strategy for covering a variety of locations frequented by protesters as well as nonparticipants in order to achieve a sample with sufficient variation in responses. Sampling at specific locations for the purpose of protest research, see Muller and Opp (1986), while not perfect, reflects the nonuniform and heterogeneous nature of collective risk taking among the population. For example, surveying protesters only in Tahrir overlooks the fact that protesters in other neighborhoods may have shown dissimilar protest behavior, or a fully uniform spatial sampling ignores the fact that protesters are often concentrated in certain public locations and uniform random sampling underrepresents the participant minority. To validate the sampling strategy, I use comparisons between media consumption statistics and participation dynamics from the survey and those in the existing literature to argue that the sample in this study shows regularities in control data that are similar to those in the other existing surveys.

The respondents were asked about their protest activity and news consumption behavior in four distinct phases demarcated by changes in media availability: January 25–27 (before the blackout), January 28 (the first day of the blackout with no cellphone and no Internet), January 29–February 1 (Internet shutdown, cellphones operating) and the final phase till February 11 after the return of both the Internet and cell communications. The memorability and trauma associated with the disruption of mass communications across Cairo helped the respondents to remember their activities at each phase of the unrest. The results of the survey confirm that the disruption of media and cell communication on the 28th was a major shock to Egyptians and left strong memories of anger, fear and anxiety; hence, the survey research strategy effectively captures the event dynamics.[76]

The respondents were also asked about their first reaction to the blackout on January 28. The sentiments expressed in the responses provide a window into the psychological processes that prompted participation or prevented action following the surprise. At the end the respondents were asked if the disruption was helpful to mobilization.[77]

SURVEY RESULTS I: VANGUARDS AT THE PERIPHERY ON THE 28TH, ... AND THE 25TH

The rate of the respondents who reported participating in the protests *outside* Tahrir was the highest on January 28. In other words, Tahrir was the least focal on the day of the blackout on January 28. The survey results confirm the dispersion analysis of protest locations in the above. Most importantly, *the vanguard*, defined as those participating in the first phase of the protests, January 25–27, were not as concentrated in Tahrir as the average protester. More importantly, during the first phase of protests, their rates of participation *outside* Tahrir were on par with

---

[76] A number of other studies examine the Egyptian protests in 2011 using survey data. Tufekci and Wilson (2012) conducted surveys on protesters around Tahrir Square itself. Beissinger et al. (2012) collected data on socioeconomic components as well as protest activity among Egyptians. Brym et al. (2014) used already existing data to study media consumption in relation to participation and finally Mourtada and Salem (2011) used an online survey to collect data on media consumption during the protests.

[77] See the Cairo survey dataset in the online appendix for a record of respondents' remarks on the blackout. Fear and anxiety are frequently cited. In addition to the scans of 500 filled questionnaires available at https://goo.gl/7keQ9O, the survey data are also available in the book's online appendix at https://goo.gl/S9Jm3e. Survey questions are included in the appendix.

Survey Results I

the rates of localization, i.e. participation levels outside Tahrir, on the day of the blackout, on January 28. See Figure (2.5).[78] The induced dynamics are different from those set in motion by centralized instigators.

A more detailed breakdown of participation statistics shows a bimodal pattern of participation frequency. Those who participated were likely to take part in action in the majority of the phases.[79]

---

[78] The initial spread of vanguards is key to the experimental explorations in Chapter (5).

[79] Table (7.1) shows the protest participation pattern among the survey participants. The rates of participation drastically rose on January 28, were sustained between January 29 and February 1 and steadily rose toward the end of the 18-day period. The rates are graphically reproduced in Figure (2.5), along with the reported rates of participation in Tahrir.

The dynamic trends in Table (7.1) in the appendix show that the overall rate of participation was increasing as time passed. For example, among participants the highest reported patterns are $(1,1,1,1)$, $(0,1,1,1)$, $(0,0,0,1)$, $(0,0,1,1)$ in that order, 1 in (ith position means participation in ith period) which clearly shows an upward trend of participation toward the defining events of February 11, 2011 among the participants.

Breakdown of protest frequency among 740 participants based on the frequency of their participation in the four periods (25–27, 28, 29–1, 3–11) below shows a bimodal distribution: the majority of the respondents were either steadfast protesters or nonparticipants. The distribution is skewed toward participation.

0	1	2	3	4
278	103	115	115	129

From 740 survey participants, 300 took part in the protests on January 28. The table below shows the protest profile of these 300 protesters in the following two periods: January 29–February 1 and February 3–February 11.

Note that the distribution of four possible outcomes is in line with a growing trend: only around 20 percent of the 28th protesters gave up on protesting, while approximately 64 percent reported continuous presence and 80 percent took part in the last and final phase.

The high rates of participation on January 28 mattered, because *stalwarts* Beissinger et al. (2012) did not revert from protesting in the streets after that day.

Total number	28	29–1	3–11	Percentage
191	✓	✓	✓	63.67
22	✓	✓	X	7.73
37	✓	X	X	12.33
50	✓	X	✓	16.67

Decentralization of Revolutionary Unrest

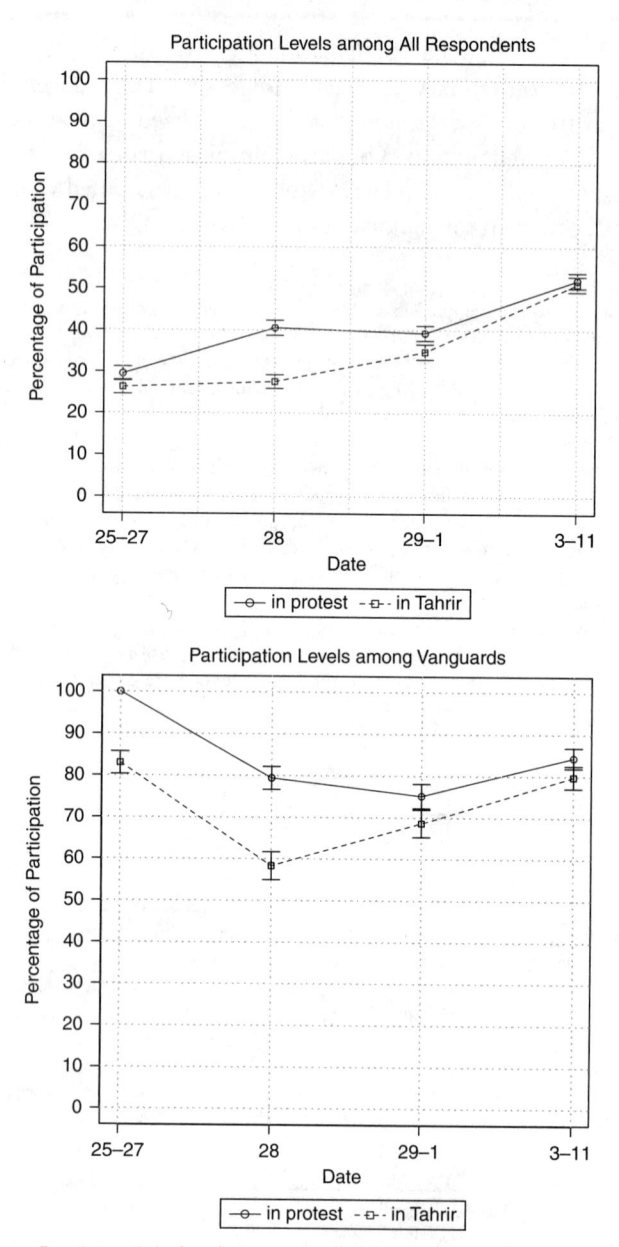

FIGURE 2.5. Participation levels among all survey respondents (top) and vanguards (bottom). Vanguards are defined as those who protested during the first phase of the protests January 25–27. Note the largest gap on the 28th (highest dispersion on the 28th) $N = 740$ for the top figure, and that the vanguard were as dispersed during the first phase of the protests as they were on the 28th, $N = 218$ for the bottom figure. Compared to the average protester, the vanguard were more likely to have started away from Tahrir.

SURVEY RESULTS II: REVERSION TO NETWORK NEIGHBORS AND LOCALIZATION OF THE PROTESTS DURING THE BLACKOUT

From the reports on participation in protests in relation to going to Tahrir, it is clear that protests were decentralized on the 28th. One significant process in brining about such a transformation of contentious social network, I would like to argue, was turning to friends and acquaintances to gain news about the events. The agitators relied on their personal network, at times face to face connections, to learn about the ongoing events. As expected, the rates of using alternative and local media were the highest on January 28, when the Internet and cell phones were not available.

The vanguard, on average, relied on friends and acquaintances to gain news on protests, more often. Such local influence, in addition to decentralizing the contention, empowered a fragmented and transient leadership from the periphery. In the survey results, many mentioned using landlines to reach out to their family and acquaintances, while others reported learning firsthand about the protests from observing the events in streets – which directly translated to participation in the events. At the beginning they were unwilling to accept the risks of engaging with the protests.

The rates of alternative media usage conspicuously grew among the vanguard on January 28, but not among the nonparticipants. Finally, and as expected, rates of the usage of state media were steadily higher among the nonparticipants.[80]

In line with the observations above, 80.7 percent of the vanguard found the disruption as helpful to the uprising, while only 57.8 percent among the nonparticipants deemed the shutdown as a catalyst during the protests. In other words, nonparticipants' subjective views of

---

[80] Comparisons of media usage profiles between *the vanguard*, i.e. those who had protested between January 25 and 27, to that of nonparticipants, i.e. those who never protested, in Figure (7.15) reveal a number of patterns: nonparticipants used satellite and private television as a news source on protests more frequently; they also relied less frequently on alternative means of gaining news ("other" category). Figure (7.15) in the appendix shows the dynamics of media usage divided into multiple categories: *state media, satellite and private television and radio, newspapers, the Internet* and *news from friends and acquaintances* in three stages of the protests: the first time the respondent heard about the protests, on January 28 when mobile and Internet communications were fully disrupted, and between January 29 and February 1 when mobile communications were restored but the Internet was still dysfunctional. The respondents were allowed to choose more than one option, if necessary. Satellite and private media became increasingly popular as a news source about the protests after January 28.

decentralizing processes at work on January 28 were not as favorable as those of the vanguard.

The respondents were also asked about their first reaction to the blackout. The words *qazab*, *khouf* and *qalaq*, i.e. anger, fear and anxiety were common terms used to express their feelings immediately after the disruption. Many expressed shock and helplessness after learning they were unable to communicate with their family and friends. They reported confusion about the consequences of the shutdown. The anger and disbelief among some of the respondents motivated them to join the protests.[81]

LOCALIZATION PROCESSES AND CONVERGENCE ON LOCAL AND GLOBAL FOCAL POINTS

In Table (2.4) I have regressed participation in protests as the dependent variable on news consumption variables. The results of the logistic regression show a positive, statistically significant and robust correlation between gaining news from one's friends and acquaintances and participation in protests. On the other hand, the results do not show a similar link between learning about protests from centralized media with contentious content and participation in protests.[82] The regression results support the importance of local influence among the ardent protesters on the first day of the blackout. The protest decentralization occurred on the same day.

To probe further, Table (2.5) shows the a similar regression with participation during the first phase of the protests (January 25–27) as dependent variable and this time an interaction term between Internet usage and gaining news from friends and acquaintances added.

The interaction term between gaining news from friends and acquaintances and the Internet is statistically significant, while gaining news from friends is not significant. This means that among the respondents, gaining news from friends and acquaintances effectively operated through the Internet, a possibility that did not exist in the next two phases of the protests (January 28 and January 29–February 1), hence the enabling of

---

[81] Many of the respondents mentioned that the disruption signaled the regime's *recklessness* and unlikely will to limit public liberties. This only worked to energize the opposition. All respondent comments are included in the book's online appendix.

[82] The word "Al Jazeera" was explicitly included in the satellite/private television option in the questionnaire. The oppositional content of the centralized media is not key here. Those who primarily watched television on the 28th, by default could not be present in protests.

TABLE 2.4. *Dependent variable: participation in the protests of January 28, logistic regression, significance codes: 0 **0.01 *0.05 †0.1 1, (Std. Error).*

	(1)	(2)	(3)
(Intercept)	−0.5846	−1.58594	−1.79256
	(0.2278)*	(0.27408)**	(0.28546)**
State Radio/TV (28) media28a	−0.5702	−0.43385	−0.52549
	(0.2513)*	(0.28355)	(0.28941)†
Satellite/Private TV (28) media28b	−0.3622	0.03678	−0.01571
	(0.2005)†	(0.23364)	0.23503
Newspaper (28) media28c	−0.3598	−0.57388	−0.44582
	(0.2556)	(0.29698)†	0.29743
Friends and Acquaintances (28) media28e	0.6580	0.64422	0.74574
	(0.1697)**	(0.19186)**	(0.19652)**
Other (28) media28f	1.8592	1.89715	1.81880
	(0.3021)**	(0.33764)**	(0.33976)**
Participation 25–27		2.39428	2.37124
		(0.20719)**	(0.20849)**
Online Survey			0.60732
			(0.20232)**
Observations	740	740	740
AIC(≈−2 x log-likelihood)	914.62	757.24	750.24

alternative modes of communication including face to face interaction in its lieu. All these tangible interactions helped to proliferate and escalate the conflict.

It is clear that communicating with one's local social network was strongly correlated with protest activity, but it is not clear if gaining news from the local social network helped the mobilization to the *global* focal point, Tahrir, the way it did for local mobilization. The results of two sets of logistic regressions in Tables (2.6) and (2.7) show that, conditioned on *participation in protests, presence in Tahrir*, in fact, does not correlate with gaining news from one's immediate social network neighbors. Interestingly enough, the significance of local communication with one's friends and acquaintances has all but vanished in both regressions, showing that, after controlling for participation itself, local processes of news sharing with friends and acquaintances did not significantly contribute to convergence on Tahrir, the global focal point, during the first two phases of the protests.

In fact, Internet communication shows a negative and significant correlation with presence in Tahrir during the first phase of the protests,

TABLE 2.5. *Estimation results: logit* participation25 *on* media1a *State Radio/TV,* media1b *Satellite/Private TV,* media1c *Newspaper,* media1d *Internet,* media1e *Friends and Acquaintances,* media1f *Other*

Variable	Coefficient	(Std. Err.)
media1a	−1.741**	(0.485)
media1b	−0.648**	(0.198)
media1c	0.379	(0.330)
media1d	0.784*	(0.345)
media1e	0.303	(0.419)
media1d#media1e	1.112**	(0.338)
media1f	0.642	(0.438)
Intercept	−1.330**	(0.338)
N	740	
Log-likelihood	−412.826	
$\chi^2_{(7)}$	71.545	

Significance level: 10%: † 5% : * 1% : **

which is in line with the report above on the nature of the initial call to the protests before January 25: Tahrir Square was not among the four destinations advertised through email lists. Instead, on January 28, news from "other" sources was positively linked to presence in Tahrir, not interaction via practiced channels or centralized media.[83]

To summarize, local news consumption influenced protest activity, but not the convergence on the global focal point of the protests.

SUBJECTIVE REACTIONS

The respondents were also asked about their opinion on the role of the blackout in escalating or de-escalating the contention. In Table (2.8) the answers to the question "Was shutting down the media on the 28th

[83] *Contagion* in space and time, exposure to the participation of strangers in spatial proximity in the absence of digital media are both candidate processes. Again, gaining news from centralized media, even with a potentially contentious message, does not show a significant correlation with presence in Tahrir, even after conditioning the dependent variable on protest participation.

Subjective Reactions

TABLE 2.6. *Estimation results: logit* `tahrir25` *on* `part25`, `media1a` *State Radio/TV,* `media1b` *Satellite/Private TV,* `media1c` *Newspaper,* `media1d` *Internet,* `media1e` *Friends and Acquaintances,* `media1f` *Other*

Variable	Coefficient	(Std. Err.)
part25	4.912**	(0.342)
media1a	−0.369	(0.568)
media1b	−0.642†	(0.343)
media1c	0.130	(0.537)
media1d	−1.156*	(0.549)
media1e	−0.214	(0.622)
media1d#media1e	−0.525	(0.523)
media1f	0.901	(0.717)
Intercept	−2.367**	(0.497)
N	687	
Log-likelihood	−166.241	
$\chi^2_{(8)}$	459.833	

Significance level: 10%: † 5% : * 1% : **

TABLE 2.7. *Estimation results: logit* `tahrir28` *on* `part28`, `media28a` *State Radio/TV,* `media28b` *Satellite/Private TV,* `media28c` *Newspapers,* `media28e` *Friends and Acquaintances,* `media28f` *Other*

Variable	Coefficient	(Std. Err.)
part28	4.781**	(0.434)
media28a	−0.245	(0.396)
media28b	−0.298	(0.290)
media28c	0.544	(0.416)
media28e	0.396	(0.257)
media28f	1.006**	(0.374)
Intercept	−4.393**	(0.521)
N	740	
Log-likelihood	−215.043	
$\chi^2_{(6)}$	441.371	

Significance level: 10%: † 5% : * 1% : **

TABLE 2.8. *Estimation results: logit shutdown helpful? on* media28a *State Radio/TV,* media28b *Satellite/Private TV,* media28c *Newspapers,* media28e *Friends and Acquaintances,* media28f *Other*

Variable	Coefficient	(Std. Err.)
media28a	−0.402†	(0.228)
media28b	−0.093	(0.215)
media28c	−0.389	(0.247)
media28e	0.348*	(0.170)
media28f	0.570†	(0.326)
steadfast	0.886**	(0.263)
Intercept	0.663**	(0.239)
N	740	
Log-likelihood	−435.507	
$\chi^2_{(6)}$	33.066	

Significance level: 10%: † 5% : * 1% : **

helpful to the movement?" is regressed over media usage parameters and an indicator on being a *steadfast* protester (those who protested during all four phases). A similar analysis with *nonparticipation*, instead of *steadfastness* is omitted for the sake of brevity. The results are similar but with an opposite sign (as expected) for the participation variable.

Those who heard the news of the protests from the state media for the first time were likely to take the blackout to be harmful to mobilization, despite the fact that many of these respondents did not take part in protests at all. Gaining news from friends and acquaintances was also a statistically significant correlate of assigning a positive role to the shutdown. The analysis with *nonparticipation* as a dependent variable, shows that lack of participation was robustly correlated with ascribing a negative role to the media shutdown in relation to mobilization. Those who did not take part in the protests were likely to see it as disruptive to mobilization. A similar speculation could have caused the disruption of communications on the side of the regime. At the same time, those who fervently took part ascribed a significant and positive role to the communication disruption.

To take stock, those who relied on the state media for receiving news about the protests and did not take part in the contention subscribed to the view that the disruption was harmful to the mobilization. In contrast, those who received news from their friends and acquaintances and actively took part in the demonstrations were likely to see the disruption as a catalyst for mobilization.

TOO MANY IN TOO MANY PLACES …

In the above I showed that the vanguard, i.e. those who protested during the first phase of the 18-day event, reported levels of protest *outside* Tahrir comparable to those of the 28th, the day of dispersed protests. Decentralization of protests during the blackout was also confirmed. Local influence was shown to be strongly correlated with participation. However, conditioned on participation, going to Tahrir was not correlated with local influence in one's social circle. These are intriguing finds. In the next chapter I introduce a theoretical formulation for the network collective action process, and demonstrate that once the decentralization happens, it promotes a specific type of social interaction in locally dense but globally sparse networks, i.e. *small world networks*, in which collective action can further benefit from lack of information. Overall, it becomes a self-reinforcing process of escalation.

I also argued that the favorable portrayal of social media in fostering unrest in the context of heterogeneous networks should be reconsidered. In other words, in the presence of a risk averse majority and a radical minority, adding more links among the majority does not necessarily help mobilization. In the absence of centralized media, crowds' risk-taking behavior becomes independent of the state's intentions. Note that even the most authoritarian regimes prefer not to systematically bomb their own population, they instead use a threat of forceful military action in order to deter. When it is impossible to communicate the possibility of a painful military retaliation, the state is unable to dissuade the crowds. In fact protests proliferate when such threatening measures fail. In reaction to a shock similar to the one exerted on the Egyptian society on January 28, the population can overwhelm the incumbent apparatus. The consequences of such an action were evident in the aftermath of the Egyptian media blockage.

The Lede blog[84] reported from Alexandria on January 28 (emphasis is mine):

---

[84] Mackey (2011).

It's clear that the very extensive police force in Egypt is no longer able to control these crowds. *There are too many protests in too many places ...* said Peter Bouckaert, emergencies director of Human Rights Watch, who observed the street battle in Alexandria on Friday.

3

Vanguards at the Periphery
A Network Formulation

Do you imagine that death, present on such occasions in a thousand forms, cannot produce in the minds of men those wild panics which [they] have such difficulty in explaining? Will you have it that in an army of a hundred thousand men there may not be single coward? Do you think that discouragement of such a one may not produce a discouragement in another? That the second influencing a third, would soon make him produce a like effect upon a fourth? No more would be necessary to cause a whole army to be suddenly seized with despair, and the larger the army, the more sudden the seizure.[1] ... *But I shall say no more about it, Nathaniel; it seems to me that it is not a subject deserving such serious treatment.*

Montesquieu, Persian Letters, Letter CXLIII

If *leading from the periphery* can result in far reaching, rapid and decentralized waves of risk taking in a society, then it is important to understand the logic of such persistent vanguardism at the margins of the network. The dynamics of its spread from the hardened and highly connected, albeit marginal, cells of contention are to be different from centralized and well coordinated collective action. Marginal cells of contention as sources of collective action induce singular dynamics. In this chapter, I introduce these dynamics in the context of a number of basic network models.

---

[1] This is clearly an explanation based on the logic of contagion. See the exposition in Axelrod (1997), where he shows the very same phase transition effect in simulations: the larger the size of the group of individuals learning from each other, the more likely a global cascade of this type occurs. Threshold models of collective action underlying such cascades are discussed in Granovetter (1978) and Kuran (1989).

There is extant evidence on the importance of marginals in inciting risky behavior and innovation adoption.[2] For some time the idea of *marginal man*, as the motivating force behind transgressions from the social norm gained ground, and gave force to qualitative evidence on the singular role played by those not burdened by assuming regularities of a well established social role.[3]

A theory of *leading from the periphery* needs to address two main issues: first, what are the conditions under which marginal instigators can sustain and preserve social innovation? And second, how such beginnings can travel far in the social network, recruiting the majority of a population into adopting a new social norm, a new technological innovation, a novel religion or ideology.

"MINIMAL CORE" INSTEAD OF "CRITICAL MASS"

Later in this chapter, I introduce the concept of *minimal core* of action, as a replacement for *critical mass* in theories of collective action. *Critical mass* theories emphasize mass mobilization based on proliferation and expansion from "one" major component of the social network, always the largest component.[4] *Minimal cores* in contrast, are the smallest cells of contention that can sustain themselves in the face of the majority's apathy toward social and political change. Collective action originating from *minimal cores* does not necessarily emanate from the largest component of the social network, instead network effects of diffusion and contagion take collective action far and wide, if conditions are apt.

Note the difference: while *critical mass* theories stress the importance of one growing community of actors which eventually would subsume the whole population in its frenzy of collective risk taking, a theory based on *minimal cores*, gives the priority to multiple, if not many, cores of action in the periphery, which sustain themselves among a majority that is not sympathetic to their action in contrast to the status quo. These *minimal cores* do not need to be coordinated via selective incentives or alike, in order to generate a far reaching cascade of collection action. The reach of such a cascade from a given *minimal core*, is the *radius of diffusion* for that dynamic flow of collective risk taking, which is basically

---

[2] See Rogers (2003) for a discussion of the role of marginals in innovation diffusion.
[3] See Park (1950) and Stonequist (1937) – both note the role of an uncomfortable situation between two societal poles. That inconvenience is taken to be the source of societal consequences.
[4] See Marwell and Oliver (1993).

the maximum extent a wave of risk taking travels from its point of origin, the starting *minimal core*.[5]

The notion of *leading from the periphery* combined with the introduction of *minimal core*s of action, represents a significant connection to a well known and extensively studied configuration of social networks, characteristic of many human connections, namely *small world networks*.[6] These are networks with short paths between any two individuals in the social network, while maintaining high clustering levels in local subgraphs. A network type frequently observed in the analyses in the previous and next chapters, with high connectivity on the local level, in the urban environment, and short paths to other centers of contention in different spatial and social neighborhoods, portrays a situation that is highly similar to the *small world networks*.[7] I will show that this type of network, observed in the empirics of civil conflict I study in the next chapter, imposes a specific type of collective action dynamics, which benefits from the disruption of a public information signal, such as national media coverage or an aggregate result of social media reportage. This means, in *small world networks* interestingly enough, collective action *benefits* from a lack of public information, not the opposite. To do so, I use a widely accepted information model, and apply the existing network-agnostic formulation to a given network.

Combined with the localization effect I demonstrated in the previous chapters, the accentuating effect I mentioned above (escalation in *small world network* in the absence of public information) turns an instance of media disruption into a potent catalyst for collective action via leaders in the margins: lack of globally acknowledged information decentralizes the network, and that very same decentralization further activates contention. The result is a fast spiral into a global awakening of contention in a given society.

---

[5] Later in the discussion of the mathematics of this problem, I will show that this formulation produces a *pointwise* version of the well known and fundamental *isoperimetric problem* for a given graph, G.

[6] See Watts (2002) for a technical layout of the network topology identified as *small world networks*. These are networks that have short average path lengths while having highly connected clusters, see Watts and Strogatz (1998) for a random graph generation model producing graphs with small world properties. However, these networks are not *scale-free*, which means the degree distribution in the Watts-Strogatz network model does not show an exponential decay with the degree size. On the other hand, the model in Barabási and Albert (1999) produces a scale-free network.

[7] Watts (2003, 2004).

The reason this result is important is that common wisdom in studies of collective action takes more information to be conducive to more action. In contrast, the models I outline here predict that more connectivity, at times, can hinder collective action, not the opposite. An approximate explanation is the following:[8] in the initial phases of a collective action cascade, the risk aversion of the majority population can drown the initial sparks of risk taking. Leaders at the margin, with few connections, are largely immune to such muting effects. They can uninhibitedly influence their network neighbors, and their actions are more effective in the small circles they lead. Furthermore, adding more links among the risk averse majority does not necessarily help mobilization. It only accentuates the dampening effects of the majority and their risk aversion.[9]

To further demonstrate the counterintuitive role of information in *leading from the periphery*, as a paradigm, I also show that in certain social network configurations, *radius of diffusion*, the farthest distance where risk taking can travel from an initial *minimal core*, decreases as the rates of connectivity increase. Not only that, in the presence of a risk averse majority, the nuclei of contention, i.e. *minimal cores*, become harder to sustain when there is more connectivity. Finally, the social value of public information, i.e. its importance for inciting social change, is dependent on the social network structure, and that dependence increases in significance and variety when the uniform reach of *public information* is disrupted.

In the previous chapter, I argued that during the blackout in Egypt, in the absence of coordination mechanisms, social facilitators such as a lack of leadership and an urge to find news forced more face to face interactions in public spaces and motivated unintended contacts with instigators of conflict already operating in the spatial neighborhood. After formulating the logic of *leading from the periphery* here in this chapter, I use another instance of civil conflict, this time in Damascus, to demonstrate the recurring mechanisms of localization in collective risk taking. In the next chapter, I show that the result of another ubiquitous blackout was local clustering and global dispersion. During the Syrian blackout, similar to the one in Egypt, contagious spillovers were aggravated during the media shutdown. This event provides yet another concrete instance of escalation as a result of decentralization.

---

[8] Later, I will elaborate on this line of reasoning using *threshold models* of collective action Granovetter (1978); Kuran (1989).
[9] Average risk propensity in human population is skewed toward risk aversion Holt and Laury (2002).

Before starting with another detailed empirical case in the next chapter, in the following I outline the basics of a decentralized theory of collective action. These models are based on two distinct formulations of collective action. One is *inward* looking, preoccupied with the psychology of engaging in collective risk taking, based on one's own intrinsic tendency to act. The other is *outward* looking, calculating the prospects of acting, versus staying put, based on two types of signals, one to oneself, and the other shared with others. Keynes used a "beauty contest" model to describe the second type. Situations in which the public wants to guess the "real" state of affairs based on available information, but at the same time individuals want their guesses to be similar to those of their social network neighbors.[10] To introduce the idea of network locations of the vanguard, I superimpose network structure on both formulations.[11] While the importance of a web of interaction on the end result of collective action was discussed before, the idea of *leading from the periphery* as a mode of collective action was scantly explored. The vanguard are assumed to be central. When decentralization becomes an intentional or derivative tactic, the leaders cannot be limited to central and globally visible celebrities.

THE NETWORK LOGIC OF VANGUARD ACTIVITY AT THE PERIPHERY

Instead of finding the requirement for generating cascades of collective action, I divide the process into two phases: first one in which local cores of action start to take shape and persist in the face of an adverse majority, and the second process in which action from these resilient starter islands permeates to the rest of the social network. Obviously, the role of information is key to both of these stages. "Sleeper cells", often invoked in the studies of clandestine collective action,[12] are stubborn islands of contention in a sea of risk averse individuals.[13]

---

[10] First introduced in Keynes (1936) and later used as a model of collective social behavior Angeletos and Pavan (2007); Bergemann and Morris (2013); Morris and Shin (2002).
[11] The addition of network structure to the first formulation, i.e. threshold models, was pioneered in Gould (1991, 1993).
[12] Della Porta (2013).
[13] Later I will show that under certain conditions, sufficient criteria for sustaining clusters of collective action in the midst of a majority of risk aversion translate to a well defined and fundamental mathematical question.

Relevant to each of the conceptions above, two parameters are the defining elements of a model of collective action originating from leaders in the periphery: first, the size of the smallest group of radicals who can sustain action in the midst of onlookers, this I call *minimal core*; second, the longest distance collective action travels starting from these *minimal cores*, I call this distance *radius of diffusion*. Both of these parameters interact with the nature of information available to the individuals in the social network.[14]

These two parameters emphasize the *itinerant* nature of collective action: it travels from the margins to all corners of the society via contagion processes; the sources of such dynamic movements are the radical cores that can sustain themselves in the periphery. As such the instigators of collective action can be an array of decentralized cells capable of maintaining their operations in various locations. It is necessary to understand the dynamics of collective action in a network of relations between the vanguard and the rest. In particular, marginal vanguard pose a case scantly discussed in the existing studies of collective action. The common wisdom of collective action studies suggests that leaders are central. Here I consider the exact opposite: the vanguard who, perhaps even for strategic reasons, are peripheral to the social network.[15]

When the vanguard are peripheral and distributed, the existence or lack of communication has unexpected influences on the results of collective action. Another common conception challenged by the new proposition is that more communication leads to more contention. Using a number of simple models, I show why this is not always the case.

PUBLIC VERSUS PRIVATE: INNATE RISK-TAKING THRESHOLDS

Public displays of power are staples in authoritarian societies.[16] Surveillance is not the only means of projecting control. Often it is important for the authorities to be seen and to be ever present. *Public information*

---

[14] *Minimal core* is related to *critical mass* Marwell and Oliver (1993); however, here the parameter of interest is the minimum sustainable size of the radical group, not the minimum size necessary for global diffusion. For further examples of structural models of social organization see Boorman and Levitt (1980); Granovetter and Soong (1983, 1986).

[15] For a recent example see Banerjee et al. (2015). I have included more examples of vanguard centrality assumption in the penultimate chapter. Here I take the opposite approach, focusing on those who start their activity from the margins.

[16] Chwe (2001).

in such situations is not a tool of liberation, but a source of deterrence and intimidation. When such sources of public information are disrupted, the local news generation mechanisms take their place, elevating *private information* about the state of the affairs. These private and local sources of information are not directly controlled or governed by the authorities. A certain structure of *correlation* among these private signals, imposed by the social *network*, can induce dynamics of network collective action that are distinct from those in a society only connected to unidirectional sources of information, such as centralized media. The basic pictorial formulation is shown in Figures (3.1) and (3.2). When centralized media sources streamline the news and individuals maintain minimum connections with their immediate local neighbors, the underlying social network is similar to the first Figure (3.1). This was the exact situation, which Adorno and others warned against as a mechanistic scheme of *culture industry*.[17] When the links between centralized sources of information and the rest of the population are severed, as they were on January 28, 2011 in Cairo and elsewhere in Egypt, news seeking individuals shape local clusters of contention. A locally dense, but globally sparse platform shapes, see Figure (3.2).[18]

Later I will show that the utility of public signals, in general, is a function of the underlying network structure, and when there exist many dense locales, loosely connected with each other, public signals often distract and suppress local dissent. To put this concisely, the process results from a decline in local utility of action from being exposed to a distracting piece of public information. The utility of being synchronized in action with one's immediate neighbors falls when one is exposed to public information. If all are already decided to act, public information can only dissuade.

The other half of the formula involves the innate affinities of each individual for risk. Threshold models of collective action[19] take the decision between maintenance of the status quo and taking action against it to be a function of the rates of risk taking among one's social network neighbors. These models assign an innate propensity for engaging in

---

[17] Adorno [1963] (1991).
[18] The same applies to "operations rooms", of the type functioning on January 25 during the Egyptian uprising, which received information and coordinated action among a number of the revolutionary vanguard, who in turn relayed the information and coordinated a number of followers.
[19] See Granovetter (1978) and Schelling (1978) for pioneering proposals of the threshold models of collective action.

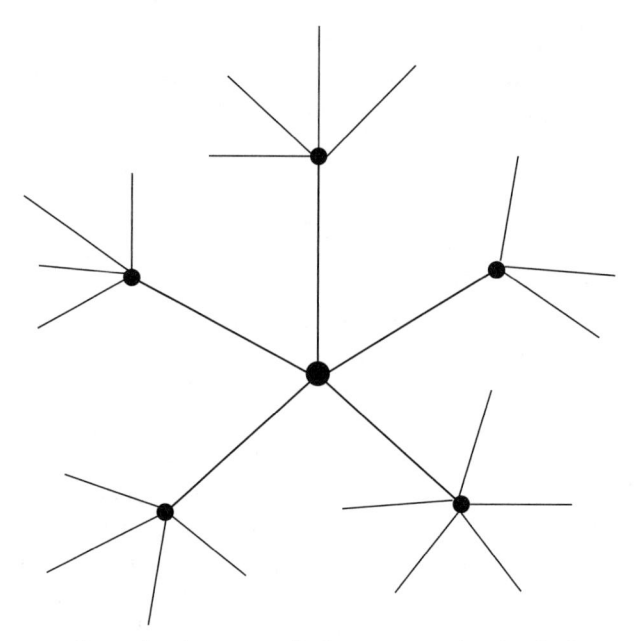

FIGURE 3.1. Centralized sources of information and individual consumers.

risk to each individual. If the level of participation in one's network neighborhood[20] is above one's personal threshold, one switches from non-action to action. If not, there would be no action.

Now, assume a dynamic version of this model, in which at each iteration, i.e. each new decision interval among individuals, they decide to act or not – based on the rule outlined above – then they update their level of personal threshold. If they see many daring actions around themselves, they become more prone to taking risks. If they see only apathy and turned backs, their tendency to taking risk plummets. These interactions, i.e. choosing to take action and updating personal tendencies, are repeated until the network dynamics reaches a steady state.[21]

In the previous chapter I argued that the existence of full connectivity does not necessarily help the diffusion of collective action when risk-takers are in the minority. An example outlined in Figure (3.3)

---

[20] Threshold and action dynamics is superimposed on a given network structure Granovetter and Soong (1983).
[21] Although there are situations in which the dynamics result in oscillation. A formalization of static and dynamic versions of the model are included in the following passages and ensuing notes.

Public versus Private 77

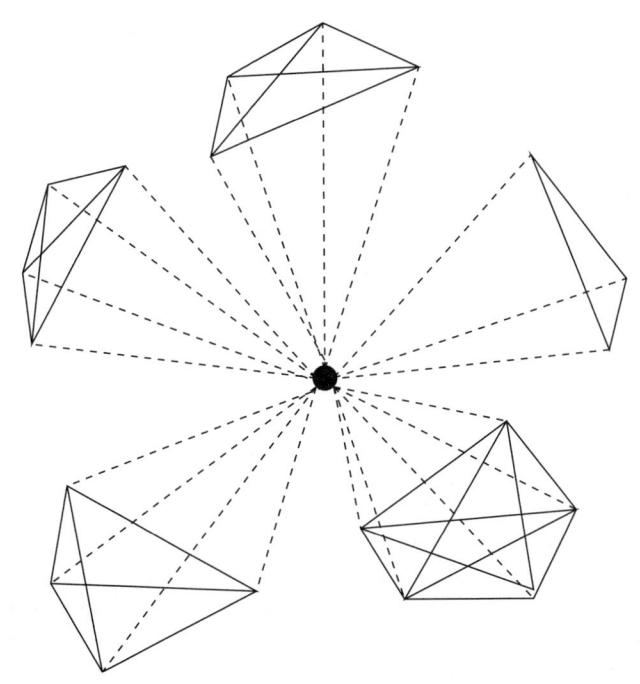

FIGURE 3.2. Same groups in the absence of far reaching communication links: new local clusters of contention take shape, are dispersed and decentralized.

illustrates why that is the case. In the simple three member network here, the node with threshold 0, i.e. the instigator, *acts* regardless of participation in the network neighborhood. The other two members of the network have innate threshold τ for action. That means they do not switch to the risky option before τ percent of their neighbors having done so. The risky option includes a range of choices, sometimes a once in a lifetime decision, at times mundane everyday dilemmas. Deciding to take part in an oppositional political campaign is one, switching from a brand of consumer electronics to another, is another, particularly if the usage utility depends on the number of people in one's social network who make the same decision.

In this example, adding a communication link between the two nodes with non-zero thresholds does not help the mobilization toward global risk taking by all three individuals. The instigator with zero threshold exerts more influence when the other two are only connected to the instigator and not to each other. In other words, more communication is not always helpful to proliferation of collective action. In Figure (3.3),

$(\tau, 2/3\tau)$ $(\tau, 0.57\tau)$

$(0, 2/3\tau)$ ———— $(\tau, 2/3\tau)$ $(0, 0.57\tau)$ ———— $(\tau, 0.57\tau)$

FIGURE 3.3. Connectivity is not always helpful to collective action, values in the parentheses: (initial threshold, steady state threshold).

the tendency to take action in the steady state is higher when the third link does not exist.[22]

DYNAMIC NETWORK THRESHOLD MODELS: COMMUNICATIVE AND OBSERVATIONAL

Other regarding models of collective action, such as the one based on personal thresholds for engaging in risk, are amenable to network formulations. The interactions, the observations of the social network neighbor's actions or knowledge of their propensity for risk, on the other hand, provide a dynamic framework for adjusting one's own personal threshold based on those of the others'.[23] The general idea, to put it in simple words, is that seeing many breaking windows, makes one more prone to breaking windows.

In the following I study the dynamics of the network threshold model in two distinct classes of *communicative* and *observational*, and show that the observational models lead to the idea of *minimal cores*. These are the structural sources of leaders concentrated at the periphery. In its

[22] The following table summarizes the dynamics of the network in Figure (3.3). The exact description of the threshold and action dynamics (*communicative dynamics*) will be fully outlined in the following. For now, the table contains the processions of the binary choices between non-action (N) and action (A), and the corresponding threshold sequence for the triplet members of the social network, from time 1 to steady state at ∞.

Thresholds	Actions
$\tau(1) = (2\tau/3, \tau/2, \tau/2)$	$A(1) = (A, N, N)$
$\tau(2) = (5\tau/9, 7\tau/12, 7\tau/12)$	$A(2) = (A, A, A)$ if $\tau < 1/2$; o.w. $= (N, A, A)$
$\tau(3) = (31\tau/54, 41\tau/72, 41\tau/72)$	$A(3) = (A, A, A)$ if $\tau < 6/7$; o.w. $= (N, A, N)$
⋮	⋮
$\tau(\infty) = (0.57\tau, 0.57\tau, 0.57\tau)$	$A(\infty) = (A, A, A)$ if $\tau < 0.875$; o.w. $= (N, N, N)$

Dynamics of the star network in Figure (3.3).

[23] See one based on *DeGroot* dynamics in Jackson (2008).

pure form, the problem of finding the *minimal cores* in a given network is a fundamental mathematical problem, which I heuristically solve for a number of network configurations central to the analysis.

The social network is comprised of individuals who decide to act or to abstain based on an other regarding formula. The dynamic model assumes that these individuals update their thresholds, i.e. inner propensity to take risks at each iteration of collective action. This can be daily decisions on joining protests, or other periodical opportunities for switching from a safe status quo to a risky option that is rewarding only if a certain number of one's acquaintances and relevant social connections have also taken the same leap of faith.

In the dynamic model the individuals' risk propensity changes with time. Before examining the connection between information and collective action in the dynamic configuration it is necessary to outline a 'static version' of the same strategic network interaction.

In the *static* model the network of individuals $i = 1,\ldots,n$, and social relations $e = 1,\ldots,m$ is represented by a graph $\mathcal{G}(\mathcal{I},\mathcal{E})$, where $\mathcal{I}$ is the set of all nodes in the network $i = 1,\ldots,n$, and $\mathcal{E}$ is the set of all edges connecting these nodes. Each node i bears the threshold for action, Γ_i. Γ_is represent the likelihood for taking action, conditioned on the actions of the others. Each of the agents is deciding between taking action (A) or abstaining (N). The decision is made based on the proportion of one's network neighbors who are acting, according to the following rules. Take p_i,[24] to be the proportion of i's network neighbors acting (self-included), and Γ_i to be i's threshold. i acts if $p_i \geq \Gamma_i$, and does not act otherwise.

Each link, e, is an informational connection: it allows for observation of others' action, or direct communication of thresholds. In the following, I propose two distinctive models based on each mechanism. Edges can be directed, i.e. some cannot see others acting, while they can be seen by others.[25] The edge weights are identical.

This defines a *static* network game. An equilibrium in this network game is defined similarly to conventional games. Here I consider only pure strategy equilibria. In addition to the two trivial equilibria of full action and full non-action, there are often multiple equilibria.

Consider the following homogeneous example, where all three individuals share a common threshold τ.[26]

---

[24] Or $p_i(t)$ in the dynamic version of this game.
[25] There is always a self-loop, because everybody is aware of what they do, or what threshold they have.
[26] Self-loops are not included in Figure (3.4), but they are implicit in the model.

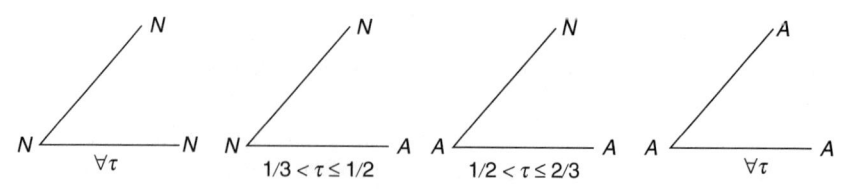

FIGURE 3.4. Equilibria for a network game, all agents have a common threshold τ.

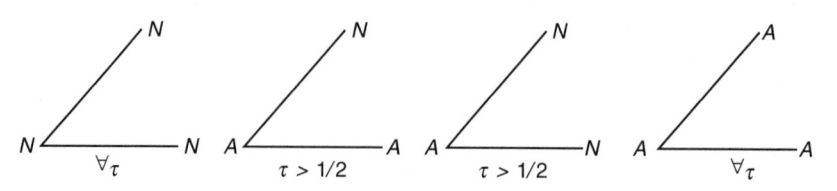

FIGURE 3.5. Equilibria for a network game, agents have thresholds (τ, ϵ, τ).

Contingent upon τ, the game in Figure (3.4) can have multiple non-trivial equilibria. For any value of $0 < \tau < 1$, all nodes acting (A, A, A), and none of them acting (N, N, N) are two equilibria of the game. There exist two other asymmetrical ones as well. For example when $1/2 < \tau \leq 2/3$, there is another equilibrium (N, A, A), the third configuration from left in Figure (3.4). The central player is in equilibrium because $\tau \leq 2/3$ (A), the peripheral ones are as well, because for the first player $\tau > 1/2$ (N), and for the third $\tau < 1$ (A).[27]

To capture the distinction between the *vanguard* and the rest, and to infuse heterogeneity, I take vanguards' thresholds to be close to zero, while others are represented by threshold τ. Consider the following case in Figure (3.5) where the radical actor has a negligible but larger than zero threshold (ϵ), while the two other players have identical thresholds τ. In this case, when $\tau \leq 1/2$, there are only two equilibria (N, N, N) and (A, A, A). When $\tau > 1/2$, there are four, (N, N, N), (A, A, A), (N, A, A) and (N, A, N) (see Figure (3.5)).

Also the third and final "heterogeneous" configuration is an asymmetric triplet, where the vanguard is at one of the prongs of the three member network. Compared to the previous heterogeneous case, it yields a very different equilibrium distribution. See Figure (3.6).

[27] Homogeneous networks were considered in detail in Jackson (2008) and Morris (2000).

Dynamic Network Threshold Models 81

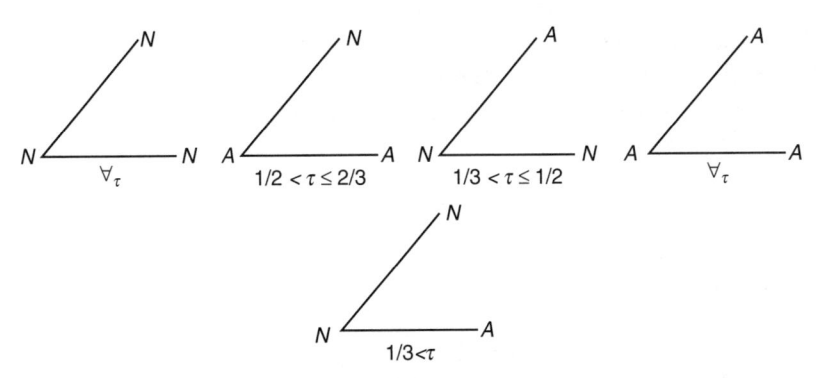

FIGURE 3.6. Equilibria for a network game with the vanguard at the periphery, agents have thresholds (τ, τ, ϵ).

In addition to decisions to act, in the following I assume that the propensities to take action, i.e. thresholds, change with time. This is a basic dynamic threshold model that also incorporates network structure into the formulation.[28] I take two distinct dynamic models into consideration, one in which the individuals are aware of each other's risk propensities: I call this the *communicative* model, based on the assumption that effective communication is necessary for sharing information about such propensities. The second case involves inferring other's risk propensities from their actions. This often happens in local street demonstrations, observations of innovation adoption by colleagues in the workplace and the awareness of cultural shifts in one's social environment.

In both cases individuals update their thresholds based on what they see in the context of their local networks, or what they hear from their network neighbors.[29] Here I examine the two updating mechanisms in turn, starting with the communicative model, based on averaging neighbors' thresholds. The observational dynamics is the basis for the definition of *minimal cores* of collective action originating from the periphery, hence it is central to the theme of vanguards starting from the periphery.

---

[28] Some computational simulations of such configurations can be found in Siegel (2009, 2011). Here I focus on analytical conclusions from the basic models in canonical network topologies instead of simulating the dynamics of the model in large networks.

[29] For an early example of endogenous threshold models with an assumption of dynamic thresholds see Granovetter and Soong (1986).

In the following I first outline the two communicative and observational dynamics. According to the communicative dynamics, individuals update their threshold as a weighted average of their own and neighbors' thresholds, then at each time t they act if their personal collective action threshold is lower than the level of activism in the social network neighborhood.[30]

In communicative dynamics, the individuals know their network neighbors' risk propensity, i.e. the thresholds, and at each update replace their prior propensity to take risk with an average of their own and their network neighbors' view of risk.[31] The dynamics of both threshold and action are of interest, specifically their asymptotic and steady state after many iterations. The communicative formulation produces a coupled dynamic model between actions and thresholds. The technical details can be found in the notes.[32] The steady state thresholds are a function of the specific network structure, as well as the initial threshold values. Later I will

---

[30] A formal representation of *action* dynamics is the following. Take $A_{n \times 1}(t)$ as the vector of individuals' action at time t. $A_i(t) = 1$ implies action, and $A_i(t) = 0$ non-action. At each time t, individuals either join in collective action or refrain. The perceived level of participation for individual i, $p_i(t)$, can be a product of their personal network, or a number known to everybody and the same for all, $p_i(t) = p(t), \forall i$. The decision to *act* or *not act* is made based on the comparison of $p_i(t)$ and $\Gamma_i(t)$. At time t, person i acts if $p_i(t-1) \geq \Gamma_i(t)$ and does not act if $p_i(t-1) < \Gamma_i(t)$. Here, I assume that $p_i(t)$ is the percentage of i's neighbors acting at time t. Note that there could be various ways of modeling $p_i(t)$. For example, we could assume a universally accepted $p(t)$ Morris and Shin (2002) or perceived participation levels, $\tilde{p}_i(t)$, that are different from real $p_i(t)$s.

[31] The formal representation of threshold dynamics for the communicative model is as follows. At time t, i updates its threshold to be a linear combination of the neighbors' thresholds and its own. Define Matrix $\Delta_{n \times n} = [\delta_{ij}]$ equal to the weight that i gives to neighbor j's threshold. Normalize the δs so that $\sum_j \delta_{ij} = 1$. Take $\Gamma_{n \times 1}(t)$ to be the vector of thresholds for individuals 1 to n at time t. The threshold dynamics is

$$\Gamma_i(t) = \sum_{j: ij \in \mathcal{G}} \delta_{ij} \Gamma_j(t-1), \tag{3.1}$$

$$\Gamma(t) = \Delta \Gamma(t-1). \tag{3.2}$$

[32] The objective is to find the values for both thresholds Γs, and actions As, when $t \to \infty$. The action vector A is a derivative of the threshold vector Γ. Define

$$D \sim D_{ij} \doteq \frac{1}{\deg(i \in \mathcal{I})} \quad \text{if } ij \in \mathcal{E},$$

the self-loops included. Another way of finding D: $D = B^{-1}J$, where B is the diagonal matrix comprised of the degrees for each node. J is the adjacency matrix. D is fixed for all t,

$$A(t) = \text{sgn}(p(t-1) - \Gamma(t))$$
$$= \text{sgn}(DA(t-1) - \Gamma(t)).$$

show that higher connectivity can in fact impede the percolation of collective action from the minority vanguard. In plain words, more connections in this model result in the suppression of the risk-taking sparks of the instigators. All is drowned in the self-reinforcing flow of the status quo.

The second class of dynamics, central to the definition of *minimal cores* is the observational formulation. Consider a threshold update mechanism based on a linear combination of one's own propensity for risk (threshold) and mere *estimates* of neighbors' thresholds based on what they did in the previous round(s) of collective action. The least demanding extrapolation would be to infer a neighbor's threshold to be zero if they acted in the previous round, and to be one if they did not. The action profile $A(t)$ is decided based on the same threshold mechanism, giving a coupled dynamic equation between the action and threshold profiles.[33] This dynamic model is *observational*, because the updating is based on

sgn(t) is the sign function, sgn(t) = 0 if $t < 0$, sgn(t) = 1 if $t \geq 0$. Therefore these two equations together characterize the Markov dynamics of this system,

$$\Gamma(t) = \Delta \Gamma(t-1)$$
$$A(t) = \text{sgn}(DA(t-1) - \Gamma(t)). \tag{3.3}$$

I take $\Delta = D$, hence

$$\Gamma(t) = D\Gamma(t-1)$$
$$A(t) = \text{sgn}(DA(t-1) - \Gamma(t)) \tag{3.4}$$

Initial conditions: $\Gamma_i(0)$s are given. $A_i(0) = 1$ if $\Gamma_i(0) = 0$, otherwise $A_i(0) = 0$. An example of the dynamics in simple networks of three nodes is depicted in Figure (3.3).

The steady state of the first equation in (3.4) is solved by putting $\Gamma(t) = \Gamma(t-1)$. If $\mathcal{G}$ is connected, all thresholds converge to one value Γ_e, which depends on network structure and initial threshold values, $\Gamma(0)$.

If d_i is the degree of the node i, it can be shown Golub and Jackson (2010); Jadbabaie et al. (2003)

$$\Gamma_e = \frac{\sum_{i=1}^n d_i \Gamma_i(0)}{\sum_{i=1}^n d_i}, \tag{3.5}$$

which depends on the degree distribution and initial thresholds. Another way of deriving the steady state threshold is through v, the left unit eigenvector of D, $\lim_{t \to \infty} \Gamma(t) = v^T \cdot \Gamma(0)$ Jackson (2008). One then could find the steady state vectors A by putting $A(t) = A(t-1)$ after substituting Γ_e for $\Gamma(t)$ in (3.3).

[33] The formal representation of the observational model is

$$\Gamma_i(t) = D_{ii} \cdot \Gamma_i(t-1) + \sum_{j \neq i} D_{ij} \cdot (1 - A_j(t-1)),$$

$$A(t) = \text{sgn}(D \cdot A(t-1) - \Gamma(t)).$$

Initial conditions are $\Gamma(0)$ and $A_i(0) = 1$ for all is for which $\Gamma_i(0)$, and $A_i(0) = 0$ wherever $\Gamma_i(0) \neq 0$.

the observations of one's neighbors' actions. The actions and propensities induced are different from those of communicative dynamics.[34] With minimal communication, stable islands of action can continue to exist among apathetic neighbors. This is the main feature of decentralized, at times dormant, centers of collective action. Observation of refusal from the neighbors does not dissuade them, until at some point the propensity for risk in the neighborhood rises and the risky option starts to diffuse through the network.

MINIMAL CORE

A decentralized theory of collective action, in addition to the dynamics of proliferation, requires a formulation of contention in dispersed but lasting clusters. For the very same purpose, I define *minimal core* as the minimal set of radicals that can sustain risk taking among risk aversion of the majority in a given social network.

To start, it is clear that in a social network the location of the vanguard in relation to the others influences the dynamics of collective action. A number of recent studies have discussed the clustering of the vanguard in the *periphery* and its role in networked proliferation.[35]

When contagion of risky action necessitates multiple reinforcements, the existence of peripheral instigators becomes increasingly important. Joining a contentious movement, with risks to life and livelihood, does not result from cursory connections. It is a result of continuing conditioning in small circles of close associates. These clusters shape more effectively in the margins of regular social networks around relations of friendship and connections of political and social importance.[36]

Peripheral vanguard can provide multiple reinforcement more easily in smaller marginal cliques. In contrast, centralized and visible opinion leaders are at the mercy of too many connections to be able to effectively act on highly risky conversions. In an other regarding process, of a type described above, marginal vanguard are likely to influence their few connections more effectively than a central figure; the majority of the population are risk averse and their conservative attitudes toward risk overwhelm the centralized leadership. In contrast, if a cluster of social

---

[34] Note that decisions based on history of actions can go farther than the previous day.
[35] See Centola (2010) and Liu et al. (2011), also Granovetter (1978) and Rogers (2003) for pioneering discussions of *marginal social innovators/deviants*.
[36] The proliferation process based on multiple reinforcements is called "complex contagion" Centola (2010).

innovation takes hold in the margins, it can effectively influence the few connections it has first, and consequently start a collective action cascade seeded away from the center. In the penultimate chapter of this book, I review an experiment of collective risk taking which demonstrates the very same proliferation dynamics from the periphery toward the center of a given social network. Despite the plausibility of these possibilities, the existing models of collective action do not examine the role of a vanguard class clustered in the periphery. It is often assumed that they are central figures.

In the following, using observational dynamics, I explore how and when clusters of radicalism can either take hold or wither way. I will show that the existence of excessive communication activity can eradicate these nuclei of contention.[37] Later, I use the conception of *minimal cores* in connection with the notion of *radius of diffusion* to argue that a combination of these peripheral centers of contention with diffusion flows of collective action in the absence of communication generate surprising waves of conversion to new social and political modes.

MINIMAL CORE IN A GIVEN GRAPH AND THE ISOPERIMETRIC PROBLEM

Minimal core is the smallest set of individuals who, given a specific set of interpersonal dynamics, are capable of maintaining their activities[38] among a majority opposed to their actions.

Given the disconnect between the *minimal cores* and the rest of the population in the steady state of the dynamics, the observational model is a more plausible platform for studying the characteristics of *minimal core* in relation to regimes of information, connectivity characteristics of the social network, compared to communicative dynamics.

At the steady state of the observational dynamics, those acting have more acting neighbors than abstaining ones. The argument is straightforward, in the steady state, for acting individuals the personal threshold is equal to the proportion of the inactive network neighbors, and this threshold needs to be smaller than or equal to the proportion of acting neighbors in the network. Hence the number of acting network neighbors, $\#A$, is larger than or equal to the number of inactive network

---

[37] Here the threshold dynamics are based on *observational learning*: one's neighbors' thresholds are not known, they have to be inferred from their actions. I take the simplest inference possible: action is equated to threshold 0, non-action to 1.

[38] This is the "Action" option in the binary game I discuss.

neighbors, $\#N$.[39] $\#(A) \geq \#(N)$, in i's neighborhood, i itself included, if i is acting in steady state. Similarly for individual j which is not acting, $\#(A) < \#(N)$ in j's neighborhood. This leads to the following definition.

Definition 1. *For each graph $\mathcal{G}$, the "minimal core" is the smallest subset $\mathcal{S} \subset \mathcal{G}$, such that $\forall i, i \in \mathcal{S}$, i has at least as many neighbors in $\mathcal{S}$ as it does in $\mathcal{G} \backslash \mathcal{S}$.*

Minimal core is a concept parallel to *"critical mass"*, instead of finding the size of radicals needed to initiate a global cascade, *minimal core* is the smallest set of sustainable action.[40] *Minimal core* is the *smallest* set of radicals that when the network collective action starts with their vanguardism, the process continues unabated, at least among the instigators.

For each graph $\mathcal{G}$, *minimal core* represents the smallest subset $\mathcal{S}$ of radicals that can sustain action in the context of social network $\mathcal{G}$. This is a well defined problem for any graph. In the following I find the size of S for a number of canonical graphs and explore the relation between levels of connectivity in network, and the size of the *minimal core*, $|S|$.[41]

Finding the smallest subset with more neighbors for each node *inside* the subset as opposed to the *outside* is similar to a fundamental question in graph theory, i.e. the *isoperimetric problem*, although the two problems are not equivalent. The isoperimetric problem, in general terms, is to find

---

[39] In this dynamic system, asymptotically,

$$\Gamma_i = \frac{\#(N)}{\#(A) + \#(N)},$$

where $\#(N)$ is the number of inactive agents, and $\#(A)$ is the number of active ones. By definition,

$$p_i = \frac{\#(A)}{\#(A) + \#(N)},$$

and asymptotically for an agent to be able to act, $p_i \geq \Gamma_i$, therefore $p_i \geq 1/2$. Also note that the dynamics in equation (3.6) can be solved in the steady state for two cases when either $A_i = 1$ or $A_i = 0$. Assume $D_{ii} = 1/n$ where n is the number of i's neighbors (self included). At the steady state $\Gamma_i = n(1-p_i)/(n-1)$ when $A_i = 1$, and $\Gamma_i = 1 - np_i/(n-1)$ when $A_i = 0$. Now obviously for $A_i = 1$, one should have $\Gamma_i - p_i \leq 0$, that gives the condition $p_i \geq n/(2n-1) > 1/2$. When $A_i = 0$, again $\Gamma_i > p_i$ gives the condition $p_i < (n-1)/(2n-1) < 1/2$.

In the limit when n is large, the point of division becomes simply $1/2$, but for finite ns, there exists a gap of $1/(2n-1)$ between the two limits. This gap does not exist in the asymptotic case. Nevertheless, $p_i \geq 1/2$ is a condition that applies to both cases.

[40] One way of thinking of the vanguard group is to take thresholds for $j = 1, \ldots, |S|$ equal to 0, and for others threshold equal to τ.

[41] I conjecture that the general problem of finding the *minimal core* in a given graph is NP-Hard.

the largest volume that can be included in a given surface area, the largest area that can be included in a given boundary length and the largest number of nodes – as a subgraph – that can be included in a boundary area intersecting a certain number of edges. The mathematical problem posed above, finding the size and characteristics of *minimal core* in a given graph is a *pointwise* version of a well known isoperimetric problem for graphs.[42] One can start with simplest possible graphs, a path, a line of individuals, each in touch with two neighbors, and a regular rectangular grid.

Example 1. *For the path graph, i.e. an infinite line of individuals, size of minimal core $|S| = 2$, for the simple rectangular grid in Figure (3.7), size of minimal core $|S| = 4$. When diagonal connections are added to the same rectangular grid, the size of minimal core grows to $|S| = 12$.*

Construction of the above examples is straightforward. Note that in these simple examples, adding edges increases the size of the *minimal core*. For example adding diagonal connections increases the size of minimal sustainable core. Adding links here does not promote mobilization. In fact, the effect is the reverse.[43]

It is possible to extend the definition in example (1). The same question, i.e. the size of the *minimal core*, can be posed for a grid of m dimensions for which the *radius of connectivity* is n. Here each node i is connected to others within n units on each dimension.[44] Each individual comes to know of the actions of its network neighbors within n hops on each of the m dimensions of the grid network. Every node in such a grid is connected to $(2n+1)^m - 1$ other nodes, hence the size of *minimal core* in the grid of m dimensions and n hop-radius of connectivity, $|S_{m,n}|$, cannot be smaller than half of this value, which is a lower bound, albeit rather approximate, on the size of *minimal core*.[45]

---

[42] Note that Cheeger inequality (used in proving results on isoperimetric problems) applies to the *sum* of outgoing edges of S in relation to S's volume, not pointwise boundary conditions at *each* individual $i \in S$ Chung (1997).
[43] These structural characteristics have implications for control and governance based on architecture. A city fully built on a diagonal grid is not as amenable to collective protest in streets compared to one built on a rectangular grid. The reason is that maintaining cores of action is more difficult in the diagonal design. For further examples of state control projection via structural elements of space see Gould (1995) and Scott (1998).
[44] See Morris (2000).
[45]
$$|S_{m,n}| \geq \frac{(2n+1)^m - 1}{2}. \qquad (3.6)$$

88   *Vanguards at the Periphery*

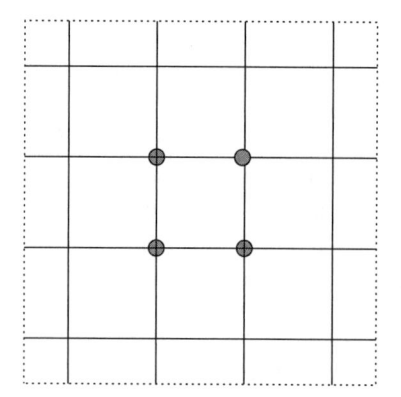

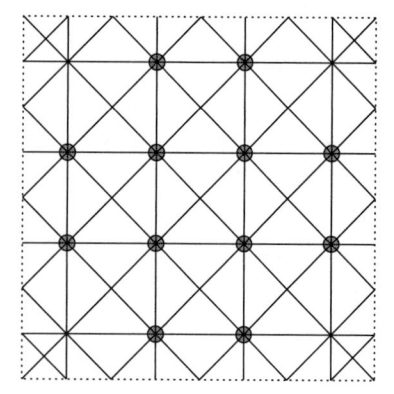

FIGURE 3.7. When diagonals are added, the size of the *minimal core* increases from 4 to 12.

Simple line and rectangular grids lead to more general connection patterns. Consider the following example.

Example 2. *By construction, for $m = 1$, the path graph, it is easy to show that $|S_{1,n}| = n + 1$. For $m = 2$, two dimensional grid of radius of connectivity $= 1$, $|S_{2,1}| = 12$. For two dimensional grid with higher radius of connectivity, $n = 2$, $|S_{2,2}| = 121$. See Figure (3.8).*

The size of the *minimal core* grows considerably with increasing n. Increasing the horizon of visibility from 1 to 2 hops in the two dimensional grid increases the size of the *minimal core* about tenfold, from 12 to 121. Here, the existence of long ties, links to individuals farther than $n = 1$ hops away, inflates the size of the *minimal core*.[46]

---

[46] It is plausible to think that the size of S increases with n, radius of connectivity in a given grid. For each node $i \in S$, located at the coordinates $(i_1, i_2, \ldots, i_m)$, decreasing the radius of connectivity, n, leaves the proportion of inside nodes on each dimension k the same, but decreases access to the outside by removing a layer of external exposure, hence fewer nodes are needed to sustain the *minimal core*.

Without loss of generality assume that the origin of the m-dimensional space lies at the center of S and define *interior* with respect to point $J = (j_1, j_2, \ldots, j_m)$ as all points I for which $\nexists k, |i_k| > |j_k|$. An attempt for the proof by induction for $m = 2$ is as follows: the statement is true for $n = 1$ and $n = 2$, see Figure (3.8). Consider reducing the radius of connectivity from n to $n - 1$. After such a transformation, access of each node to observations from the interior is unchanged, because $n - 1 < n$ and all that was visible before is still accessible, but access to the outside is more limited, because $n > n - 1$, and for each node access to the farthest nodes on each dimension in the external direction is impossible. Here the proportion of interior nodes has increased. In other words, the

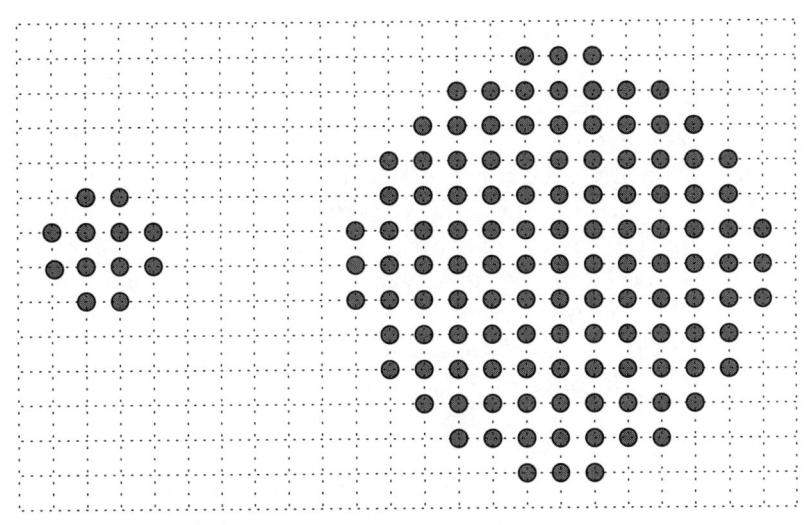

FIGURE 3.8. A comparison between the size of the *minimal core* for $m = 2$ dimensional grids, radius of connectivity $n = 1$ (left) and $n = 2$ (right). $|S_{2,1}| = 12$, $|S_{2,2}| = 121$. Increasing radius of connectivity by one unit increases the size of the *minimal core* from 12 to 121.

The diffusion of collective action from the peripheral hotbeds of clandestine, radical vanguardism is the next topic needed for formulating a theory of network collective action. In the following, using the same dynamic models used above, I show that increasing connectivity can impede proliferation of collective action from the vanguard minority. In that sense, the results on the effect of connectivity on *minimal cores* is in line with the influence it has on *radius of diffusion*.

RADIUS OF DIFFUSION

When the early adopters of a social practice, a political cause or a new defining idea are at the margins, increasing links for visibility is to the detriment of the collective cause. It makes circles of contention wither way, but that is not the only procedure through which collective action is impeded through an overwhelming flow of information. Furthermore, the adverse effects operate on the *diffusion* of action from the cells of contention to the other parts of the social network. Interestingly enough,

proportion of connections to the inside vis a vis the outside has grown. Fewer nodes are required to sustain action.

this is not a trivial effect at all. Adding communication links can help radicalism traverse across hardened islands of status quo, which is the effect often identified: at the same time, it can stop the step by step stream of collective action on its way from the leaders at the periphery to the other parts of the social network. In that sense, communication and connectivity influence the dynamics of *leading from the periphery* in ways different from those in centrally orchestrated collective action. For a few cases of canonical networks, the net direction of the combination of the two forces, I will show, is negative.

Radius of diffusion is defined as the farthest distance *taking action* can travel from an *instigator* (or a group of instigators forming a *minimal core*). Combined with the idea of *minimal core*, radius of diffusion explains the nature of network collective action dynamics in a given web of interactions. To start from a simple and basic example, consider a ring network where individuals are aware of the actions of their two immediate neighbors. There is one instigator with threshold zero, and n others with threshold τ.[47] Consider a system of *communicative* dynamics of the type described above implemented in this simple topology. Figure (3.9) depicts *radius of diffusion* in a ring network with $n = 100$ nodes for all pertinent thresholds τs. For threshold values smaller than $1/3$ a complete diffusion of collective action takes place, everybody in the network starts to act in due time and the *radius of diffusion* is at its maximum possible value, i.e. 50. For $1/3 < \tau < 1/2$, collective action partially spreads through the ring network.

Increasing connectivity through adding communication links to the simple ring configuration can change the dynamics of diffusion in two ways: first, it can extend the reach of action, an effect which can help the diffusion of collective action; second, it can impede collective action by exposing the *minimal core* to an inactive majority. In the following, I examine an increase in the connectivity through two distinct procedures, first, adding local network *bridges* traversing over multiple individuals. The bridges are defined as links between individuals far apart, who are not already connected, in the ring.[48] The second procedure is increasing the local connectivity for each individual via adding to the *radius of connectivity*. This means each individual is in touch with more than just

[47] A ring with $n+1$ vertices, $n > 1$. The vertices are labeled 0 to n clockwise. At $t = 0$, the personal thresholds $\Gamma_0(0) = 0$ and $\Gamma_i(0) = \tau$, $0 < \tau < 1$, for $i \in \{1,\ldots,n\}$. Individual 0 is the radical instigator. In this case, the initial value of action variables are $A_0(0) = 1$ and $A_i(0) = 0$ for $i \in \{1,\ldots,n\}$.
[48] These are links characteristic of digital communications. See Centola and Macy (2007).

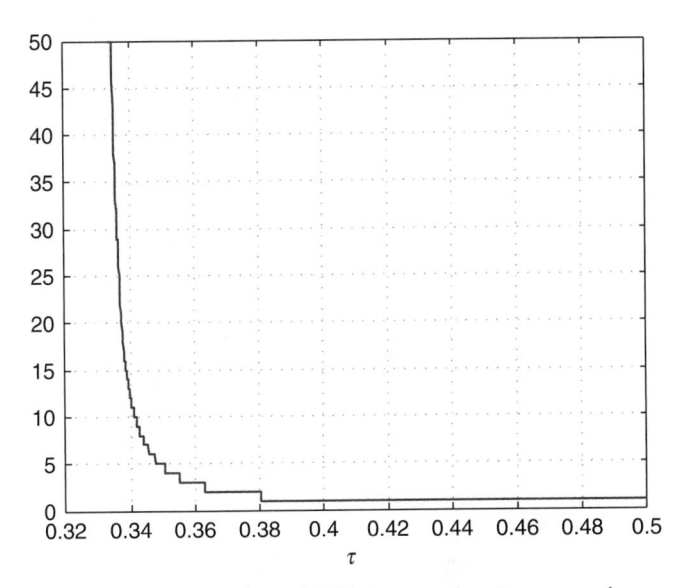

FIGURE 3.9. *Radius of diffusion*, regular ring network.

immediate neighbors. I will show that, when the diffusion of collective action is originating from a single source on the ring network, both procedures for increasing connectivity impede the spread of collective action.

First, consider adding local bridges (see Figure (3.10)) between nodes that are diagonally apart.[49] When there is one bridge of this type, as expected, the structure of diffusion changes. With *communicative* dynamics $r = 1$, a global cascade does not happen at $\tau = 1/3$ as in Figure (3.9), but it takes place at higher thresholds, τ.[50]

Adding more and more diametrical bridges (as in Figure (3.10)) further decreases the set of τs for which a global cascade, i.e. maximum *radius of diffusion*, 50 in this example, is possible. Asymptotically, adding many local bridges turns the network to a *fully connected* graph for which complete diffusion happens when $\tau < 1/(n+1)$. This means the range of

---

[49] i.e. i and $i + \lfloor \frac{N}{2} \rfloor$.
[50] Approximately $\tau = 0.25$. In these simulations $n = 100$, and the bridge is between nodes 25 and 75. A similar simulation with two bridges yields a similar dampening effect on the diffusion of collective action. For the simulation with two diametrical bridges, the local bridges are between nodes 13 and 63, and 37 and 87. The simulations are run long enough for the system to reach the steady state.

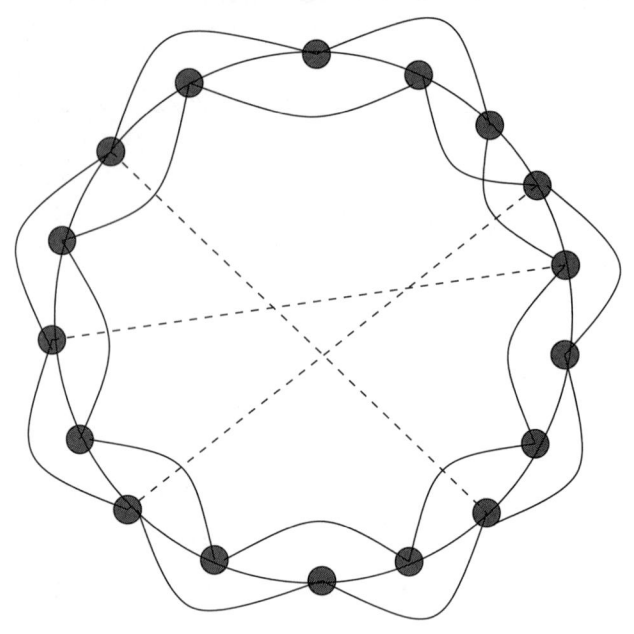

FIGURE 3.10. A ring network with bridges (dashed) and connectivity radius $r > 1$, here $r = 2$.

τs, for which complete diffusion occurs, decreases from $1/3$ to $1/(n+1)$, $n > 2$. All this means adding local communication bridges does not help the diffusion of collective action. To the contrary, in a ring network it effectively blocks the proliferation of risk taking spreading from a single instigator to the rest of the network.

Another possibility for adding connectivity is to increase the number of neighboring individuals. Consider a case in which each individual has access to neighbors other than those only one step away on the ring; this is a ring network with *connectivity radius* $r > 1$.[51] Adding farther reaching links to each node increases the ring graph's connectivity. See Figure (3.10) for a depiction of a ring with $r = 2$. Similar to the case of $r = 1$ outlined above, I look for the *radius of diffusion*.

It is possible to show that the range of threshold for which complete diffusion happens *decreases* linearly with the radius of connectivity, r.

> If $\mathcal{G}$ is a ring graph with $n + 1$ vertices $i \in \{0, 1, \ldots, n\}$, connectivity radius $r > 1$, with "communicative" dynamics and initial threshold values $\Gamma_0(0) =$

[51] In the regular ring $r = 1$.

0, $\Gamma_i(0) = \tau$, $i = 1,\ldots,n$. Then for all τs, such that $\tau \leq 1/(2r)$, all nodes in the ring act in finite time. All nodes will be inactive for $t \geq 1$, if $\tau > 1/(2r)$.

Proof of the above statement can be found in the notes.[52]

Again note that adding to connectivity in the general ring graph with connectivity radius of r decreases the range of τs for which complete diffusion is possible. Increasing reach of communication does not facilitate diffusion, it does the opposite.[53]

WHY "VISIBILITY IS A TRAP": MINIMAL CORES AND RADIUS OF DIFFUSION AMONG SMALL WORLDS

Public and grandiose landmarks are economizing tools of political power. They keep the governing stature ever present in sights and minds. Such means of collective mobilization are central to any governance project. In contrast to centrifugal forces of official politics, *leading from the periphery* does not benefit from more visibility. In the following, I will show that *public* information is, in fact, detrimental to the sustenance of action in small circles of contention, loosely connected in a larger web of social contacts. Panopticons of state power are not of much use when the instigators of social change reside in the periphery. This is a condition specific to certain network configurations and vanguard locations. The oft cited *small world networks*, which bear the marks of the platform

---

[52] At time $t = 1$,
$$\Gamma_0(1) = \Gamma_1(1) = \ldots = \Gamma_r(1) = \frac{2r\tau}{2r+1}.$$
For nodes $i = 0, 1, \ldots, r$, $p_i = 1/(2r+1)$. If $2r\tau > 1$, no one acts at $t = 1$, this is the non-action steady state. As long as $2r\tau \leq 1$, all of these $r+1$ nodes act at time 1. I will show that this is sufficient for having all nodes $i = 1,\ldots,n$ act in finite time. First note that if a node starts acting, it never reverts to non-action, because p_i for such a node is $(r+1)/(2r+1)$, which is always larger than the highest possible value for thresholds, i.e. τ, because $\tau \leq 1/(2r)$ and $(r+1)/(2r+1) > 1/(2r)$ for any $r \geq 1$. This is true for both a simple ring $r = 1$ and those with $r \geq 2$. Now consider the case in which only a subset of nodes is acting, therefore there is an intersection between acting and non-acting nodes. $A_i = 1$ for $i = 0, 1, \ldots, k$, and $A_i = 0$ for $i = k+1, k+2, \ldots, m$, but this is impossible because for the node $i = k+1$,
$$p_{k+1} = \frac{r}{2r+1} > \frac{1}{2r} \geq \tau > \Gamma_{k+1} \quad \text{for} \quad r \geq 2,$$
this is a contradiction. Hence the only possible equilibrium is all action. □

[53] In contrast to the gradual increase of *radius of diffusion* between $\tau = 1/2$ and $\tau = 1/3$ in the case of $r = 1$, the transition is sharp for $r > 1$. For $\tau \leq 1/(2r)$, all nodes act, otherwise they all become inactive after $t = 1$. The action region, in terms of τ, is smaller, because $1/(2r) < 1/3$ for $r \geq 2$, and decreases *linearly* with local connectivity radius, r.

I have been outlining in this chapter, are the closest candidate: they are locally dense, but globally sparse. The locally dense clusters are loosely interconnected with a number of far reaching connections.

This is not a mere coincidence, the semi-random rewiring of social conditions, in the aftermath of a cataclysmic shutdown of the means of culture industry, is likely to recast the social network in the image of a new network akin to the *small world* configuration.[54] The transition from centralized and semi-centralized media to friends, acquaintances and neighbors reported by the Egyptian protesters are marks of a similar transition.

PUBLIC/PRIVATE INFORMATION AND NETWORK COLLECTIVE ACTION DYNAMICS

In the above, I used dynamic threshold models of network collective action to show that, in contrast to the existing theories of centralized collective action, increasing connectivity derails mobilization from the margins. In the following I use another formulation, a division of information available to the social network into two distinct classes of public and private to show that a disruption of public information can set small and densely connected clusters of the marginal vanguard, and their risk averse disciples, into motion. This is a formulation that relies on the distance structure of private signals between each pair of individuals, i.e. the geometry of signal space, to impose a network structure on the oft studied public/private formulation of the role of information in collective action.

The imposition of network structure on the existing models of collective action is paramount, because each structure yields a distinctive outcome, even with similar mobilization tactics. An important example is the dissonance between platforms of civil contention. The structure of the social networks underlying urban conflict is drastically different from those in rural civil wars. Patterns of information propagation are superimposed over neighborhood patterns. Dense local social networks are embedded against a substrate of weak ties[55] between each of these information neighborhoods. This is very different from the dispersed and

---

[54] See a description of the rewiring algorithm, and an analysis of network characteristics of the resulting *small world* webs in the pioneering work of Watts and Strogatz (1998).
[55] Granovetter (1973).

highly programmed webs of insurgency often studied in the collective action literature.[56]

In the following I contrast the consequences of losing a public signal in locally dense environs vis a vis the results of the same information shutdown in more evenly dispersed network configurations. It will become clear that rates of mobilization in relation to communication depend heavily on existing and ensuing social network patterns.[57]

Building on a model of public and private information usage,[58] here I demonstrate sufficient network conditions under which lack of public information results in higher rates of collective action, compared to the status quo. I will show that the social value of public information is contingent on the underlying social network structure. This connection had not been explored in the context of models of collective risk taking in the format of global games based on Keynes' notion of "beauty contests".[59]

WHY PUBLICITY IS NOT ALWAYS CONDUCIVE TO COLLECTIVE ACTION

A model of collective action based on the well known Keynesian *beauty contest* takes the utility of collective action to be the function of two terms. One depends on the proximity to the reality of the situation, for example a precise assessment of the state power, the prospects of the new and risky venture and the like. The second term is a function of the "social" component of the act: to gain the most, it matters to act similar to the acts of the social network neighbors; the same is true of rebellions, innovation adoptions and cultural transformations. The decision is made based on two distinct *signals*. One is publicly shared among all; one is strictly personal.[60]

The formal representation of the model is as follows. Consider a situation in which each individual i is receiving two signals, one public y, and the other private x_i. Each of these signals is a noisy version of the

---

[56] See Weinstein (2007) and Wood (2003), two studies of coordinated insurgent contention. A theory of *coordinated* collective action based on selective incentives is included in Lichbach (1995).
[57] For computational results on the connection between network structure and mobilization see Siegel (2009).
[58] Introduced in Morris and Shin (2002).
[59] See Keynes (1936).
[60] This distinction can clearly be extended to include semi-private or semi-public signals. I have utilized the conventional clear distinction between public and private to make the point. It is sufficient.

state of affairs θ.[61] The signals are a combination of the state of affairs θ and noise, $y = \theta + \eta$, and $x_i = \theta + \epsilon_i$.[62]

There is a continuum of individuals, each indexed on the unit interval [0, 1]. Each individual i chooses action $a_i \in \mathbb{R}$. The state of the world, e.g. an indicator of state power, θ, is distributed uniformly on an interval in $\mathbb{R}$. If the action profile for the whole population is taken to be **a**, then the utility of action a_i in state θ for individual i is a function of two terms, the first is a penalty based on the distance between a_i and the state of the world θ. The other is a "conformity" utility term. The utility structure is $u_i(\mathbf{a}, \theta) = -(1-r)(a_i - \theta)^2 - r(L_i - \bar{L})$, where $0 < r < 1$, and $L_i = \int_0^1 (a_i - a_j)^2 dj$, $\bar{L} = \int_0^1 L_j dj$.

Individual i gains higher utility from acting if the action distance profile (from others) captured in the scalar parameter L_i is close to the average distance profile $\bar{L}$. Each individual is trying to guess other contestants' guesses, while staying close to the real state of affairs. Every individual i decides between the utility from participation in the collective action setup, i.e. gaining the utility in the formulation above, based on action a_i at the equilibrium, or abstaining from it altogether ($u_i = 0$).

Now, introduction of network structure into global games can be done in multiple ways. For example, it is possible to show that imposing a network correlation ρ_i between private signals x_is and y does not alter the linear equilibrium strategy.[63] The proof is straightforward and is omitted for the sake of brevity. ρ_i, the correlation factor between the signals, is a proxy for structure, i.e. network edges, based on signal proximity.[64]

Furthermore, in this general case, the distance between private signals $|x_i - x_j|$ imposes an underlying network structure upon the strategic

---

[61] Assume that the noise is additive. Similar assumptions exist in Bergemann and Morris (2013) and Morris and Shin (2002).
[62] $\eta \sim \mathcal{N}(0, \sigma_\eta)$, and $\epsilon_i \sim \mathcal{N}(0, \sigma_x)$.
[63] In this formulation (x_i, y) are jointly Gaussian.
[64] In this case the unique action equilibrium is

$$a_{i\text{-eq}} = \frac{\alpha_i y + \beta_i (1-r) x_i}{\alpha_i + \beta_i (1-r)} \tag{3.7}$$

where

$$\alpha_i = \frac{1}{\sigma_\eta^2} - \frac{\rho_i}{\sigma_x \sigma_\eta}$$

$$\beta_i = \frac{1}{\sigma_x^2} - \frac{\rho_i}{\sigma_x \sigma_\eta}.$$

ρ_i is the correlation factor between the public signal y and the private signal x_i. The addition of the correlation factor ρ_i allows for the study of a more involved information structure.

collective action game based on public/private signals.[65] The private signals, x_i and x_j, of close network neighbors are statistically alike, while those of distant network neighbors are statistically disparate.

In the following, I outline an appraisal of the relation between *lack* of the public signal and rates of participation in network collective action. It becomes apparent that such a removal of public signal in a specific type of network, i.e. *small world networks* plays an important role in the escalation of network collective action. Later in the next chapter, using empirics from urban conflict in Damascus I detect patterns similar, in topology, to those commonplace in *small world networks,* i.e. local concentration of collective activity in highly dispersed clusters.

Proposition: In *small world networks*,[66] with the network collective action framework outlined above, removing the public signal increases the rates of participation in collective action.

Proof is included in the notes.[67]

---

[65] Note that (x_i, y) are jointly Gaussian, and according to the prior lemma, they produce the same equilibrium actions as the simpler game.

[66] These are networks in which the mean distance between nodes is small compared to the size of the network Watts and Strogatz (1998).

[67] I compare the two utility terms, $u_i(\mathbf{a}, \theta) = -(1-r)(a_i - \theta)^2 - r(L_i - \bar{L})$, in two situations: (a) with public *and* private signals, y and x_i, both available; and (b) with only private signal, x_i accessible. I will show that the utility from taking action is dependent on the quality of signals and the distribution of signals dictated by the network structure (through its effect on pairwise distances between private signals). In making a decision to act, each agent i is comparing the utility outlined above to 0 – the utility from abstaining. Positive changes in utility incite taking action a_i. Negative changes in utility result in abstaining from taking action. I examine the two terms of the utility, conformity and fidelity equations, in turn.

There are two sources of utilities:
1. *Utility from conformity (consensus)*, $-r(L_i - \bar{L})$:
a. *When there exist private and public signals, x_i and y*
Actions at the equilibrium are a linear combination of y and x_i Morris and Shin (2002). See equation (3.7). It is easy to show that when an individual decides to take action, the absolute value of conformity utility $|L_i - \bar{L}|$ is a sum of terms of the following form,

$$\gamma (x_i - x_j)^2 = \left(\frac{\beta(1-r)}{\alpha + \beta(1-r)} \right)^2 (x_i - x_j)^2.$$

When the public signal is removed (e.g. in the case of a blackout), the above term is multiplied by $1/\gamma$, $\gamma \leq 1$.

b. *When only private signals x_is exist, and the public signal, y, is removed*
In this case, actions $a_i = x_i$ and the absolute value of the conformity utility term scales with the difference between the private signals $(x_i - x_j)^2$.

The consequences of the removal of the public signal are noteworthy. If the term $L_i - \bar{L}$ is negative, the absence of the public signal increases the overall utility by an order of $1/\gamma$, making it more likely for the agents to participate in action. If the term $L_i - \bar{L}$ is positive then removing the public signal makes it less likely for the relevant agent i to take part in action on either side. However, the sign of $L_i - \bar{L}$ is a function of signal

To summarize, the distribution of signals in one's social network effectively influences one's participation mechanism. The participation rates of those in close-knit communities, where distances between private signals are below the average of the whole network, are more likely to engage in network collective action in the wake of an omission of a public signal. Hence, in communities with strong communal and local connections media disruptions incite action, while in loosely connected

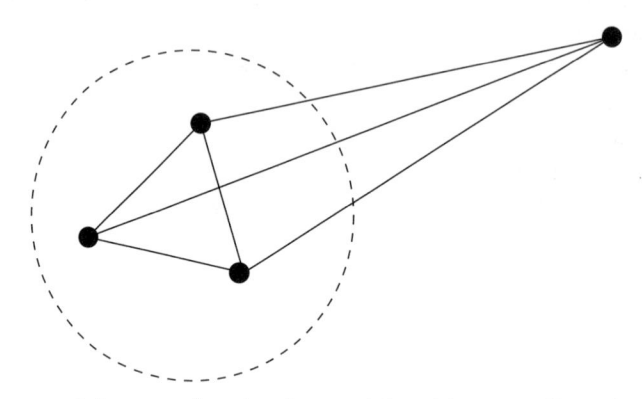

FIGURE 3.11. A four-member signal space (of x_i s) in a two-dimensional space. Consider the above illustration of a four-member signal space (of x_is) in a two-dimensional space. There is a close-knit community on the left, members of which all have L_is that are smaller than $\bar{L}$, hence they benefit from suppression of the public signal. The change in utility after the signaling intervention is in the opposite direction for the node on the right. It is possible to extend this analysis to general signal spaces.

distribution in one's network. For node i in close-knit subcommunities where signals are closely related and highly similar, the term L_i that is a linear function of $\sum_j (x_i - x_j)^2$ is smaller than $\bar{L} = \mathbb{E}_i(L_i)$.

2. *Utility from fidelity term,* $-(1-r)(a_i - \theta)^2$:

Similarly one can show that the change in the average difference between the equilibrium action and the state of the world, $(a_i - \theta)^2$, averaged over noise terms η and ϵ_i, when the public signal is removed, is equal to (u_{f-p} for utility only with private signal, u_{f-pp} for the case with both public and private signals): $\Delta u_f = u_{f-p} - u_{f-pp} = (1-r)(2r - 1 - \sigma_\epsilon^2/\sigma_\eta^2)$.

As expected the loss of utility resulting from the blackout is considerable when the public signal is of high quality, i.e. σ_η^2 is small. When that is not the case, the removal of public signal does not drastically change the decision calculus. Assuming $\sigma_\eta > \sigma_\epsilon$ and putting $r = 1/2 + (1/2)(\sigma_\epsilon^2/\sigma_\eta^2)$ suffices to do away with the change in the fidelity term. □

subcommunities – as it is often reported in classic collective action theory – the result is the opposite. See Figure (3.11).

COLLECTIVE ACTION IN *SMALL WORLD NETWORKS* BENEFITS FROM DISRUPTION OF PUBLIC SIGNAL

Using the same comparisons I applied between situations with and without public signal, one can show that in highly interconnected local communities sparsely spread around in the structural context, the exclusion of public signal promotes network collective action. Consider the following two examples.

Scheme 1. Dense locales Consider a version of signal network in Figure (3.11) where there are two locales: one community in which all n signals are equidistant with distances d_1, and a similar community is located D signal units away, with all n members of that community being d_2 units apart from each other, assume $d_2 > d_1$, i.e. compared to the first one, the second community is loosely connected. It is clear that the members of the first community have signal distances, L_is, smaller than the average distance $\bar{L}$, while all the members of the second community bear signal distances, L_js, larger than the total average. Hence when the public signal is shut down, the members of the first community become more likely to take part in network collective action, while the opposite will be true of the second community: their loosely connected members were highly reliant on the public signal for deciding to take action or to abstain.

The above straightforward argument paves the way for the next conclusion.

Scheme 2. Small world networks These webs of interaction resemble spatially confined social networks among individuals.[68] Each person is connected to a few neighbors, while some individuals are connected to others across the universe of all individuals, i.e. if r is the radius of connectivity, everybody is connected to $2r$ neighbors, while there are a small number of random diametrical bridges in the network, see Figure (3.12). Take the signal distance ($|x_i - x_j|$) between neighbors in local neighborhoods to be d. It is clear that the average signal distance in the whole network is $d + \epsilon$, where the small positive term ϵ exists because of rare diametrical bridges. Also for the majority of individuals in a *small world network*, $L_i = d < \bar{L}$, which means in a *small world network* an

---

[68] See Watts (2002).

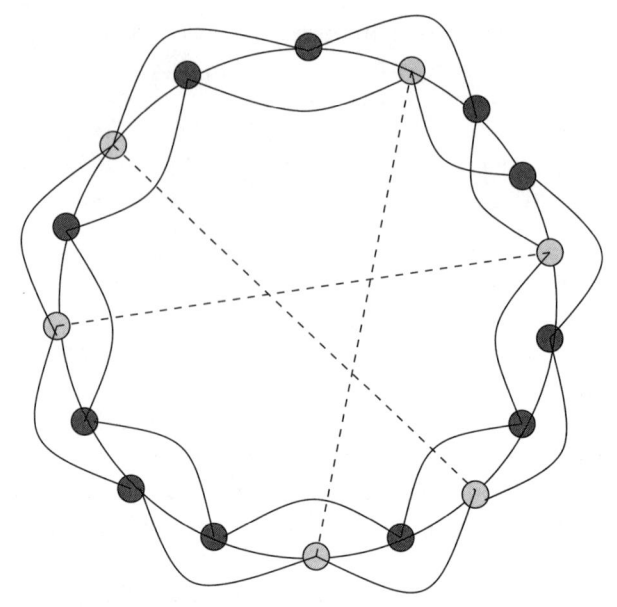

FIGURE 3.12. A *small world network* with random bridges (dashed) and connectivity radius $r > 1$, here $r = 2$.

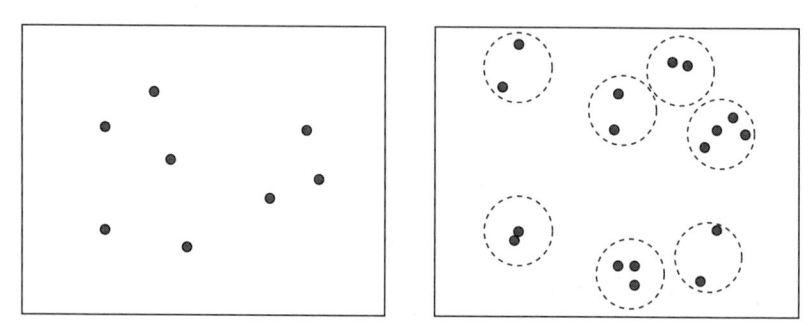

FIGURE 3.13. Schematic depiction of decentralization and localization processes after the disruption (from left to right), each dot represents a conflictual incident.

absolute majority are more likely to take part in collective action in the case of a public signal blackout.

In the next chapter, detailed daily distributions of conflict locations in Damascus before and during a complete shutdown of communications in late 2012 demonstrate spatial characteristics similar to the hallmarks of *small world networks*. I have used a detailed geolocated list of conflictual incidents to show that further dispersion of contention clusters (c.f.

minimal cores), close-knit on the local and widespread across the city of Damascus, occurred during the Syrian blackout of late November 2012. Such transformation of social network represents a situation similar to that in Figure (3.13). In the absence of routine public signals it is likely that the decentralized escalation was exacerbated based on the logic I outlined above: lack of public signal in *small world networks* promoted collective risk taking, not the opposite.[69]

All of these patterns are only the initial steps in detailing the dynamics of *leading from the periphery*. Later using behavioral experiments of collective risk taking I ponder the speed and trajectory of the agitations originating from the periphery. The results of network experiments portray fast moving waves of risk taking in networks, the failure or success of which are more frequent and more rapidly diffusing than those originating from the central vanguard. However before tending to these two corroborating studies, it is necessary to examine the dynamics of decentralized leading from the margins, in relation to one of the better known procedures in network theory for generating *small world networks*.

REWIRING TO *SMALL WORLD NETWORK?* NETWORK MODELS AND FURTHER EMPIRICAL EVIDENCE

Finally, it is important to note the effect of media disruption on an existing social network, and close this analytical chapter with an exploratory idea. Note that during a blackout the social network edges, the broken links among friends, acquaintances and media users and their sources of information have to be *rewired*. During the chaotic conditions of a complete media shutdown the process of rewiring is at times random. The results of the Cairo survey in the last chapter show that many of those affected reported seeking alternative modes of communication, taking to the streets and asking onlookers about the situation. Now this process of *rewiring* of an existing status quo network is similar to the well known Watts-Strogatz algorithm for producing *small world networks* from regular grid networks. The result of rewiring each edge with a given fixed probability is shown to produce variations of *small*

---

[69] Note that according to the model, the disruption itself is not a public signal, as it can either alarm the population about an imminent strike or spread the impression of a weak state. The net psychological effect of such rare and consequential events is not clear. It certainly does not promote an accurate *public signal*, among the disconnected public, instead it causes public signals to wither.

world networks which are locally dense, and are linked across highly connected locales via far reaching *bridges*.[70] Now, after three chapters, the idea of collective action as a product of *leading from the periphery* is starting to take shape: such processes are overshadowed by the hardened means of centralized power and communication. During complete and abrupt shutdown of existing social networks, the alienated individuals quickly start seeking new links in the information vacuum. Local clusters take shape, new network formats that are conducive to action from the periphery are formed. Their propensity to take risk is sharpened in the absence of public information and in the presence of the newly shaped social network. The exacerbating effect of the two processes escalates the decentralized network collective action to new levels, and empowers the local vanguard.

Later, in a series of experiments, I will show that these waves of network collective action from the periphery, are abrupt and ubiquitous.

---

[70] Watts and Strogatz (1998).

4

Civil War and Contagion in *Small Worlds*

> In the literature on social protest, organizations matter principally as mechanisms for coordinating action and mobilizing resources (human and otherwise) through the application of incentives; their impact on social interaction tends to go unnoticed
>
> Roger V. Gould, *Insurgent Identities*, p. 21

Edward Snowden, a fugitive former system administrator for the Central Intelligence Agency (CIA) and a previous National Security Agency (NSA) contractor,[1] ascribed the only multi-day countrywide disruption of the Internet and fast cellular communications in Syria in 2012, and the longest during the conflict,[2] to the US National Security Agency. This claim, if true, provides a unique opportunity for studying the effects of information and communication technology on the course of urban conflict in the form of an experiment run in Syria by the NSA. Snowden claims[3]

> One day an intelligence officer told him that TAO – a division of NSA hackers – had attempted in 2012 to remotely install an exploit in one of the core routers at a major Internet service provider in Syria, which was in the midst of a prolonged civil war. This would have given the NSA access to email and other Internet traffic from much of the country. But something went wrong, and the router was bricked instead – rendered totally inoperable. The failure of this router caused Syria to suddenly lose all connection to the Internet.

---

[1] Alexander (2013).
[2] To date.
[3] Bamford (2014).

Comparing the above with a description of the disruption from a data science and open intelligence company, which monitored the Syrian Internet at the time, is intriguing:[4]

> In Syria all backhaul for cell networks is done on IP and … we were able to notice all IP infrastructure went down in Syria. That means the cell networks did not go down because the physical layer went dark, but because the IP layers stopped functioning[5] (core routers were off, and DNS was down).[6]

The above email provides support for the statement on tampering with routers. No physical disruption took place, it was a software malfunction which caused the collapse of main routers and the Internet Protocol (IP) layer.

While Snowden's claims cannot be independently verified, the incident provided a unique opportunity to study the dynamics of conflict in relation to means of communication in either case: if disruption in Syria's countrywide communications was an accident, or it was intended by the regime, as was the case in Egypt. Either way, the situation is another unique, countrywide, albeit unfortunate, experiment run by those who have means to disrupt or control the means of streamlined communication.[7]

In particular, it is important to see if the disruption activated the same decentralization processes that I outlined in the Egyptian case. More importantly, the proliferation processes in these clusters of dispersed contention are of interest. The dynamics of spread of the conflict is related to the nature of contention, coordinated or not, and provides insights into the role of information in collective risk taking during bouts of contentious activity against the state. *Leading from the periphery* is expected to spread via *contagion*, i.e. spillovers in space and time, not through projections of authority from collective action's centralized command. These patterns, if present at all, are discernible in the detailed daily data on conflict I will present later in this chapter. If collective violence in Damascus was solely a product of centralized coordinations, then contagion from one spatial unit to another should not take place. On the other hand, if the contention is the product of stoking contention by

---

[4] Sec Dev (2012).
[5] Distracting typos in the original email are fixed in the quotation.
[6] Rohozinski (2013), personal correspondence with SecDev. IP stands for Internet Protocol (layer), DNS represents Domain Name System.
[7] In the following, I will argue that there is strong evidence for the singularity of the Syrian media disruption in November 2012.

peripheral leaders in a variety of locations, then the flow and trajectory of their spread, and the spatial correlations created by such step by step proliferation from each corner to the next, should be detectable in the data. If the spread of collective action took other routes in the social network, for example if it spread from a central leadership to all, close and far, then a significant correlation in the spatiotemporal micropatterns of daily violence should not exist. In that sense, microlevel data on conflictual evidence, which I will present and analyze in this chapter, can verify the existence of *leading from the periphery*, and network collective action from the margins. More importantly, in the absence of all means of communication, during the shutdown, these processes should escalate, these are the effects one can seek in the data.

This chapter continues on the notion of highly clustered versus loosely connected locales, as well as the dynamics of contention (coordination and contagion based) and how they interacted differently with the blackout.

In this chapter, I put the predictions of the logic of *leading from the periphery*, outlined in the previous chapter, to the test. The spread of violence in local spheres of contention, that are globally dispersed, but locally concentrated, should be, at least partially, evident in the data. Furthermore, I will show that the patterns I detect are not forms of governmental action. Routine and coordinated acts of violence follow trajectories distinct from the processes I have discussed in the previous sections of the book. A separation between government induced versus oppositional activities will help to make this point clear.

In contrast to an orchestration of action from the center, mobilization from the periphery, as a collective action mechanism, operates over ephemeral, short-lived and contagious connections. The detection of contagion processes – simply the impersonal proliferation of action from one spatial quarter to an adjacent one – can provide an explanation on why a mass movement seeded in the margins of the society can take it over.

As I argued for the Egyptian case, modes of communication can emphasize one mode of proliferation, contagion or coordination, over the other. A complete shutdown of communications in the second year of the Syrian Civil War provided a unique opportunity to put the *Dispersion Hypothesis* to the test yet again. The findings in this chapter test the existence of three distinct, but interconnected, features of *leading from the periphery*: first, contagion as a process of proliferation; second, escalation during a blackout – a reaffirmation; third, local clustering and global dispersion of collective action, akin to the structure of *small world networks*.

COMMUNICATION AND CONFLICT IN THE MARGINS

Modes of mobilization based on coordination and contagion operate on different dynamic patterns and, based on the very same division, the role of information and communication technology in conflict is at best dichotomous. The introduction of mobile communication to the African continent is shown to have increased the levels of civil violence,[8] while there are reports on Iraqi rebels destroying cell towers in an attempt to diffuse the flow of information to the authorities. The existence of cell communication on the regional level in Iraq is linked to lower levels of conflict.[9] A potential resolution to these seemingly contradicting findings is impeded by empirical difficulties, as highly detailed data on communication and violent transactions in the volatile context of a live conflict are rare. Randomized experimentation in the field on such occasions are obviously impermissible.[10] In such situations, the best one can do is to extrapolate sudden, far reaching and – ideally – exogenous changes in modes of communication and identify significant effects in the spatiotemporal dynamics of the conflict as a result of the shock. The results help to explore the processes that underlie such effects. An opportunity for such a study represented itself during the Syrian Civil War in late November 2012.

During the Syrian Civil War the Assad regime frequently used local disruptions of communication as a means of war.[11] This is in line with novel usage of means of communication and grid connectivity in conflict. Any tools of connection which can be switched on and off become means of war in such situations. However, on November 29, 2012, Syria experienced an unprecedented and complete shutdown of the Internet and fast cell communications[12] that lasted for at least two days.[13] During the blackout, the daily fatalities of the war in the whole country increased.[14] Later I will show that the disruption was also accompanied by an increase

---

[8] Pierskalla and Hollenbach (2013).
[9] Shapiro and Weidmann (2015).
[10] I will present the results of a controlled laboratory experiment of collective risk taking in the next chapter.
[11] Personal interviews with Damascus residents in southern and eastern Damascus, also see Chozick (2012).
[12] Syrian Observatory of Human Rights (2012).
[13] Connectivity was restored on December 1, the incident was the longest of its type during the conflict. Source: Google Transparency Report, www.google.com/transparencyreport/.
[14] Daily counts based on reports in Syrian Observatory of Human Rights (2012) show an uptick in the number of fatalities. Gohdes (2015) demonstrates a similar surge.

in the geographical dispersion of conflictual incidents in the city of Damascus proper and its suburbs.[15] A theory of civil conflict based on coordination,[16] selective incentives[17] and punishing ambivalence[18] alone cannot explain the increase in the intensity and dispersion of conflict during the blackout. In fact, resource mobilization theories predict a *deescalation* in the absence of communication.[19] Not surprisingly, and based on a similar logic, authorities often disrupt communications in an attempt to diffuse rebellion.[20]

Furthermore, if the Syrian government wanted to strike the rebels at certain areas, it could have done so on a local level, as it had been doing for the total length of the civil war to that date. The blackout, even as an ominous signal, does not motivate abrupt and colossal participation on the side of the rebels, instead it informs the population of an imminent strike. A similar blackout of only a few hours on July 19, 2012 prompted flights from volatile neighborhoods in Damascus:[21] "Damascus: The Basateen al-Mezzah area is witnessing a large-scale migration out of the area, they are fearing military operations from the syrian [sic] forces who have surrounded the area."

In the asymmetric conditions of the Syrian Civil War such signals discourage direct *coordinated* engagement. An answer to the puzzle of decentralization and escalation during total blackouts merely based on a logic of *coordination* is incomplete. Instead, marginal and ephemeral vanguard on the contagious grounds of total blackout take the helm, and the traces of the process are verifiable in the spatiotemporal trajectory of the conflictual process.

In this chapter, I outline a design which employs the Syrian media disruption of November 2012 as a tool for studying the dynamics of leading network collective action from the periphery, specifically in the urban environment. After identifying a significant increase in the geographical dispersion of conflict in the Syrian capital during the disruption, I characterize the processes of *contagion* in Damascus in 2012, simply defined as proliferation of conflict from one spatial unit to an adjacent one, and detect proxies for both dispersion and contagion.

---

[15] Similar decentralization processes were reported during the complete media shutdown of the 2011 Egyptian Revolution Hassanpour (2014).
[16] Olson (1971).
[17] Lichbach (1995).
[18] Kalyvas and Kocher (2007).
[19] Marwell et al. (1988).
[20] Howard et al. (2011).
[21] Syrian Observatory of Human Rights (2012).

TABLE 4.1. *Four possibilities, coordination and orientation, quadrants of interest, (I) and (III), contain the majority of the events. The signs show the effect of the two parameters on clustering (distance from nearest incident) of conflictual events. + represents an increase in the nearest distance, – a decrease*

	Coordination	No Coordination
Anti-Regime	+ + (II)	+ – (I)
Pro-Regime	– + (III)	– – (IV)

Based on a detailed account of conflict in Damascus in the course of the last nine months of 2012, I construct a dataset that documents the daily existence of violent conflict at a mile-by-mile resolution in an area of 252 square miles covering Damascus and its suburbs from April to December 2012, in conjunction with the geographical elements of Damascus' urban landscape. I use the pertinent GIS (Geographical Information System) dataset to detect processes of spatial contagion during the conflict. The Damascus GIS dataset is available in the online appendix at https://goo.gl/ZCjY9b.

A nearest incident analysis of the location of violent conflicts shows two utmost important findings: first, that on average, premeditated and coordinated violent incidents were less clustered in space and time compared to the rest of the conflictual events. Second, compared to regime induced atrocities, anti-regime violent incidents were more dispersed.

A combination of both effects constitutes a dispersed insurgency that was also locally clustered. See Table (4.1). In other words, lack of coordination meant more clustered violence, and oppositional violence was more dispersed in general, i.e. two conflicting characteristics of locally clustered and globally dispersed contention. These are defining qualities of *leading from the periphery*.

Furthermore, I find the existence of conflict in the neighboring spatiotemporal units to be significantly linked to the occurrence of violence in a given unit of analysis, i.e. a day-spatial window. This provides an estimate for the average counts of conflict at time t based on the number of violent incidents in the spatial neighborhood at time $t-1$. I show that existence of one additional incident in the immediate spatial neighborhood in the previous day translated to a 25 percent increase in the average possibility of conflict on a given day.

One last, and important at that, finding is that while both *contagion* and *disruption* parameters in the dataset are significant predictors of violent incidents in the spatiotemporal window of interest, adding the *interaction term* between the two (*contagion* and *disruption*) reveals that the significance of communication disruption as a facilitator of conflict is through its activation of contagion processes. Contagion was effectively activated during the blackout.

In the previous discussion on the role of the underlying signal structure on network collective action, I showed that only certain types of social networks become more contentious when public signal is removed. Was the Syrian case also similar in nature to such networks? Posing this as a dilemma, I hypothesize that if the Syrian contentious network had been of a hierarchical or highly connected type, then the removal of the public signal should have quieted the conflict, but if it was of the type shaped in small and clustered circles of action, dispersed far apart, and mainly driven by contagion, then a removal of these widely shared signals on danger, coordination and planning should have resulted in an exacerbation of the whole conflict, further decentralization of the contention and an escalation. After controlling for the regime's activities, regularities of the conflict and the regularities of the rebel movements in each zone of the urban theater, I show that it is the case.

WHAT ARE THE PROCESSES OF "LEADING FROM THE PERIPHERY"? GEOMETRY OF *CONTAGION* VERSUS CALCULUS OF *COORDINATION*

The role of digital communication in conflict can be cast in two distinct molds: communication links can be used to facilitate collective action via *coordination*,[22] digital communication can also create long social *bridges*[23] that are known to interact with the proliferation of social processes in *small world networks*.[24] *Long bridges* hinder diffusion via stifling action when the contagion of collective action requires multiple reinforcements to become viable.[25] The existence of further communication links can prevent clustered reinforcement of risk taking,

---

[22] Marwell et al. (1988).
[23] Links between highly connected clusters of a *small world network* facilitated by means of virtual communication.
[24] These are networks that show high levels of local clustering, but they are globally sparse, see Watts and Strogatz (1998).
[25] That means when contagion is of a *complex* kind Centola and Macy (2007). In complex contagion, induced by other regarding processes, for example, the threshold models of

simply because the majority are risk averse. In this setup, too much exposure to the average sentiment of the network via excessive communication only overwhelms deviations from the norm.

Another important difference between the two modes of collective action involves group size in relation to intention to act. Contagion is facilitated in larger groups, and is suppressed in smaller ones.[26] For coordination, however, the provision of public goods for preventing free-riding becomes more difficult as the size of the group grows.[27] Coordination in the open requires safe havens from the authorities such as higher geographical elevation, as well as means for far reaching communication via digital means. These are all characteristics of civil conflict in more sparsely populated areas. In contrast, contagion benefits from interactions in closed and crowded urban spaces in the plains. Contagion processes from radical *minimal cores* suffer from long communication ties provided by excessive usage of digital communication.[28] When there is a possibility of observing others' action in close quarters and close-knit social networks, *contagion* processes become prominent. The dichotomy between the two processes leads to a research plan that is informed by the geography of conflict as well as the nature of the means of digital communication. The logic of civil conflict in urban environments combines insights from civil war studies with those of contentious politics, at times violent, in urban spaces.[29] The urban staging

collective action Granovetter (1978), often multiple social reinforcements are required for triggering action. The results of the dynamics are clearly the opposite if the contagion is of a simple kind, i.e. when a single contact between two individuals is enough for transmitting a behavior Watts and Strogatz (1998). For examples of diffusion in heterogeneous institutional networks see Strang and Tuma (1993).

[26] Axelrod (1997).
[27] Olson (1971).
[28] The debate between those who take communication technology to be a catalyst of rebellion, e.g. Pierskalla and Hollenbach (2013) and others who find communication media to be an *opium of the masses* of sorts Kern and Hainmueller (2009) is best understood under a framework that distinguishes *coordination*-based explanations from those which explain contention as a result of *contagion* processes. Cell communication eased coordination among African rebels, hence it increased the level of rebel conflict under the watch of weak African states; it also opened conduits for reconnaissance and intimidation in other contexts. By targeting cell towers Shapiro and Weidmann (2015), Iraqi rebels disrupted information channels to the authorities and at the same time enabled local network relations among potential recruits, a communication network that was far from the eyes of the Iraqi state.
[29] The topology of geographical terrain is known to influence the odds of insurgency Fearon and Laitin (2003). Urban planning has been used as a means of political control. Urban arrangement, as a mode of visibility Scott (1998), was a salient component of mobilization during the Paris Commune. The *Haussmannization* of Paris' landscape

of the Syrian Civil War, particularly in Damascus, along with variations in the communication regime during the conflict, provide a plausible testing ground for theories of coordination and contagion in urban conflict. In contrast to resource mobilization theories of collective action in civil wars fought in open terrains, the results invite more attention to network processes at work in civil warfare in dense urban quarters.[30]

THE SYRIAN CIVIL WAR, SYRIAN CULTURE OF VISUAL AUTHORITY, STRUCTURAL COMPONENTS OF CONFLICT AND CONNECTIVITY

The Arab Spring reached Syria in March 2011.[31] Civilian protests in mostly Sunni areas faced uncompromising military response that soon escalated to an all out war. In suppressing the protests without mercy, Bashar Al Assad was replicating a similar episode from 1982, when his father Hafez al-Assad responded to a rebellion in the city of Hama with full force leaving fatalities in the order of thousands.[32] Following the indiscriminate killings in 1982, the authorities remodeled Hama: "Heavily damaged old quarters were bulldozed away, roads were cut through where once no car could pass, squares and gardens were laid out. The whole of Hama was reshaped on a grand scale."[33]

Subsequent to the protests in 2011, violent conflicts occurred both in rural and urban areas and the newly salient ethnic and religious allegiances fueled local contention.[34]. Dense urban areas in Damascus, Aleppo, Hama, Homs and Dara became grounds for clashes. Rebels used digital means of communication for organization; simultaneously these tools became venues for surveillance and tracking on the side of the regime.[35] Both sides implemented an array of communication strategies to gain the upper hand in a conflict that relied on mediated narration as a

---

and population shifts around the city ensured the Commune resurrection in 1871 was different from the one in 1848 Gould (1995). Social networks also transform during civil wars Lyall (2010); Wood (2008), and the underlying social network structure influences the nature of collective action Metternich et al. (2013); Parkinson (2013).

30 The Syrian Civil War is shaped by both the public urban terrain and digital means of publication Lynch et al. (2014). The emblems of authority were present in each and every aspect of Syrian life Wedeen (1999). The ubiquitous presence of authority in Hafez Assad's Syria was an economizing replacement for the actual use of violence Scott (1990).
31 Lynch et al. (2014).
32 Seale (1988); Van Dam (2011).
33 Seale (1988, p. 334).
34 Christia (2013); Holliday and Lynch (2012); Petersen (2013).
35 Chozick (2012).

means of war.[36] Less than a year after the start of the uprising, Damascus itself became a scene of clashes between the rebels and the regime's forces. A fragile ceasefire between the two sides was in place between April and June of 2012, the end of which culminated in a rebel offensive in Damascus starting on July 14. On July 18, a bomb attack against the National Security headquarters killed the Syrian Defense Minister, his deputy, a former defense minister and Syria's national security chief. The Syrian government staged the Battle of Damascus against the rebels in the following two weeks. Southern and eastern areas of Damascus endured the regime's counterattack in the ensuing two months. The second major rebel offensive in Damascus in 2012 occurred in November when the rebels attempted to capture Damascus International Airport in the southeast of the city on November 28. On the 29th major clashes happened in the east of Damascus and both sides of the conflict claimed they had the airport under their control.[37] The clashes continued and escalated in December.[38]

The communication disruption referred to by Edward Snowden as a technical glitch enacted by the NSA occurred during the clashes over the airport in the southeastern corner of Damascus. Internet communications were shut down all together across Syria around noon local time (GMT+2) on November 29[39] and did not return to normal till the afternoon of December 1. Along with Internet access, fast mobile communications were also disrupted during the blackout,[40] influencing rebel communications; e.g. for mobilization and coordination purposes rebels extensively used Skype[41] which relies on network protocols distinct from those used for voice calls. The software on mobile devices could not operate in the absence of fast cellular communications.

In the following, I exploit the very same nationwide intervention in communications in late November along with the geolocated daily account of atrocities during the Syrian Civil War in Damascus in 2012 as an identification instrument for exploring the communication–conflict nexus.

---

[36] Lynch et al. (2014).
[37] Reynolds (2012).
[38] The time line of the atrocities is quoted from the *New York Times* and Syrian Observatory for Human Rights' Facebook page. For an account of the regime's counterinsurgency see Holliday (2013).
[39] SecDev (2012).
[40] All backhaul for the Syrian cell networks flows through the Internet Protocol layer, and a disruption of the Internet means a simultaneous shutdown of the 3G cell network Rohozinski (2013).
[41] Chozick (2012). Skype is a voice over IP software.

CONTENTIOUS "SPACES OF FLOWS AND SPACES OF PLACES"[42]

I parsed Damascus' urban sprawl and its main suburbs into a 1-mile by 1-mile grid approximately 18 miles long and 14 miles wide. On this grid, I superimposed a detailed geolocated dataset of violent conflict locations in Damascus and its suburbs on a daily basis during 2012.[43] The data cover the date, the high resolution longitude and latitude for each event, as well as information on the orientation (anti- or pro-regime), type of the conflictual incident (see below) and the precision of the available information on the event. For each incident to be coded once per day per location, it had to involve at least one of the following "types":

> 1) Direct fire engagement between regime and rebel forces (fire fight with two parties involved), 2) Bombing attack against regime troops or facilities, 3) Airstrikes, 4) Indirect fire (i.e. shelling) only if reported casualties are greater than 15, 5) Assassinations or kidnappings of regime personnel, 6) Regime raids or arrests that involve a major troop movement.[44]

I intersected the conflict data with the available information on the levels of connectivity[45] in the spatial window under consideration. Figure (4.1) depicts the spatial distribution of conflictual incidents in Damascus and its suburbs (Reef Damascus). Total monthly counts of conflictual events from April to December 2012 were 29, 29, 43, 81, 50, 87, 53, 82 and 173, respectively.

High resolution spatiotemporal data on connectivity in Damascus neighborhoods on par with the detailed conflict location information are difficult to obtain.[46] I conducted interviews on the nature of local disruptions that could not be captured in an aggregate measure such as the countrywide traffic. The interviews provided qualitative data on the nature of *local* disruptions the Assad regime applies in conjunction with military tactics. It became clear that neighborhoods in the south

---

42 Castells (2009*b*).
43 Holliday (2012)'s two main sources for coding conflict locations were Syrian Observatory for Human Rights, as well as the state-sponsored Syrian Arab News Agency (SANA).
44 Holliday (2012).
45 Using a strategy similar to Pierskalla and Hollenbach (2013) and Shapiro and Weidmann (2015), albeit with a much higher resolution.
46 I tried to extrapolate daily average connectivity for each of square mile spatial windows in Figure (4.1) based on geolocated tweets produced in Damascus, but an inquiry showed that the number of geocoded tweets in the spatiotemporal window of interest was too few.

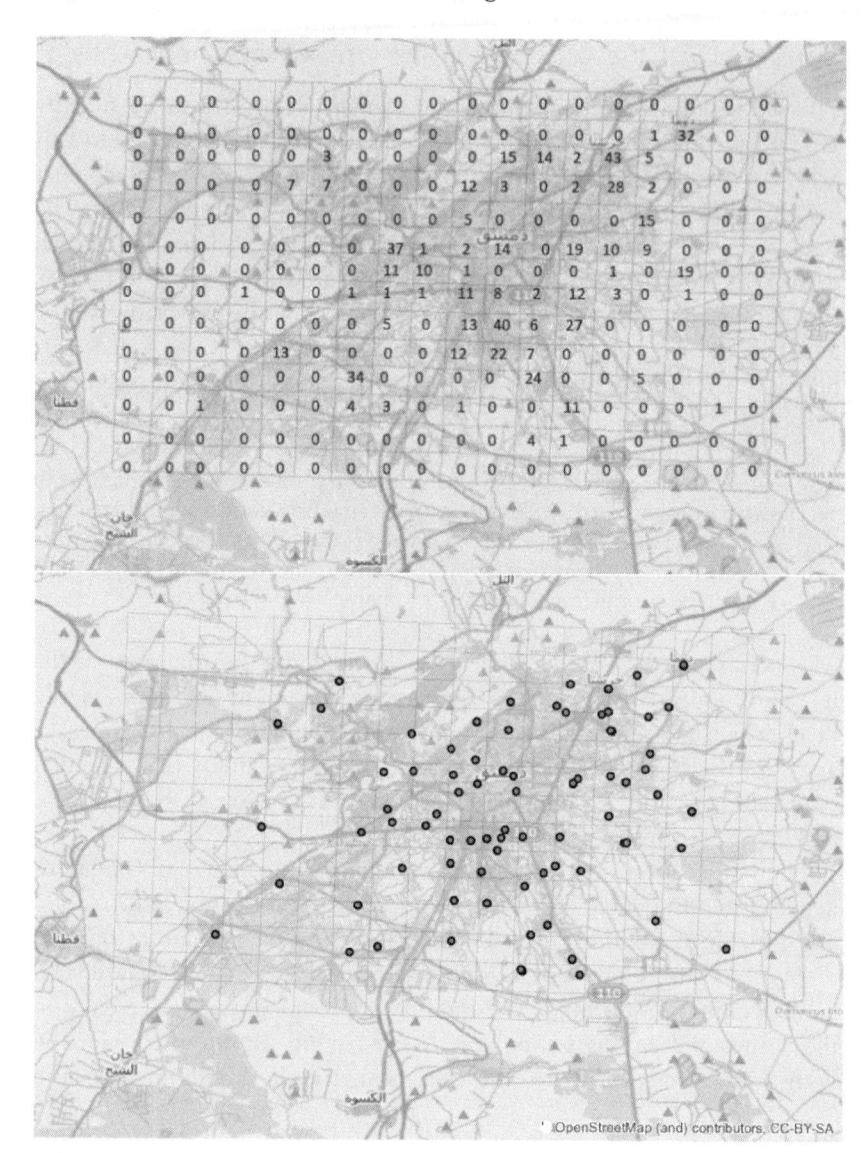

FIGURE 4.1. Top: Number of distinct conflictual incidents in each 1-square mile cell, June–December 2012, Damascus and suburbs. $N = 600$, April and May not included. Bottom: Conflict locations January–December 2012 across Damascus, superimposed on the 1-mile grid and an OpenStreetMap baseline. Some locations contain more than one incident.

and east of Damascus, such as Dayr el Asafir, Yarmouk, East Ghouta and Daraya endured extended and selective disruptions of mobile and Internet communications, at times for months, particularly those close to military facilities and those under an ongoing military attack.[47]

In the absence of daily and mile by mile data on connectivity I exploited nationwide disruptions of cell and Internet media as the intervention of interest. There were two incidents of countrywide Internet and mobile disruptions in Syria in 2012. One occurred on July 19 and lasted for approximately an hour. The extended disruption mentioned in Snowden's interview occurred on November 29. Prior to the disruption of November 2012, the only daylong blackout occurred on Friday June 3, 2011 at the beginning of the Syrian uprising, shortly after the Egyptian experimentation with a nationwide blackout in January 2011. The disruption in November 2012 is the longest in the 2011–2014 period, and the only multi-day blackout in 2012.[48] A comparison between the two occasions of countrywide blackout depicted in Figure (4.2) demonstrates technical differences. While the one in 2011 went into effect gradually, the disruption on November 29 was abrupt. A gradual switching off of communication links is unlikely to have caused the global failure of communications in November 2012.

---

[47] Personal interviews with ex-rebels who spent the year 2012 in Damascus were conducted via Skype. Interview transcripts provide limited neighborhood-level topical data on connectivity disruptions in Damascus in 2012. Because the data are not complete on a daily basis and in all quarters of Damascus, it is impossible to draw definitive inferences merely from qualitative accounts. In my search for reliable connectivity proxies, I examined the statistics of geocoded tweets generated in the spatial window containing Damascus and its suburbs with the hope of creating data on the levels of online activity on a daily basis and to detect irregularities on both spatial and temporal levels. This strategy, if applicable, could yield the most detailed account of connectivity trends in the Syrian capital. However, a preliminary inquiry (historical tweet search by Gnip Inc. on the author's behalf.) showed that the total number of geocoded tweets generated inside the 14 by 18 mile rectangle containing Damascus and its suburbs during the whole year of 2012 did not exceed 4000. Nevertheless, with the rise of geocoded online publication, more network patterns of collective behavior are coming to light. Such detectable spatiotemporal patterns are expected to promote the analysis and prediction of collective behavior on a massive scale. This study utilizes the available data from the Syrian conflict in order to detect processes of contagion and escalation, similar methods can effectively apply to the increasingly rich information on closely watched conflicts in the urban terrain.
[48] For a complete list of traffic disruptions of Google products and services and by proxy the Internet, see www.google.com/transparencyreport/traffic/disruptions/.

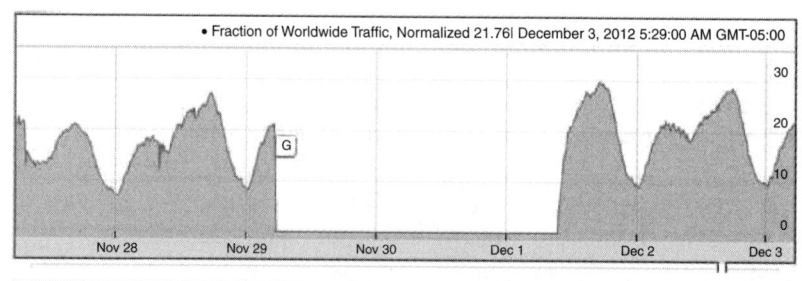

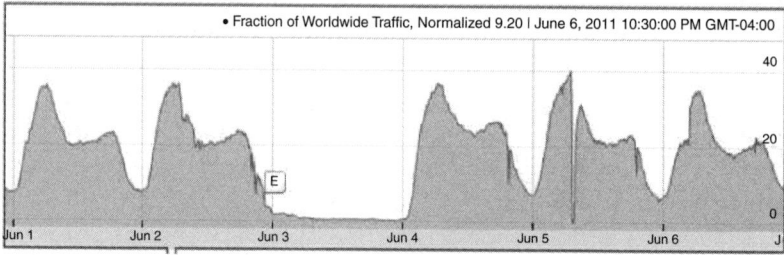

FIGURE 4.2. A depiction of full Internet disruption on November 29, 2012 (top) and June 3, 2011 (bottom). Google services, fraction of worldwide traffic, normalized. Source: Google Transparency Report http://goo.gl/5sNjN and http://goo.gl/7Go89, respectively. Mobile communications were shut down in parallel to the Internet. Comparing the two disruptions shows they were of different technical nature.

DISPERSION HYPOTHESIS REAFFIRMED: DECENTRALIZATION OF CONTENTION

The first of the predictions of a theory of network collective action based on the marginal vanguardism paradigm is that in the absence of communication media collective risk taking is decentralized. In the following using the daily geolocated data on violent clashes, I show that, similar to the Egyptian case outlined in Chapter (2), the full disruption of communication in November 2012 coincided with an unprecedented increase in the *dispersion* of the conflict in Damascus. To demonstrate the effect, I define three different measures of conflict dispersion (see equation (4.1)) and examine the temporal profile of the dispersion measures before, during and after the blackout in November.

Using the longitude and latitude of the incidents on each day I calculated the daily sum of pairwise distances between every possible pair of incidents that happen on the same day. For all incidents, i and j on day t, the pairwise distance is defined as $d_{ij}(t)$; this gives the first definition of dispersion in equation (4.1). One can also normalize the sum of pairwise distances using the daily count of incidents, N_t; finally the count on every day itself can be used as a measure of conflict dispersion, this is the same quantity used in Chapter (2) to estimate the dynamics of protest dispersion in Cairo during the Egyptian Revolution of 2011. The first two definitions capture the effect of both the distance between incidents and their counts as measures of dispersion: the farther any given pair of incidents are from each other, the more dispersed they are; every additional incident also increases the dispersion of the whole set, because every additional incident means conflict exists where it did not exist before.[49]

Figure (4.3) shows the temporal profile of the geographical dispersion of violent incidents in Damascus and Reef Damascus (Damascus suburbs) based on the three definitions in equation (4.1). All three definitions portray an unprecedented increase in conflict dispersion during the blackout. A simple examination of temporal correlations using Ordinary Least Squares (OLS) regressions in Table (4.2) shows that dispersion at time t is correlated with dispersion at $t - 1$, and days of full disruptions (coded as dummies on November 29, 30 and December 1) are robustly linked to a decentralization of the conflict. The Fridays do not induce an increase in dispersion, and their effect is not statistically significant.

The increase in the dispersion of conflict during the blackout mirrors the same phenomenon during the Egyptian Revolution. The escalation of violence during the blackout is similar to the proliferation and exacerbation of revolutionary unrest on January 28, 2011.

In the absence of definitive evidence on the verity of Snowden's claims, one could ascribe the decentralization to at least two other elements: the ongoing normal trend of the conflict, and the regime's decision to escalate. I examine both explanations in the following and show that they do not provide convincing alternative reasons on why the conflict was decentralized on the scale seen in Figure (4.3) in the aftermath of the disruption. First, one could argue that the increase in dispersion would have happened regardless of the disruption. Later, I will examine such a possibility in detail by constructing a predictor of conflictual incidents

---

[49] The normalized definition ensures clustering does not exponentially increase the dispersion. Three definitions of dispersion I have used:

$$D_1(t) = \sum_{ij}^{N_t} d_{ij}(t), \quad D_2(t) = \sum_{ij}^{N_t} d_{ij}(t)/N_t, \quad D_3(t) = N_t. \qquad (4.1)$$

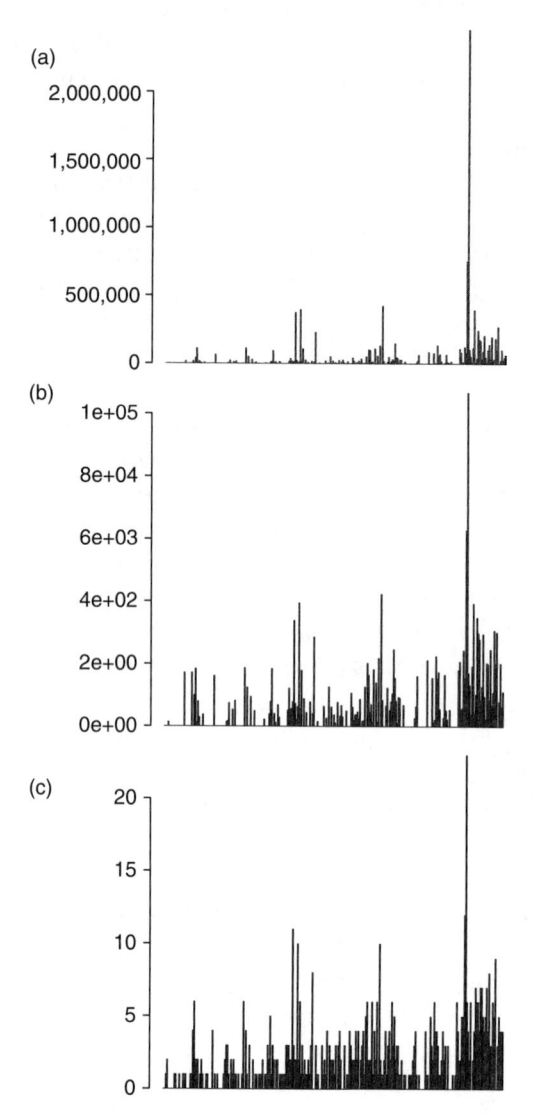

FIGURE 4.3. Dispersion of conflictual incidents in meters, Damascus and suburbs, April 1, 2012 to December 31, 2012 for three dispersion definitions in equation (4.1). The three days in which Syria was experiencing a complete blackout, November 29, 30 and December 1, show the highest levels of dispersion in all three definitions.

TABLE 4.2. *Dispersion level at time t: three definitions, OLS regressions*

	(1) Dispersion at t Sum Distance	(2) Dispersion at t Sum Distance Normalized	(3) Dispersion at t Count
Dispersion at time $t-1$	0.166***	0.261***	0.315***
	(0.0447)	(0.0510)	(0.0518)
Disruption	1025193.1***	49011.8***	9.683***
	(71164.5)	(5402.1)	(1.272)
Fridays	−21675.6	−1773.2	−0.582
	(21098.7)	(1550.4)	(0.371)
Intercept	25656.7**	4356.2***	1.537***
	(8056.0)	(656.1)	(0.179)
N	275	275	275
adj. R^2	0.474	0.339	0.298

Standard errors in parentheses
* $p < 0.05$, ** $p < 0.01$, *** $p < 0.001$

based on spatiotemporal as well as socioeconomic patterns of conflict, and show that even after controlling for socioeconomic, temporal and spatial trends, *disruption* is a statistically significant independent variable in engendering conflict.

One could also ascribe the increase in dispersion to a coordinated campaign by the regime to stifle rebel activity on the 29th, 30th and 1st. Based on this explanation, the regime decided to disrupt communications and preempt rebels in different areas of Damascus afterwards. However, there are two issues that cast doubt on such a solution to the puzzle: first, the significant increase in dispersion did not happen on the first day of disruption, i.e. November 29. Instead, it took a day for the clashes to spread to different parts of the city. If the regime had planned to ambush the rebels in different areas of the city immediately after the disruption, it should have done so on November 29 simultaneously with the full disruption going into effect, not during the next two days. The second issue is based on the temporal pattern of *first incidents*. *First incidents* are defined as those occurring for the first time during the year 2012 at a certain location. Among all first incidents occurring in 31 days, November 1 to December 1, 64 percent, i.e. nine out of 14, happened between November 29 and December 1, in three days alone, when the cell and high-speed Internet communications were absent. From the total 13 neighborhoods experiencing conflict on December 1, five of them had never seen conflict during that year. Similarly, out of nine neighborhoods experiencing conflict on November 30, three locations were the scene of violence for the first time in the past 330 days.[50] If the regime was planning to attack rebel strongholds beforehand, conflict would have been more likely to happen in areas with a history of violence during the past 11 months, not in an unprecedented number of new locations. The same pattern as the rest of November should have prevailed. Furthermore and finally, although the main battles in late November 2012 took place over the Damascus International Airport,[51] the majority of clashes in the ensuing blackout did not happen in the vicinity of the airport. Clashes had spread to other parts of the city on November 30 and December 1. Table (4.3) includes the neighborhoods experiencing clashes before, during and after the blackout.[52]

In the above, I argued that the urban uprising in Damascus during the November blackout demonstrates structural features that are distinct from those of coordinated rebellions merely based on selective incentives. If communication is beneficial for coordination, then disruptions in connectivity should have resulted in hindrance of rebellious activity, not the escalation of it. Processes other than intentional coordination based on selective incentives were likely to have operated in Damascus on November 30 and December 1. In the following, I use the dynamic profile of daily conflict locations to demonstrate the contagion processes at work during escalation. The shaping of *minimal core*, and the conditions for the activation of contagion processes are of special interest in the following. I show that coordination-based acts of collective violence show spatiotemporal characteristics different from the rest. The same is true for

---

[50] The pattern of first incidents during the month of November and the first day of December is depicted in Figure (7.16) in the appendix. Including the conflict history of the 10 months prior to November allays concerns for temporal boundary effects. The temporal distribution of the 14 first incidents that happened in November and December 1 in Figure (7.16) shows the unprecedented concentration of these incidents during the final days of the blackout, November 30 and December 1. These are locations that had not experienced violent conflict during the past 11 months at all.
[51] Reynolds (2012).
[52] Sources: Holliday (2012); Syrian Observatory of Human Rights (2012).

TABLE 4.3. *Major neighborhoods in Damascus and suburbs experiencing violent incidents, late November–early December*

Date	Conflict Locations
November 26	2: Set Zaynab/Darayya
November 27	2: Jaramana (approximate)/Darayya
November 28	5: Douma/Harasta/Beit Sahem/Set Zaynab/Darayya
November 29	5: Irbin/Babbila/Beit Sahm/Kafarsouseh/Jisreen
November 30	9: Al Mouadamyeh/Darayya/Kafar-Sousah/Yalda/Beit Sahem/ Az Zyabeyeh/ Jisreen/Saqba/Douma
December 1	13: Mouadamiya/Douma/Jisreen/Saqba/al-Thiyabiya/Daraya, Bebila/Yalda/ Beit Sahm, Aqraba(2)/Kafarsouseh/A'sh al-Warwar
December 2	4: Jisreen/Maliha/Nashabiya/Deir al-Sleiman
December 3	4: Beit Sahem/Daraya/al-Nabek/Barzeh
December 4	2: Tadamun/al-Fahama

government initiated atrocities compared to the acts of collective violence by the rebels.

DETECTING CLUSTERING, CONTAGION, PROCESSES OF ESCALATION: SPATIOTEMPORAL PATTERNS OF URBAN CONFLICT IN DAMASCUS

The rest of the chapter is an appraisal of the main themes of network collective action, using contentious collective action data from the Syrian conflict. In particular, I will calculate the clustering characteristics of the conflictual events, in order to detect signs of contagion. Based on the arguments in the previous chapter, these contagious processes sustain *minimal cores* in *small world networks*. The phenomenon of local clustering and global dispersion is shown to be central to network collective action processes.

In the following, I parse the geographical and temporal elements of the conflict in Damascus in 2012, in three steps, in order to detect localization and contagion patterns in time and space. First I use nearest past incident data to detect clustering patterns during the conflict. In particular, I use the distinction between coordinated acts of violence and the rest of the incidents to show that coordinated incidents were less clustered. Along the same lines, pro-regime incidents show higher levels of spatiotemporal continuity. Anti-regime activity was more dispersed. Second, I employ a dataset of 252 × 275 geographical cell-days to show that after controlling for structural parameters such as population, elevation, density of throughways and ethnic and economic composition, as well as spatial indices, still the disruption, and the events in neighboring locales in space and time, had a significant impact on the occurrence of violence in a certain location. Such ties across space and time were not endogenous results of some overarching spatiotemporal process. Even after controlling for both time and geographical locations, as well as regular structural components of conflict, disruption shows a significant impact on the escalation of conflict. Finally, using interaction terms between a spatiotemporal lagged index of conflict and the disruption variable I demonstrate the role of disruption in staging contagion from one geographical unit to the other resulting in escalation of the conflict. In particular, the contagion is shown to have been activated during the disruption.

THE CONSTRUCTION OF THE DAMASCUS GEOGRAPHICAL INFORMATION DATASET

I used the conflict data in Damascus in 2012 in conjunction with Damascus Geographical Information System (GIS) processing and a survey study of socioeconomic factors in Damascus to build the dataset I use in the following analysis.[53] The distance from the nearest incident in space and time, as well as the number of incidents in the immediate spatial and temporal lag neighborhood of each unit of study (cell-day) provide efficient ways for measuring the *spatiotemporal contagion* of conflict from time $t - T$ to t and from a cell to its neighboring vicinity. I calculated both of these parameters for each conflictual incident, and each cell-day respectively.

For building a spatiotemporal predictor of conflict, a rectangular 1-mile grid was superimposed on the area under study. For parsing the spatial domain the goal was to choose a grid size capable of capturing the effects of background components such as population and sum length of throughways in each grid cell. The 1-mile grid was the best fit.

---

[53] The final product of the GIS analysis, the Damascus GIS dataset is available in the online appendix at https://goo.gl/ZCjY9b. Geographic information embedded in event data facilitates detection of conflictual patterns Cederman et al. (2011), and prediction of conflict in space and time after further deconstruction to spatial and temporal elements Gleditsch and Weidmann (2012); Ward and Gleditsch (2002). For the purpose of event modeling and regression analysis, spatial regression methods take the inherent correlation between units of analysis into account Ward and Gleditsch (2008).

The average elevation for each cell, a measure of population on a mile-by-mile basis, and the total length of roads situated inside each cell comprise the main structural elements of interest: the elevation level influences the nature of insurgency in each area; the size of population in urban areas influences the organization of collective action; finally the density of roads in neighborhoods represents proxy levels for visibility in the geographical terrain, furthermore, roads are spatial conduits for street battles and their density is expected to have a significant role in altering the dynamics of contagion.[54]

Elevation shows a negative correlation with urban conflict in Damascus across the board with the three grid sizes in Table (4.4). Unlike rebellions that are more likely to take root in remote and inaccessible terrains, urban warfare was more likely to happen in the plains amenable to human construction. Total population is expected to be positively correlated with rebellion: the denser a neighborhood's population is, the more likely it is to experience urban conflict. Implicit in this conclusion is the higher likelihood of contagion processes that potentially contributed greatly to the conflict in Damascus' urban areas. Along the same lines, total length of streets in each grid cell is robustly linked to the number of incidents in the relevant area. Streets are conduits for proliferation of open air conflict, as well as links of visibility in the urban space. A spatial window with no population and no streets is unlikely to produce any violent incident during the Syrian Civil War. Based on the same criterion, I found the 1-mile grid preferable to the 2 and 0.5-mile grids, because the latter two did not capture the significance of the two main control variables of interest (population and total street length) on par with the 1-mile grid. The 1-mile grid is the only parsing mechanism among the three that simultaneously captures the significance of elevation, population and the sum length of streets in engendering urban conflict in each geographical unit.

On the 1-mile grid average control parameters are the following. The average elevation was 761.7 meters, average total population in each cell was 11,546 for a total population of approximately 2,900,000 (this includes the suburbs as well as the city). Note that the official figures were approximately 2.6 million in 2004. Finally, an average of 16,382

[54] Average elevation and total length of streets were calculated using the ArcGIS software and digitized maps of Damascus available on OpenStreetMap: www.openstreetmap.org/. Total population in each cell was calculated using a proxy for population via LandScan project: http://web.ornl.gov/sci/landscan/ Dobson et al. (2000); LandScan (2013).

TABLE 4.4. *Dependent variable: number of violent incidents in each cell, Poisson count regression*

	(1) 2-mile Grid	(2) 1-mile Grid	(3) Half-mile Grid
Average Elevation in each cell	−0.00353*** (0.000493)	−0.00390*** (0.000528)	−0.00378*** (0.000401)
Total Population in each cell	0.00000139 (0.00000103)	0.0000125*** (0.00000212)	0.0000227*** (0.00000624)
Sum Length of Streets in each cell	0.0000138*** (0.00000147)	0.0000312*** (0.00000342)	−0.0000294* (0.0000134)
Intercept	3.549*** (0.356)	2.828*** (0.382)	2.184*** (0.294)
N	84	252	1188
Log-likelihood	−569.3	−1034.3	−2205.8
χ^2	631.6	649.1	126.2

Standard errors in parentheses
* $p < 0.05$, ** $p < 0.01$, *** $p < 0.001$

meters of throughways exist in each cell. In the year 2012, an average of 5.1 violent incidents happened in each 1-mile by 1-mile cell covering Damascus and its suburbs.

Table (4.4) contains Poisson count regressions for grids of size 2, 1 and half-mile. Figure (4.4) contains patterns of population density and elevation for the spatial window of interest.

The socioeconomic condition of each neighborhood is also a cogent component of the civil conflict. The lower income areas are expected to experience more conflict,[55] and the ethnic composition of the areas under study influences the rates of conflict in each geographical unit.[56] Lacking official data on socioeconomic parameters on the microlevel,[57] I surveyed Damascus' current and previous residents on these parameters. The ethnic composition, as well as an approximate income profile of Damascus and

---

[55] Collier and Hoeffler (2004).
[56] Horowitz (2000).
[57] There are datasets such as G-Econ Nordhaus (2006); Nordhaus et al. (2006) that provide economic data on the microlevel, however the highest resolution of the dataset was in the order of 50 miles, which did not apply to the 1-mile resolution employed here.

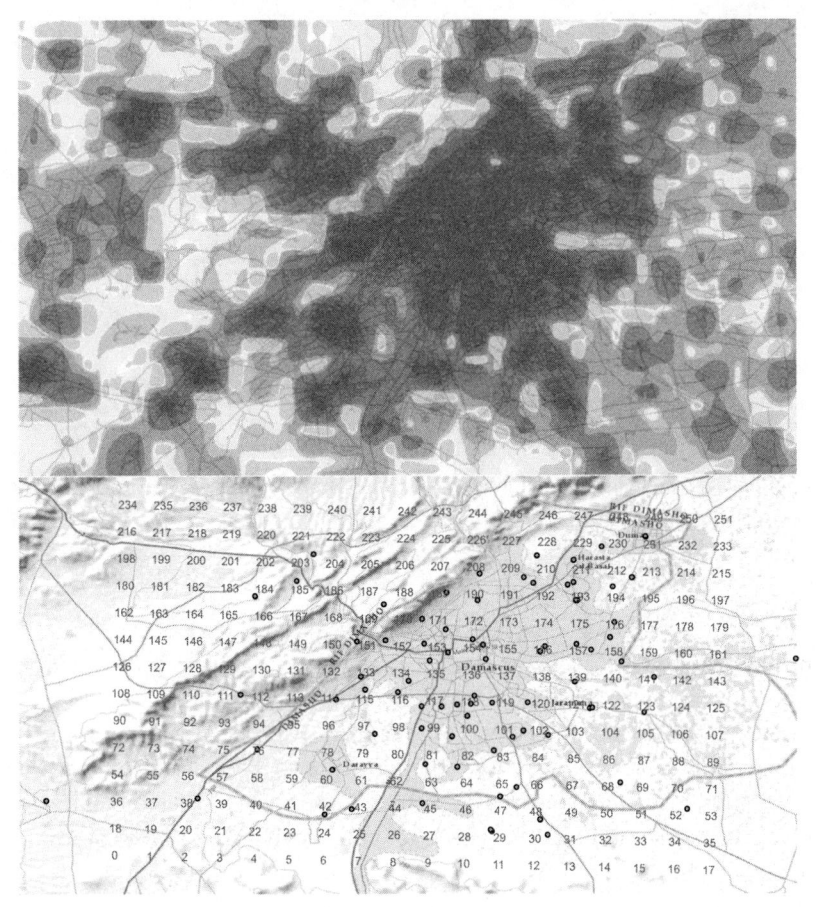

FIGURE 4.4. Top: Population proxy from LandScan (2013), baseline roads from OpenStreetMap are also included. Bottom: Elevation patterns of the spatial window.

surrounding area were coded by a number of Damascus natives. Fourteen respondents with an in depth knowledge of Damascus coded ethnicity and income levels for each neighborhood. Ethnicity–Religion was chosen among categories *Sunni, Alawite, Shia, Christian, Druze* and *Kurdish*. The income level was coded on a tripartite level *Rich, Middle Class, Poor*. I was also cognizant of the fact that Syria was witnessing large scale intra and international migration[58], hence I emphatically asked the survey respondents to answer these questions for the year of interest,

[58] Khaddour and Mazur (2013).

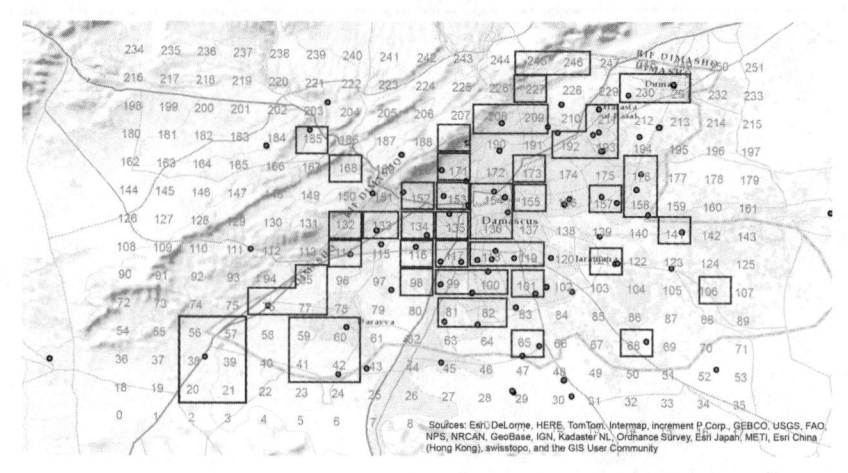

FIGURE 4.5. Damascus, 1-mile grid with the approximate neighborhood delineations superimposed.

2012, alone.[59] The socioeconomic survey questions were asked on the neighborhood level to provide the best level of cognition for our survey subjects. The neighborhoods themselves were outlined based on the existing maps of Damascus and the output from Damascus resident-experts. The map in Figure (4.5) shows the imposition of these neighborhoods on the 1-mile grid. Later, I used the same patterns to cluster the standard errors in Poisson regressions based on neighborhoods, or control for the neighborhood effect.[60]

CLUSTERING AND CREATION OF *MINIMAL CORES*: DETECTING SPATIOTEMPORAL LOCALIZATION

To further illustrate the spatiotemporal dynamics of the conflict I calculated the distance between each violent incident with the nearest event, *both* in time and space, in that sequential order, and used the

---

[59] There is no detailed and recent information on the ethnic composition of Damascus available similar to what exists for Baghdad in Izady (2013).
[60] Among the neighborhoods included in the coding were *Al-Midan, Al-Qabun, Al-Salihiyah, Al-Shaghour, Barzeh, Dummar, Jobar, Kafr Sousa, Mezzeh, Muhajreen, Old City, Qadam, Qanawat, Sarouja* and *Rukn Eldin* in Damascus proper and *Al-Assad, Aqraba, Darayya, Douma, Hajar-al-Aswad, Harasta, Irbin, Jdaydet, Jaramana, Mazzeh 86, Mouadamiyah, Qudssaya, Saqba, Sayyida Zeinab, Yalda, Yarmouk, Zabdean* and *Zamalka* in Reef-Dimashgh (suburbs).

Clustering and Creation of Minimal Cores 127

Histogram of Min_Distance

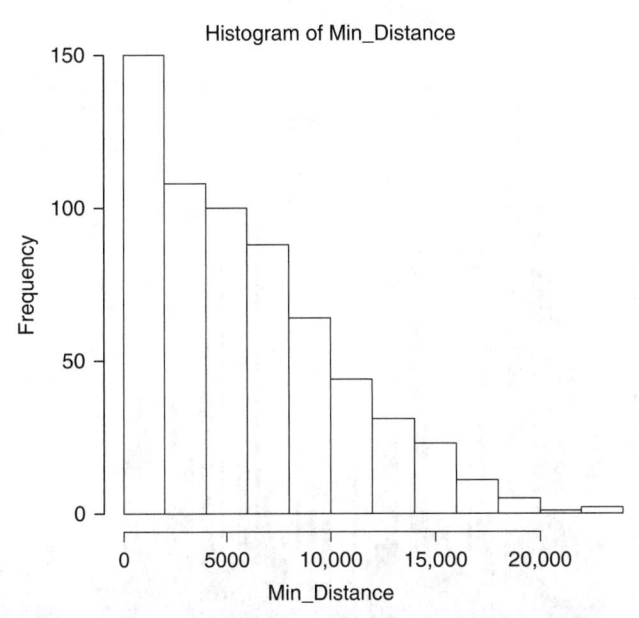

FIGURE 4.6. Histogram of distances from the nearest incident in space and time, Damascus, April to December 2012.

distance as a measure of clustering in the spatial domain.[61] For each of the 627 incidents in the dataset, this measure provides a proxy for the spatiotemporal correlation in the course of the process in the last nine months of 2012. A histogram of minimum distances in Figure (4.6) shows that the distribution is far from a Poisson distribution which is characteristic of a random spatial distribution.[62] The most frequent distances in the histogram are concentrated below 2 kilometers.

Furthermore, Figure (4.7) shows the temporal profile of the minimum distances across the last nine months of 2012 in Damascus. There is a conspicuous anomaly on November 30 and December 1. Although these two days presented the highest levels of geographical dispersion in Figure (4.3), they show a bipolar distribution concentrated in unusually large and small distances. The daily average values for distance from nearest incident as a proxy for spatial clustering is depicted in Figure (4.7). The dominance of small nearest distances, in conjunction with high levels of dispersion suggest that dense but dispersed conflictual clusters were prominent during the disruption.

[61] Clark and Evans (1954); Diggle (2013).
[62] Diggle (2013).

128   *Civil War and Contagion in Small Worlds*

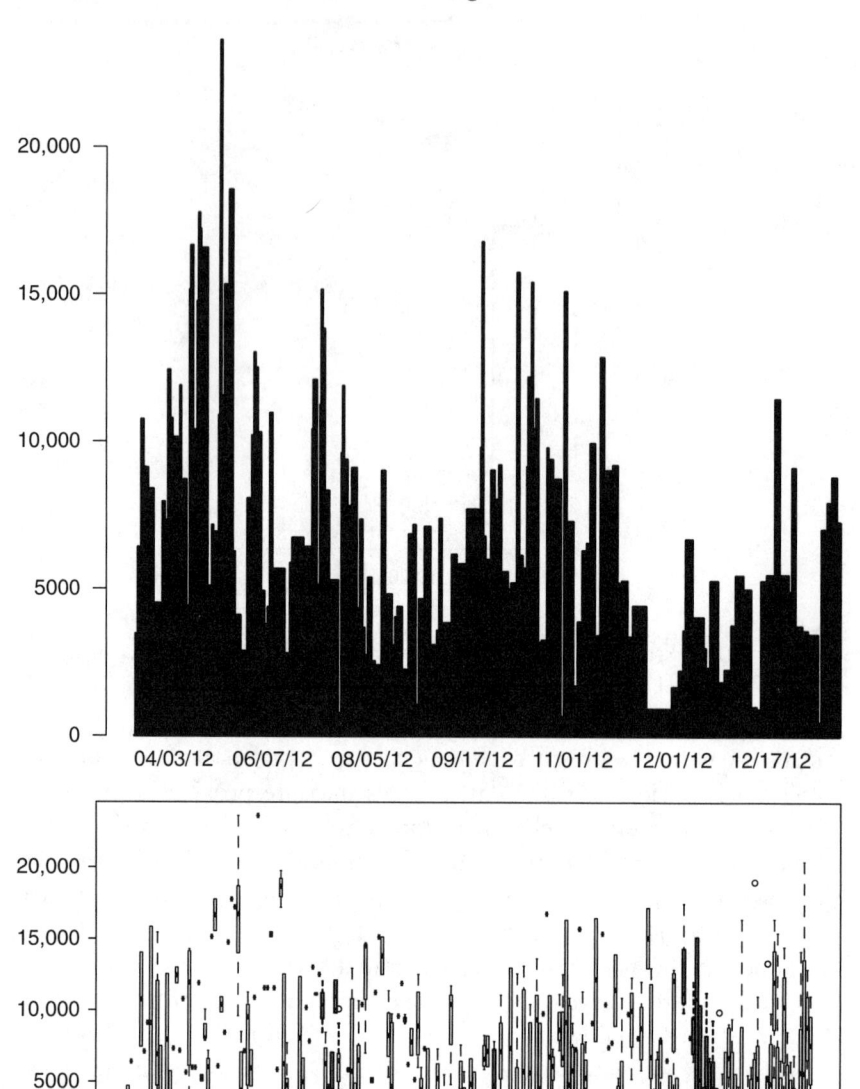

FIGURE 4.7. Average distance from nearest neighboring incident in meters, April to December, 2012. Daily average values represent a measure of spatial clustering of conflictual incidents. Note the small average values, i.e. high clustering, during the disruption, dates on x-axis weighted by the number of daily events, also the overall decreasing pattern, and the plateau at the end of November. Top: daily averages. Bottom: daily values all included.

The results of simple OLS regressions with distance from the nearest past incident as the dependent variable ($N = 627$) and two indices on the orientation of events, and the level of pertinent premeditation are included in Table (4.5). For each of the violent incidents included in the dataset, orientation_index determines if the incident was anti- or pro-regime. Furthermore, coordination_index provides a measure of coordination in the context of each of the conflictual incidents. The incidents are identified as "coordinated" if they are in one or more of following categories: *Assassination, Execution, Improvised Explosive Device (IED), Ambush/Raid, Rotary wing strike* or *Car bomb*. In contrast, instances of *direct fire* are coded as a category separate from the aforementioned classes. The main aim of such a classification is to use this crude proxy of coordination in conjunction with the spatiotemporal dynamics. The distinction lends itself to a meaningful distinction between the dynamics attributed to the coordinated events versus the rest. There are statistically significant differences between the dynamics of coordination and contagion processes.

The results of regressions in Tables (4.5) and (4.6) – disruption index included, an indicator showing if the event occurred during the disruption – show two intriguing qualities of the events in relation to the spatiotemporal dynamics: first, in line with the dispersion analysis above, *anti-regime* incidents were more spread in space and time. In contrast pro-regime attacks showed higher levels of continuity in space and time. Second, non-coordinated incidents were more clustered in space and time. Both of these effects are statistically significant on the 5 percent level or less. Figure (4.8) shows the regression multipliers, and that all 95 percent confidence intervals are above zero.

To summarize, clustering is linked with non-coordination, and anti-regime activity is more dispersed. Coordinated and government-based attacks are likely to show more continuity in space and time. Compared to the rebels, the regime was more likely to strike at the same place in short durations of time.[63] Table (4.8) includes a summary of the findings.

There is also a negative and significant relation between coordination and anti-regime nature of an event, i.e. coordinated events were likely

---

[63] This property facilitates the rejection of alternative hypotheses, other than processes of *leading from the periphery*, I discussed before; because this means controlling for regularities in space and time does away with explanations of escalation based on pro-regime activity.

TABLE 4.5. *Components of distance from the nearest incident, OLS regression*

	Coef.	Std. Err.	t	P > |t|	[95% Conf. Interval]
			(1) min_dist_t_i		
orientation_index	631.5734	243.5537	2.5932	0.0097	[153.2892,1109.8580]
coordination_index	537.8554	222.3852	2.4186	0.0159	[101.1413,974.5695]
N	627				

TABLE 4.6. *Components of distance from the nearest incident, disruption index included, OLS regression*

	Coef.	Std. Err.	t	P > |t|	[95% Conf. Interval]
			(1) min_dist_t_i		
coordination_index	462.1994	219.3350	2.1073	0.0355	[31.4739,892.9250]
orientation_index	476.8578	241.8253	1.9719	0.0491	[1.9664,951.7492]
disruption_index	−3564.9670	760.5896	−4.6871	0.0000	[−5058.5970, −2071.3370]
N	627				

to be pro-regime, see Table (4.7).[64] Therefore, in Table (4.8) the two quadrants (I) and (III) represent the main pertinent combinations of coordination and orientation indices and their impact on distance from the nearest incident. In both of these situations, there are two processes that simultaneously work in two opposite directions. For example, anti-regime incidents tend to induce events with higher nearest distances, while events that are not coordinated show more spatiotemporal proximity to the nearest incident. The tension between the two effects is also on display in the conflict data during the communication disruption, which shows more clustering on the local level accompanied with an increase in the dispersion of incidents. The end result is escalation on the local level, and increasing dispersion of the clusters on the global level.

[64] The indices are not multicollinear, $1 - R^2 = 0.82$.

TABLE 4.7. *The relation between orientation and coordination indices, OLS regression*

	Coef.	Std. Err.	(1) orientation_index t	P > |t|	[95% Conf. Interval]
coordination_index	−0.3895	0.0330	−11.7917	0.0000	[−0.4544,−0.3246]
intercept	0.4294	0.0314	13.6828	0.0000	[0.3678,0.4911]
N	627				
R^2	0.182				

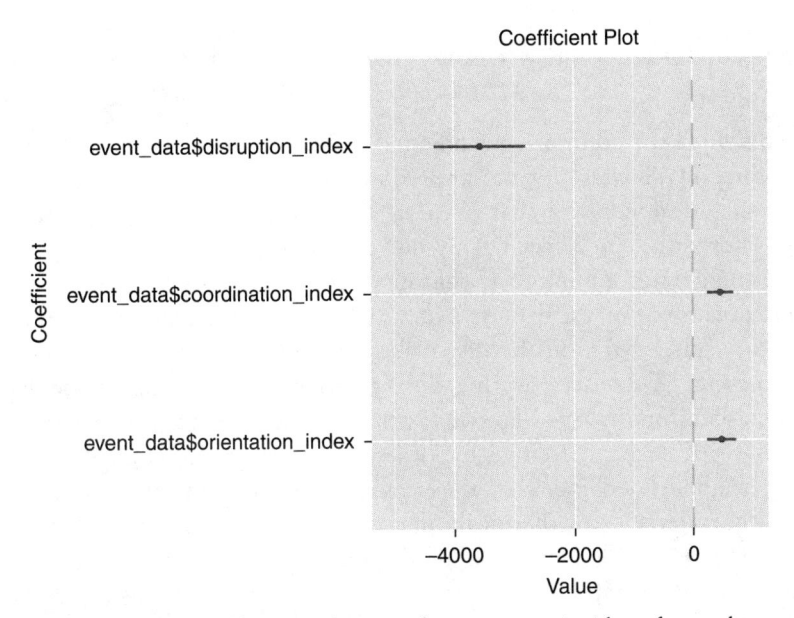

FIGURE 4.8. OLS coefficients, distance from nearest incident for each event ($N = 627$) regressed over indices for coordination, orientation (pro-anti regime), communication disruption.

As the next step, I test for the existence of spatial contagion in the time series data. The previous analysis examined the shaping of *minimal cores*. In the following, I study the nature of the diffusion of network collective action from these dispersed *minimal cores*.

TABLE 4.8. *This is a reproduction of Table (4.1) for emphasis. Four possibilities, coordination and orientation, quadrants of interest, (I) and (III), contain the majority of the events. The signs show the effect of the two parameters on clustering (distance from nearest incident) of conflictual events. + represents an increase in the nearest distance, − a decrease*

	Coordination	No Coordination
Anti-Regime	+ + (II)	+ − (I)
Pro-Regime	− + (III)	− − (IV)

DETECTING CONTAGION IN MOORE NEIGHBORHOODS AND RADIUS OF DIFFUSION[65]

I combined the account of conflictual incidents with spatial controls to produce a GIS dataset of size $252 \times 275 = 69{,}300$ entries. The dependent variable is an indicator that is 1 if at least one incident happened inside the relevant cell on a specific day, and 0 otherwise.

I enumerated a number of confounding parameters which complicate the conclusions on the definitive impact of the communication disruption in November 2012 on the dispersion and escalation of conflict across Damascus. A dataset covering the 252 square-mile spatial window in Damascus for the 275 days in April to December 2012 can test the validity of such alternative hypotheses. For example, controlling for the neighborhood index of the cells does away with concerns about the characteristics of the locale that may have caused certain patterns of conflict. The examination of the dataset also provides a test for the alternative hypothesis of *preplanned attacks*. I demonstrated that pro-regime attacks showed high degrees of continuity in space and time, therefore controlling for spatiotemporal trends of the conflict can capture such endogenous components. Note that the government's decision to attack a certain neighborhood relies on the history of the unrest, a decision made based on the pattern of the previous and ongoing rebellious activity in the area. Moreover, controlling for a lagged version of the

---

65 In a rectangular grid, Moore neighborhood for a given cell is the collection of eight cells surrounding it. The Damascus GIS dataset is available in the online appendix at https://goo.gl/ZCjY9b.

dependent variable as well as indices for both spatial window and temporal unit (square mile and day) ensures that regularities in space and time are deduced away from the treatment of interest, i.e. communication disruption.

The results of the Poisson count regressions are included in Table (4.9). The existence of conflict (as a binary index) is regressed over a number of control variables, including indicators for communication disruption and the existence of conflict in the previous day in the immediate Moore neighborhood. Across all four models the results on the controls, i.e. a daily lagged version of the dependent variable, an index for the spatial cell index, the date index, average elevation of the square-mile cell, population and sum street length, a neighborhood index (ranging over 36 neighborhoods) and the ethnic and income composition of these neighborhoods are robust.

An examination of control variables in Table (4.9) shows that unlike coordinated rebellions in the open[66] urban conflict in Damascus in 2012 was less likely to occur in high elevations. Instead lower altitudes were more likely to be a scene of conflict. The effect is robust and significant across all models. The sum street length in each cell expectedly showed a robust and significant positive impact on conflict. The index for neighborhood location is also positive and significant, showing that the borders of the 36 neighborhoods capture the building blocks of a conflictual puzzle. The significance of neighborhood indices in the presence of other control variables suggests that the civil war in Damascus was framed on the level of local urban life. The results confirm the importance of spatial neighborhood composition on the intensity and nature of civil conflict.[67] Ethnicity, defined as the difference between the Sunni and Shia population proportions, does not show a significant effect. Poor neighborhoods are more likely to experience conflict.

The results in Table (4.9) show that the spatiotemporal lag parameter[68] was significantly correlated with the likelihood of conflictual incidents. Finally, the impact of the disruption on the likelihood of violent conflict is also positive and statistically significant, even after controlling for spatiotemporal lags, neighborhood index and temporal trends. The government's decisions to attack certain neighborhoods are based on their history of unrest, their overall geographical characteristics and

[66] Fearon and Laitin (2003).
[67] Gould (1995).
[68] Defined as a binary variable indicative of the existence of conflict in the previous day in the Moore neighborhood, i.e. eight squares surrounding each square mile.

TABLE 4.9. *Poisson count regressions, unit of analysis: cell-day*

	(1) vid	(2) vid	(3) vid	(4) vid
vid_lagged	1.656*** (0.123)	1.638*** (0.123)	1.605*** (0.126)	1.592*** (0.125)
cell index	0.00417*** (0.000879)	0.00413*** (0.000879)	0.00420*** (0.000881)	0.00416*** (0.000881)
date	0.00547*** (0.000579)	0.00519*** (0.000588)	0.00529*** (0.000585)	0.00503*** (0.000593)
average elevation	−0.00389*** (0.000734)	−0.00386*** (0.000735)	−0.00379*** (0.000734)	−0.00377*** (0.000735)
population	0.0000143*** (0.00000259)	0.0000144*** (0.00000259)	0.0000143*** (0.00000259)	0.0000143*** (0.00000259)
sum street length	0.0000165*** (0.00000418)	0.0000166*** (0.00000419)	0.0000161*** (0.00000418)	0.0000163*** (0.00000418)
neighborhood index	0.0209*** (0.00536)	0.0211*** (0.00535)	0.0205*** (0.00540)	0.0207*** (0.00539)
ethnicity	0.0900 (0.146)	0.0881 (0.145)	0.0888 (0.146)	0.0867 (0.146)
income	1.647*** (0.143)	1.644*** (0.143)	1.631*** (0.143)	1.630*** (0.143)
disruption		0.764*** (0.218)		0.753*** (0.218)
spatial_temp_lag_d			0.262* (0.114)	0.254* (0.114)
intercept	−4.829*** (0.521)	−4.817*** (0.521)	−4.881*** (0.521)	−4.869*** (0.521)
N	69300	69300	69300	69300
Log-likelihood	−2567.2	−2562.2	−2564.7	−2559.8
χ^2	1237.2	1247.2	1242.2	1251.9

Standard errors in parentheses
* $p < 0.05$, ** $p < 0.01$, *** $p < 0.001$

their history of violence. These parameters are included as control variables. Despite the significance of all these parameters, communication disruption shows a positive and significant influence on the counts of conflict. Figure (4.9) shows the effect of multipliers in Table (4.9). All 95 percent confidence intervals, other than those of the *ethnicity* parameter, are distinctly above or below zero and are significant.

To ensure that the proliferation from a square-mile cell to the neighboring ones was not a usual endogenous trend, I examined the nine-month average statistics to show that unlike the time series data, the merely spatial information, averaged in time, does not show significant contagion patterns in Moore neighborhoods. This observation is highly important, because they demonstrate that spatial spillover is not a discernible phenomenon in the average data. If that were not the case, the contagion analysis on the spillover of contention from one spatial window to another could have been caused by a latent or implicit process simultaneously facilitating conflict in adjacent cells. The results in Table (7.2) in the appendix show that on average it is not the case. Significant components of conflict in the dataset result from the temporal dynamics, not from latent parameters.[69]

Similar results hold when instead of a binary indicator for the existence of conflict,[70] the *number* of conflictual events in the Moore neighborhood in the previous day is used. To further illustrate the importance of spatiotemporal lag as a predictor for political violence, Figure (4.10) shows the increase in the likelihood of conflict in a square-mile cell as a function of the number of incidents in its Moore neighborhood in the previous day. One more conflictual incident in the vicinity in the previous day translates to an approximately 25 percent increase in the likelihood of a violent incident in a given cell.[71]

---

[69] To ensure the identification of contagion in the data was not confounded by parameters existing beyond the temporal dynamics of the events during the nine months covered by the analysis, I checked the insulation of each of the 1-square mile geographical cells from its neighbors *in temporal average*. Table (7.2) in the appendix provides the results of Poisson regressions on the number of conflictual incidents in each of the 14×18 cells of 1 square miles over the same control variables used in other regression analyses, and a dummy for the existence of conflict, as well as total number of conflictual incidents, both in the Moore neighborhood of a given cell.

The spatial lag index is insignificant, and the value of the multiplier for count lag parameter is negative and small.

[70] spatial_temp_lag_d.

[71] The number of previous incidents in the Moore neighborhood varied between 0 and 4.

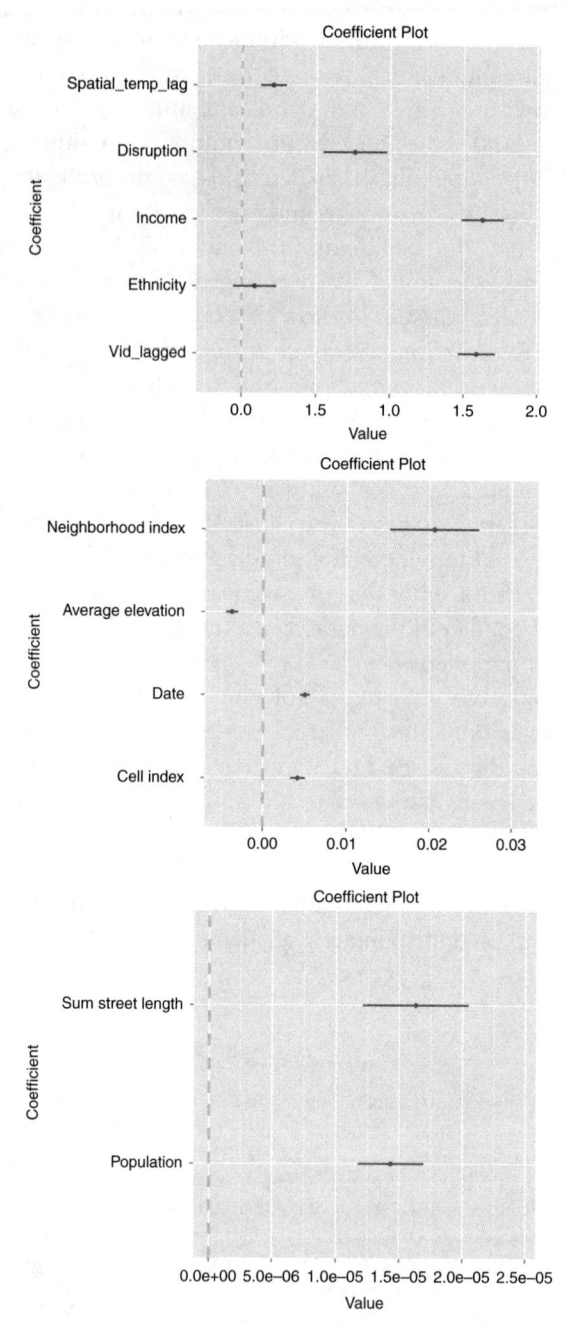

FIGURE 4.9. Coefficients from Poisson regressions in Table (4.9).

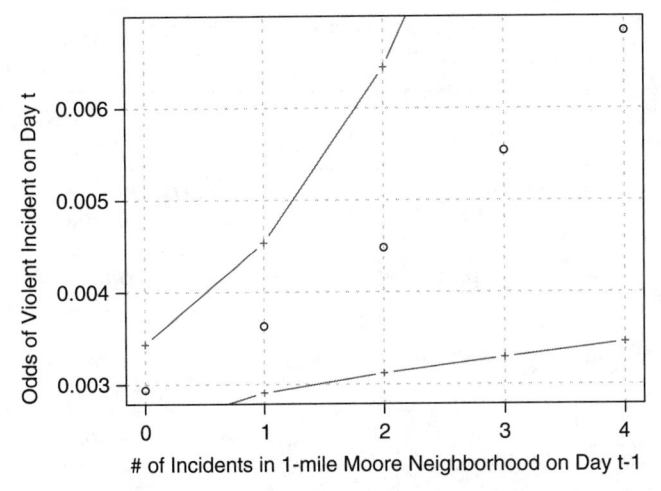

FIGURE 4.10. An increase of one in the number of neighboring incidents in the previous day translates to approximately 25 percent higher counts of a violent incident in one's locale.

CONTAGION IN *SMALL WORLDS* WAS ACTIVATED BY MEDIA DISRUPTION

Finally, for examining the potential influence of communication disruption on patterns of contagion across space and time, I included an interaction term,[72] (spatiotemporal lag × disruption), along with explanatory parameters in Table (4.9). The interaction term is a proxy for the influence of disruption as a treatment on the likelihood of violent incidents, this time via *contagion processes*. The results are included in Table (4.10). All control variables in Table (4.9) are also included in the analysis, the results on controls are similar and omitted for the sake of brevity.

The results in Table (4.10) culminate in a noteworthy finding. While in the absence of the interaction term both the contagion proxy and the disruption index are significantly influencing the odds of conflict, when the interaction term is included, it is *only* the interaction term that is significant. This means the influence of disruption on the conflict count in this regression is captured through its interaction with contagion. In

---

[72] Kam and Franzese (2007).

TABLE 4.10. *Poisson count regressions, unit of analysis: cell-day, interaction*

	(1) vid	(2) vid
disruption	0.753***	0.557
	(0.218)	(0.286)
spatial_temp_lag_d	0.254*	0.217
	(0.114)	(0.119)
disruption# spatial_temp_lag_d		1.304***
		(0.324)
N	69300	69300
Log-likelihood	−2559.8	−2559.1
χ^2	1251.9	1253.4

Standard errors in parentheses
* $p < 0.05$, ** $p < 0.01$, *** $p < 0.001$

other words, the media disruption exacerbated revolutionary unrest via activating spatiotemporal contagion.[73]

The results here are in line with the findings in Chapter (2) on the nature of social interaction and conflict tendency: those more inclined to rely on the local neighborhood were also more likely to decouple from the main narrative of power, engage in circles of contention in different locales and initiate risky acts of collective protest in Cairo. Similarly in Damascus, during the blackout, the spillover of violent contention in the adjacent spatial cell was aggravated during the blackout. The procedure is best understood in conjunction with the findings on the spatial dynamics in general, i.e. local concentration in *minimal cores*, which became globally more dispersed. It is likely that in each of these small concentrated cliques of contention, face to face interactions replaced virtual connections, and the radical vanguard became more effective on the local levels.

[73] Fixed effect regression results yield similar results and corroborate the evidence on the significance of the variables of interest, regression tabular reports are omitted for the sake of brevity.

VANGUARDS AT THE PERIPHERY AND THE SURPRISE FACTOR

In the above it became clear that the social value of information depends on the social network structure. During bouts of disconnect, the nature of conflict in Damascus changed. The results of the detailed GIS study in this chapter provided further evidence for the significance of spatial spillovers in the absence of routine means for communication. The detection of contagion revealed why the blackout should have influenced the contention the way it did. The next step in an inquiry into modes of *leading from the periphery* would be to examine the latency and frequency of collective risk taking originating from the borders of the social network, as opposed to those starting from the highly visible elite.

The role of clustering of contention in the margins, in the catastrophic escalation of late November in Damascus, also became clear. Fast diffusion of contention, in contagious ways, to new locations demonstrates dynamics that are familiar patterns in popular revolutions in politics and society. The speed with which some of these processes take place, often take central and established observers by surprise. The majority of the cohort of ephemeral leaders in the margins do not rise to fortune and fame. They may not even be cognizant of their role in the chain of historic events they set into motion. The information vacuum which facilitates their prominence, also obscures their tracks. The *surprise* element often referred to, in the case of marginal rebellions, is partly a product of the nature of instigation itself.

The next chapter proposes an experimental solution to ameliorate this lack of information on marginal leaders. In an attempt to observe both success and failures in attempts to start network collective action from the most marginal corners of the network, the behavioral experiments in the following differentiate among individuals based on their individual affinity to risk, and arrange situations in which the potential vanguard are marginal in the social network.

5

Peripheral Influence
Experimentations in Collective Risk Taking

The secret of my influence has always been that it remained secret.[1]

Salvador Dalí

In the aftermath of the Petrograd rebellion of February 1917, Trotsky wondered about the leaders of the February insurrections: *who led the revolution? Who raised the workers to their feet? Who brought soldiers into the streets?*[2] After quickly repudiating the idea of a "spontaneous" revolution, he fittingly moved on to ascribe the success of the rebellion to the teachings of *the party of Lenin*.[3] In this chapter, I examine the same puzzle of spontaneous, seemingly leaderless revolutions. I show that in a series of experiments on collective risk taking, the peripheral vanguard trigger cascades of collective action – or apathy – that are more frequent, and conditioned upon occurrence, faster in their convergence to total action or apathy. The same network experiments with the risk-taking vanguard at central positions of the experimental network yield fewer cascades of risk taking and apathy, and whenever they happen, they take longer to encompass an absolute majority of the social network. The results of these behavioral experiments on network collective action

---

[1] I start this chapter with the same quote opening as that of Banerjee et al. (2015). Interestingly enough, the next phrase in that paper is "Knowing who is influential, *or central* ..." (emphasis is mine). Clearly, the reading of Dalí's statement here is the opposite, the same interpretation is the basis for the formulation of *leading from the periphery* as a logic for network collective action.
[2] Trotsky (1937, p.161).
[3] Ibid. p. 171.

provide a resolution for the paradox of *leaderless* and *spontaneous* revolution. Those who lead are not the leaders.[4]

In the synchronous network experiments of collective risk taking I detail in this chapter, the subjects are ranked based on an individual risk propensity measure, the most risk seeking are placed in the most central, the most peripheral and random network locations and the subjects repeatedly enact a collective lottery which rewards global risk taking if the majority takes action, and penalizes taking risk if the attempt at mobilization fails.

The results of the experiments emphasize the significance of revolutionary vanguards' distribution across the underlying social network. The radicals' arraignment is shaped by spatial and social confines alike. Clearly the distribution of the revolutionary vanguard in the geographical expanse of Petrograd in February 1917, or Paris in the summer of 1789, is unavailable, but the same is not true for Cairo in 2011. All these historical events constituted spontaneous uprisings dispersed across major cities subsuming civilians and armed forces alike.[5] For the Egyptian case, in Chapter (2) I showed that the spatial dispersion of the revolutionary vanguard, defined as those who protested at the beginning of the unrest, was higher than the ordinary protester. The results of the Cairo survey, are in line with the findings of the network experiment: the vanguards of the Egyptian Revolution were more dispersed than the typical protester,

---

[4] A more recent explanation for the puzzle of revolutionary spontaneity and lack of leadership takes the disparity between public and private preferences among the population as a source of revolutionary cascades. As Leipzig Monday Demonstrations grew in size in 1989, more protesters found it permissible to reveal their private preference against the status quo and join the protests Kuran (1989). In Kuran's formulation, personal decisions to act are based on individual utility calculations where utility constitutes of two terms of selective incentives Opp et al. (1995): a monotonous function of the percentage of the *total* population that participates in the contention, and the distance between one's private preference and public action. These calculations result in a personal threshold for personal participation in protests based on the participation of others. In particular, each individual bears a personal *threshold* for engaging in collective action: one joins in the contention if the percentage of participants in the whole population surpasses one's personal threshold Granovetter (1978). The distribution of these fixed personal thresholds among the population dictates the end point of system dynamics. It can end in ubiquitous action, a successful social reversal, or can end in abject failure, at times widespread suppression. As mentioned in Chapter (3), Kuran's formulation does not take the structure of underlying social network into account. The overall rate of participation is visible to all. Such a model is skewed toward global visibility of contention and the centrality of its leaders. The spontaneity of revolution is framed under a *sui generis* disparity between public and private preferences, the puzzle of its obscure leadership is left unanswered.

[5] Doyle (2002); Hassanpour (2014); Wade (2005).

starting from the first phase of the protests. In retrospect, the experiments outlined in this chapter show that such high levels of initial dispersion of the vanguard influenced the Egyptian process' meteoric diffusion and spontaneous nature, eventually its success.[6]

Centrality is often equated with influence,[7] but the role of *peripheral* agents of change in engendering network collective action from the margins has only recently come to light.[8] Detecting the logic of mobilization from the margins is a worthwhile project, because networked promotion of political participation is now a possibility on social media and online platforms;[9] nevertheless, existing experimental studies do not consider employing the underlying network structure to mobilize from the periphery. Traditional methods of social promotion via centrally located and highly visible users is the norm.[10] The dynamics of mobilization from the margins is expected to be different from that of mobilization from the center. The experiments I outline in the following are an attempt to

---

[6] These findings contribute to the scholarship on collective action with positive externalities Schelling (1978) in at least two ways. First, as for mechanism design for social influence maximization, the results emphasize the utility of decentralized mobilization for inducing cascades of collective action. In network formulations of collective action, the position of the vanguard is a significant parameter of the model. Rather than altering the *structure* of interactions between actors, or the *payoffs* for such interactions Valente (2012), one can arrange the *placement* of actors in the space of social networks. The idea of deliberately positioning vanguards in the periphery, when it comes to risky adoption of new behavior (as compared to safe choices) comports with observational insights from classic findings on the relation between network location and "innovativeness" Becker (1970). The way influence processes originate from the margins is distinct from how influence arises from the center Katz and Lazarsfeld (2006). Second, these results are in line with frequent and puzzling observational findings in the context of social revolutions regarding the lack of centralized leadership and the spontaneity of mass rebellions. During the early phases of the 2011 Egyptian Revolution, the vanguards were found to be more geographically dispersed vis a vis the typical protester Hassanpour (2014).

[7] See Wasserman and Faust (1994).

[8] See Bakshy et al. (2011); Liu et al. (2011); Watts and Dodds (2007) for examples. Liu et al. (2011) argue that *driver* nodes are not high degree nodes. Centola (2010) argues that peripheral conversion is easier. Bakshy et al. (2011) argue that a critical mass of easily influenced individuals can be as important as central *influentials*.

[9] Coppock et al. (2015); Karpf (2012).

[10] See Coppock et al. (2015) for an example of central enticement. The arrangement of risk-takers in the periphery, however may facilitate collective action, and its dynamics are not well understood Centola and Macy (2007). The problem of finding the most influential group of k agents that can affect the highest number of other agents in a given graph G is NP-Hard Kempe et al. (2003), and even if the dynamics of the diffusion of risky behavior (itself a subject of multiple experimental and observational studies, e.g. Aral and Walker (2012); Bond et al. (2012); Kearns et al. (2006); Watts and Dodds (2007), were known, the network location of influencers during collective cascades of risk taking in heterogeneous networks is still an open problem.

explore and formulate the distinct features of network collective action that originate from instigators in the least central locations. The results demonstrate the possibility of decentralized influence maximization, and suggest novel paths for social organization.[11]

HIGH RISK COLLECTIVE ACTION AND LEADING FROM THE PERIPHERY: INFORMATIONAL CONSIDERATIONS

Many have argued that recruitment to high risk collective action is a product of strong links and effective central leadership.[12] The argument takes lengthy conditioning and strong connections as the main drivers of recruitment to high risk collective action, not the weak ties from the types shown to be necessary to the diffusion of collective behavior.[13] The missing element in this argument is simply *information*. The volunteers in Freedom Summer were fully aware of what they were to do. The same is not true of limited information regimes, particularly under fully authoritarian supervision of information flow. Local information available to individuals signifies the type of social network they are embedded in, and generates patterns of collective risk taking that are categorically different from those of complete information regimes. Examples of this divergence were evident in the previous chapters. I argued that limited information situations in fact enabled waves of high risk collective action in Damascus and Cairo. The models I outlined were demonstrations of the same logic: eliminating information at times motivated higher rates of participation, not less. To take stock, weak ties and haphazard encounters in the margins do enable consequential collective action, but the instigators in such situations are not as well informed about their role in it compared to those involved in strongly connected and highly exercised networks of activism. That intention to act upon the ideals of the movement is not always available to leaders in

---

[11] In contrast to prior synchronous experiments on cooperation Centola (2010); Enemark et al. (2014); Judd et al. (2010); Rand et al. (2011); Suri and Watts (2011); Wang et al. (2012) which did not differentiate subjects (e.g. based on their propensity to cooperate), I deliberately take heterogeneity in the attribute of interest, i.e. risk-taking propensity, into account so that I can turn the *network location* of the early adopters into an experimental treatment. Using an individual risk-propensity measurement Holt and Laury (2002), I ranked the experimental subjects based on their risk aversion, and then assigned the potential instigators (i.e. those prone to taking risk) to peripheral, random or central locations in experimental social networks.

[12] See a prominent example in McAdam (1986).

[13] Granovetter (1973).

the periphery. Their horizon of vision is limited, and the irregularities of their local information influence their decisions.

The experiments I describe in the following enact similar differences in amounts of information available to the vanguard. When the vanguard are positioned at the most central positions, they acquire the highest amount of information about the status of collective action in the network, and their acts are communicated to the highest number of connections in the network. In contrast, when risk-taking leaders are placed at the most peripheral locations, they have very little information about the global status of collective action in the social network, and their influence is limited to the few disciples in the periphery. Interestingly enough, the results show that the limited information does not preclude collective risk taking, when the most risk-prone individuals are the most peripheral ones. Part of this phenomenon can be attributed to the fact that, while conviction at times motivates high risk collective action, absence of information on dire prospects of high risk collective action can prevent defections. In Chapter (3) I showed that high levels of connectivity can be detrimental to *minimal cores*.

The experiments I outline below manipulate the level of information available to the vanguard by positioning them in two extremes of information availability, i.e. their assignment to the most peripheral and most central positions in random networks, and a third baseline configuration, where they are randomly assigned to network locations. The likely vanguard are the "first movers". I will show that the collective action cascades which the *partially* informed vanguard generate are more frequent, and when they happen they occur in fewer iterations of the collective lottery the network enacts.

A noteworthy outcome is the prevalence of "apathy" cascades – in addition to collective action cascades, in the peripheral assignment. The *average* rates of action are not much different between the two peripheral and central assignments of the vanguard, but the peripheral assignment yields a distribution of collective action that is more bipolar than the central assignment. The bipolarity is averaged out in the mean value, but it is evident in a comparison among all of the experimental sessions for each of the two treatments.

Next in this chapter is the description of the network experiments and their results. It will become clear that the outcome is in line with the empirical findings in the previous chapters and the theoretical models of *leading from the periphery*.

NETWORK EXPERIMENTS OF COLLECTIVE ACTION: THE SUMMARY OF THE DESIGN

A total of 720 subjects completed two consecutive phases of synchronous experiments in 45 experimental sessions,[14] 15 sessions for each of the three network treatments, i.e. central, random and peripheral assignment of the potential instigators on an online labor market, Amazon Mechanical Turk (AMT).[15] During the first phase of the experiment, I measured each subject's individual level of risk preference using a standard procedure based on the subjects' preference between distinct lotteries.[16] Subjects were initially ranked based on their individual preference for risk;[17] as expected the distribution was skewed toward risk aversion. The subjects were primarily young (aged 20 to 35), more likely to be male than female (57 percent male) and were likely to have some college education or higher. As such, the demographics of the subject pool were congruent with the commonplace representation of participants in collective acts of contention, paving the way for the ensuing experimental analysis.[18]

Before initiating the second phase of the synchronous network experiment, I generated an Erdös-Rényi (ER) random network of the same size as the experimental session.[19] Then the nodes in each network realization were ranked based on their *betweenness centrality*,[20] a measure of their centrality in the diffusion of action,[21] then the subjects were assigned to each node in the experimental network based on one of the three network treatments. In central, random and peripheral assignments, the network nodes were assorted based on betweenness centrality, and the subjects were ranked based on their risk aversion; afterwards the most risk seeking were assigned to the most central, random and most peripheral

---

[14] Average size of a session $\mu = 22.69$, with a Standard Deviation, SD = 2.57.
[15] Each session lasted 33 minutes on average (Standard Deviation, SD = 3.48).
[16] Holt and Laury (2002b).
[17] On a scale of 1 to 10 (Mean, $\mu = 6.8$, Standard Deviation, SD = 1.9, $N = 1168$ total recruits), with score 10 representing the highest level of risk aversion.
[18] For an appraisal of the usage of online labor markets for experimentation in the social sciences, see Berinsky et al. (2012).
[19] The size of the network was between min = 17, and max = 27, with 40 percent density of possible ties. The construction of these random graphs was similar to the procedure in Watts and Dodds (2007), yielding a Poisson distribution of *degrees* with mean, $\mu = 8.94$, and Standard Deviation SD = 2.49, min = 3, max = 17 in 45 network realizations.
[20] Mean of betweenness centrality in these networks, $\mu = 4.90$, SD = 4.86, min = 0, max = 26.73.
[21] See Kempe et al. (2003) and Wasserman and Faust (1994) for a description of the utility of *betweenness centrality* in diffusion of ego attributes.

nodes, respectively. The assignments of subjects to the three experimental categories were random and *balanced* in terms of their individual risk seeking scores.

FIRST PHASE OF THE EXPERIMENT: ALLOCATING THE VANGUARD

During the first phase of the experiment I measured subjects' individual level of risk propensity. The measurement process was comprised of a number of consecutive risk elicitation lotteries. For each individual, the choice was between a safe lottery, and a risky one with a higher reward and a higher penalty. Each individual made repeated choices among the lottery pairs, during which the risky lottery became progressively less risky, and the safe lottery turned riskier at each round;[22] each *rational* subject would switch from the safe lottery to the risky one at a certain iteration point, which is their *risk rank*. Those who switch in early stages are likely *vanguards*. Their switch from the status quo to the risky option does not require much effort. These are the experimental subjects who are inclined to move first.[23] As expected, the final distributions of risk ranks for the three treatments follow similar trends.[24]

Once all the subjects finished conducting the lotteries, they were sorted based on their *risk ranks* and were assigned to their locations in a

---

[22] Eleven rounds total, based on the canonical design in Holt and Laury (2002).
[23] During the first phase of the experiment each subject chose between two lotteries:

$$A = (\$2.00 \text{ w.p. } x, \$1.60 \text{ w.p. } 1-x)$$

and

$$B = (\$3.80 \text{ w.p. } 1-x, \$0.10 \text{ w.p. } x).$$

In 10 consecutive steps, x changed from 1 to 0, decreasing 0.1 at each round of the experiment. The subjects made 11 decisions between the two options. The first and the 11th choices were trivial. Subjects that answered questions 1 and 11 incorrectly were screened out. Eventually all subjects switched from A to B. The first switch from A to B is the *risk-taking rank* of the subject. Those who switch more than three times were excluded from the second phase. The eventual assignment to three experimental groups was balanced in risk rank.
[24] The subject risk rank statistics are balanced among the three groups. See the table below.

	Mean	Std. Dev.	No. of Obs.	No. of Subjects
Central	7.61	1.85	10228	380
Random	7.89	2.01	10535	403
Peripheral	7.91	1.86	10463	385

Summary statistics of subject's rank ($N = 1168$).

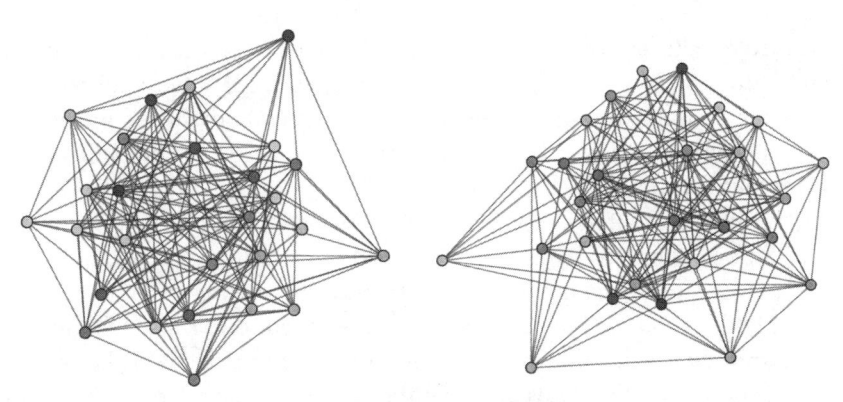

FIGURE 5.1. Two realizations of the Erdös-Rényi graphs used in the second stage, $r = 0.4$.

realization of an Erdös-Rényi random network. The networks underlying the experiment were $3 \times 15 = 45$ realizations (15 for each treatment), with connectivity parameter $r = 0.4$, and average size of $\mu = 22.69$ nodes.[25] Two illustrative network realizations are depicted in Figure (5.1). Darker nodes are of higher betweenness centrality.

In the second, and main, phase of the experiment, the subjects were placed in the pertinent experimental network based on their propensity for risk, and later enacted a collective game of risk taking.

MAIN EXPERIMENTAL PHASE: COLLECTIVE LOTTERIES WITH LIMITED INFORMATION

During the second and main stage of the experiment, the subjects engaged in repeated binary lotteries that rewarded risk taking only if more than a certain threshold of the total population chose the risky option over the safe one in a given round. The lotteries' reward parameters were similar to the one executed in the first stage. However, the payoffs for both choices, safe and risky, were conditioned on the *total* number of subjects in the network who chose *the risky option*. If the attempt at collective risk taking succeeded, i.e. the number of risky choices made in the total social network was above a certain threshold, all who had taken risk were rewarded, but if the attempt at majority had failed, they gained only a small amount. In contrast, choosing the safe option ensured a safe but not considerable payoff that was slightly higher when the majority

[25] Standard Deviation, SD = 2.57.

decided to take the risky route. In repeated rounds of the collective lottery, and before making a decision at the given round, the subjects observed only the actions of their immediate network neighbors, in the previous round. The subjects enacted this collective lottery for 15 rounds when the game suddenly ended.[26]

The network interaction was a game of collective risk taking with *local* information, in which each individual's payoff was a function of the *global* levels of action in the whole network. The situation simulated the real life dilemma of joining a rebellion: if enough join, those who took part are rewarded, otherwise rebelling has repercussions. On the other hand, continuing the status quo guarantees a smaller but sure payoff and a possibility for free-riding.[27] Each individual has to make this decision relying on the local information they have. The interaction simulates the real life situations in limited information regimes, common to the majority of contentious collective action situations.

As mentioned above, the choices of the ego network were the only information available to the subjects during the repeated rounds. Technically speaking, this is a design choice that best captures the importance of network structure and heterogeneity in risk propensity in the experimental networks.[28] Each of the two phases of the game were preceded by training sessions. Figure (5.2) shows three snapshots each, from rounds 1, 8 and 15, for three sessions pertaining to the peripheral, random and central network treatments.[29]

[26] The payoff structure of the repeated collective lottery is as follows,

	$N > TH$	$N \leq TH$
Red	$3.80	$0.10
Blue	$2.00	$1.60

Risk taking is rewarded only if it is the choice of the majority, threshold $TH = 67$ percent.
[27] Lichbach (1995).
[28] See Centola (2010); Judd et al. (2010); Kearns et al. (2006); Rand et al. (2011).
[29] In the second phase the subjects were shown the rules of the game according to the utility structure of phase two. Choosing the risky option paid off only if the rate of risk-takers (choosing the risky option) in the population was above a threshold, $TH = 0.67$ here in this iterative lottery. In the experiment the choices are simply called A and B. The players were only shown the choices of their immediate network neighbors. At each session the collective lottery was repeated $N = 15$ times without a warning for the end of the game. Note that the utility parameters for the second stage game are the same as those used in the two lotteries implemented in the first phase of the experiment for measuring individual risk propensity. Before each phase (1 or 2), the subjects went through practice sessions. A snapshot of the instructions shown on the subject console during the "second" phase is included in Figure (7.17) in the appendix. A complete reconstruction of the network experiments' dynamics in more than 45 experimental

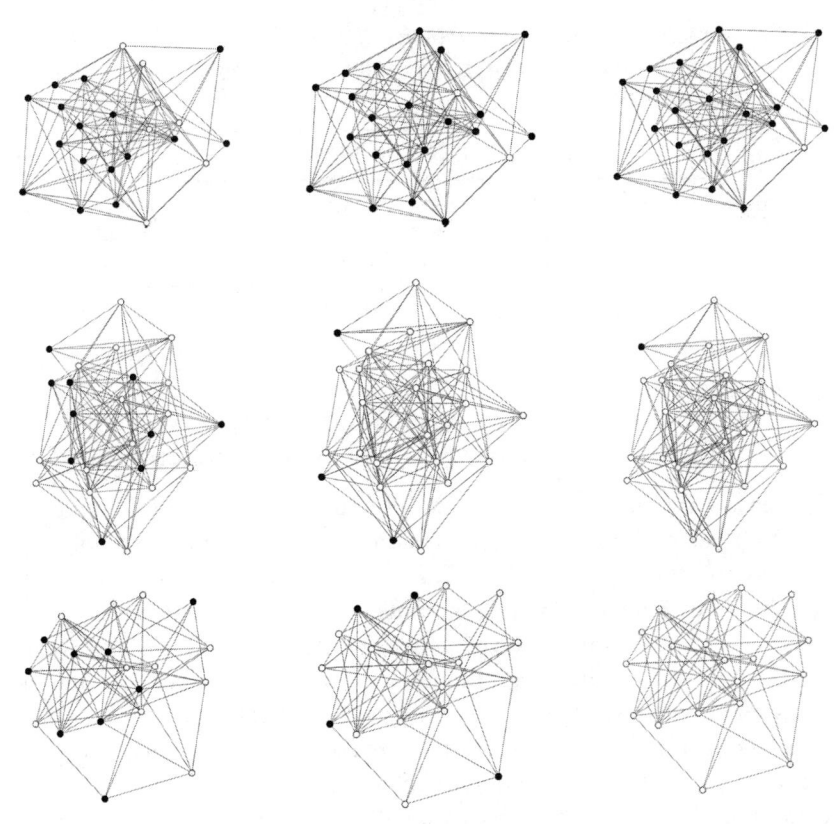

FIGURE 5.2. Rounds 1, 8 and 15 for peripheral, random and central assignments (sample realizations, top to bottom). The acting nodes are differentiated from non-acting ones with their darker color. The complete set of network visualizations, is available in the online appendix at https://goo.gl/Dr7mW6.

The summary statistics of choosing the risky option are included in Table (5.1). Note that the total average rates of choosing the risky option is *higher* for the central assignment of the vanguard compared to the peripheral assignment. In the following, I show that the comparison's direction is the opposite, when it is between the "extreme" rates of action and inaction. Peripheral assignment of the vanguard induces more cascades of network collective action in the experimental sessions.

sessions, in the format of network visualizations, is available in the online appendix at https://goo.gl/Dr7mW6. The network experiment dataset itself is included in the online appendix at https://goo.gl/FQ6PE0.

TABLE 5.1. *Summary statistics of choosing the risky option in each session-round in the second stage (N = 720)*

	Mean	Std. Dev.	# of Obs.	# of Subjects
Central	0.554	0.497	3555	237
Random	0.471	0.499	3525	235
Peripheral	0.504	0.500	3720	248

FREQUENCY AND LATENCY OF COLLECTIVE ACTION CASCADES IN THE PERIPHERAL ASSIGNMENT

To measure the frequency and latency of bouts of collective risk taking or apathy, I looked for experimental sessions in which the rates of choosing the risky option, or status quo for that matter, was above a certain threshold for extended periods of time. *Cascade sessions* as such are those in which risk taking stayed above or below a limit for k time units (first definition), or for the *rest* of interactions (second definition). Action cascades closely resemble encompassing waves of collective risk taking[30] which constitute social revolutions and mass opinion reversals; however, this time some of these cascades originate from the margins.[31] With both definitions the frequency of network collective action cascades is higher when the risk prone vanguard are assigned to the periphery of the social network.

Consider a definition of a cascade session as one in which the proportion of risky choices among the subjects is above (or below) a certain threshold TH for at least k *consecutive rounds*. In Figure (5.3) the proportions of sessions in action cascade status are plotted in terms of parameter k, the number of consecutive rounds above the threshold needed to establish a cascade. It is clear that for the majority of k values, total number of rounds needed for establishing a cascade, the peripheral assignment of instigators is the network treatment with the highest numbers of sessions in the cascade status. The high frequency of action cascades in the peripheral assignment is robust to changes in threshold TH (75, 80 and 90 percent in Figure (5.3)), and a good variety of possible k values. See Figure (5.3).

[30] Kuran (1989); Marwell and Oliver (1993).
[31] All of the methods and analyses described below apply to failure cascades as well.

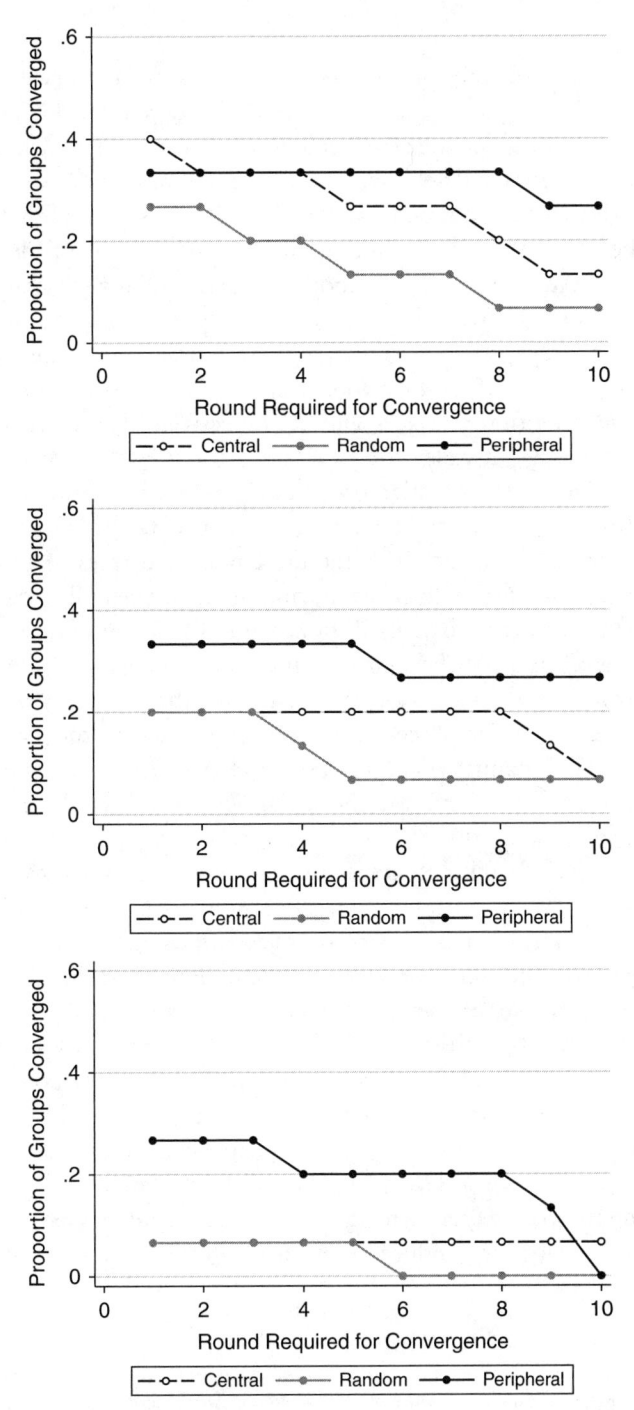

FIGURE 5.3. Proportion of sessions in *action* cascade status for each treatment, with thresholds 75, 80 and 90 percent (top to bottom). The conducive effect of peripheral assignment of the vanguard is robust.

The results on the rate and speed of convergence to action cascades are also robust with respect to more substantive changes to the definition of a cascade. Consider a "prospective" definition of cascade in which cascades defined as experimental sessions in which rates of action go above (or below) a threshold and remain higher than the chosen threshold for the rest of the game. For this definition, and for each treatment (peripheral, central and random assignments), both rate of risk taking (or apathy), and the number of sessions in the cascade are important. With a threshold set of (0.75, 0.25) one can show that the number of action cascades for *peripheral, central* and *random* assignments of instigators, with the prospective definition, are 5, 4 and 2, respectively. There are a similar number of apathy cascades for 5, 3 and 7 for *peripheral, central* and *random* assignments of instigators. Taking rates of risk taking in each round of these cascade sessions into account it is possible to show that the peripheral assignment yields the most polarized rates of action and non-action of the three treatments during the experimental sessions.[32]

Similar to the definition I used to measure dispersion of decentralized conflict, here I propose *the sum rate of action among all sessions in the cascade status, in each round,* as a measure for the frequency of cascade status for each of the three treatments according to the prospective definition. This quantity captures both the frequency and intensity of extremes of collective action in the social network. A similar parameter can be defined for apathy cascades. Figure (5.4) includes a comparison of this sum rate of action (or inaction) per round for all sessions in action cascade status (the top triplet), and all sessions in apathy cascade status (the bottom triplet), with the (0.75, 0.25) cascade thresholds. Note that in the comparison between *central* and *peripheral*, the peripheral vanguard engender higher rates of action, and inaction, starting from the first round to the end of the interaction. The gap between sum action rates of the two network treatments stabilizes after a few initial rounds, for both types of treatments, and it is similar for action and inaction cascades.

Given the higher rates of "average" action in session-rounds for the *central* treatment (see Table (5.1)), this is a remarkable result, showing that in the network experiments, peripheral agents of change, compared to the central vanguard, induce more extreme rates of action and apathy.

---

[32] With the same threshold set of (0.75, 0.25), the total numbers of session-rounds in action cascade status for the three treatments of *peripheral, central* and *random* assignment are 63, 42 and 16, respectively.

Risk Taking in Action (Top) and Apathy (Bottom) Cascades

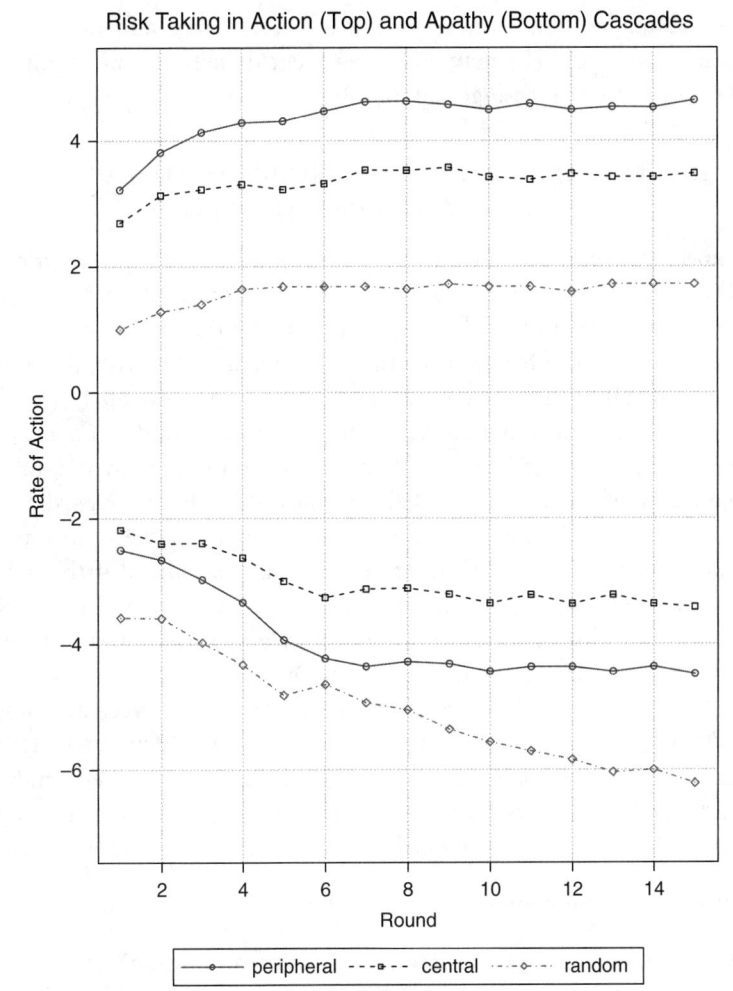

FIGURE 5.4. Sum of action rates in all sessions in cascade status for action (top) and apathy (bottom) cascades. Note that peripheral assignment generates higher rates of action and apathy in cascades. The results are more extreme when the vanguard are assigned to the periphery. Total number of subjects in the experiment $N = 720$.

With the prospective definition of cascade, similar results confirming the higher frequency of action cascades hold for a range of cascade cut-offs, from 75 percent to 90 percent and from 25 percent to 10 percent. Compared to the two other mechanisms, *random* assignment consistently yields the smallest number of sessions in action cascades, and highest rates of failure cascades. The network experiment dataset is available in the online appendix at https://goo.gl/FQ6PE0.

THE CENTRALITY MYTH? A SESSION'S INITIAL ACTION CENTRALITY AND CASCADE STATUS

As expected, because of the random assignment, the average *initial* rates of choosing action per session are similar: 0.55, 0.56 and 0.53 for *peripheral*, *central* and *random* assignments, and there is no statistically significant difference between the three treatments. Moreover, the initial rate of risk taking in a given session is positively correlated with the action cascade status, as expected, and this effect is uniform across all three treatments. That is, if, by chance, a session had many risk-takers at the beginning, it was more likely to end in "rebellion", regardless of treatment status. To further explore the dynamics of the centrality of action vis a vis the network treatment factor, I wondered if the initial average of "betweenness centrality" among risk-takers in a given session influences the possibility of an action cascade in ways that are distinct from one network treatment to another. Ordinary Least Squares (OLS) regression results in Table (5.2) gauge the correlation between a session's action cascade status in each round "Cascade" (a dummy for action cascade status for the pertinent session-round) for each treatment, and the average centrality of risk taking in the first round of the relevant session, "InitCent".[33] The robust standard errors are clustered based on session.

$$\text{InitCent}_i = \alpha \text{Treatment}_i \times \text{Cascade}_i + \beta \text{Treatment}_i + \gamma \text{Cascade}_i + \epsilon_i \quad (5.1)$$

It is expected that the average centrality of "action" in the first round influence the action cascade status of a given session. In line with the treatment-level findings, both of these correlates are negative for *peripheral* and *central* assignments, and statistically significant for *peripheral* assignment. *Random* assignment, the treatment with the smallest number of action cascades, shows a positive correlation.

In *peripheral* assignment whenever the initial acts of risk taking occurred in more peripheral locations, on average there existed a *higher* rate of session-rounds in action cascade status, peripherality was instrumental in engendering higher levels of risk taking. *Random* assignment, on the other hand, resembled an expected outcome more

[33] Total $N = 15 \times 15 \times 3 = 675$.

TABLE 5.2. *Estimation results: OLS regression, average centrality of risk taking in the first round on action cascade status by treatment*

Variable	Coefficient	(Std. Err.)
Central × Cascade (binary)	−0.680	(0.916)
Random × Cascade (binary)	1.480**	(0.386)
Peripheral × Cascade (binary)	−1.023*	(0.454)
Intercept	4.963**	(0.251)
N		675
R^2		0.072
$F_{(3,44)}$		8.917

Significance level: 10%: †5% : * 1% : **

closely: when subjects are randomly assigned to network locations, more central acts of risk taking, on average, instigate more action cascade session-rounds, an observation in line with seedings that are agnostic to the location of potential risk-takers. When centrality is equated with influence, it is merely because the positioning of the vanguard is not a part of the thought model. Random allocation of experimental subjects would create a positive and significant correlation between cascade status at the end and average centrality of the vanguard at the beginning. The nature of the correlation is different when there is a relation between risk propensity and network betweenness centrality.

Counterintuitively, for *peripheral* assignment of the vanguard the more central the initial risk taking in an experimental session is, the less successful is the attempt at a global action cascade. These observations are indicative of dynamics that are distinct from those of centrally orchestrated cascades of collective risk taking.

LATENCY TO CASCADE STATUS

Not only were the success and failure cascades more frequent when the risk seeking subjects were positioned at the periphery, on average they also began *earlier* during the sessions. Based on the prospective (second) cascade definition with thresholds (25 percent, 75 percent), the average points of entry to "action" cascade were 2.3, 5.0 and 7.0 for the *peripheral, central* and *random* assignments. Similar averages for inaction cascades were 4.2, 8.3 and 8.7 for the three treatments. Furthermore, the three nonparametric Kaplan–Meier estimators showcase the temporal

Convergence to Action Cascades

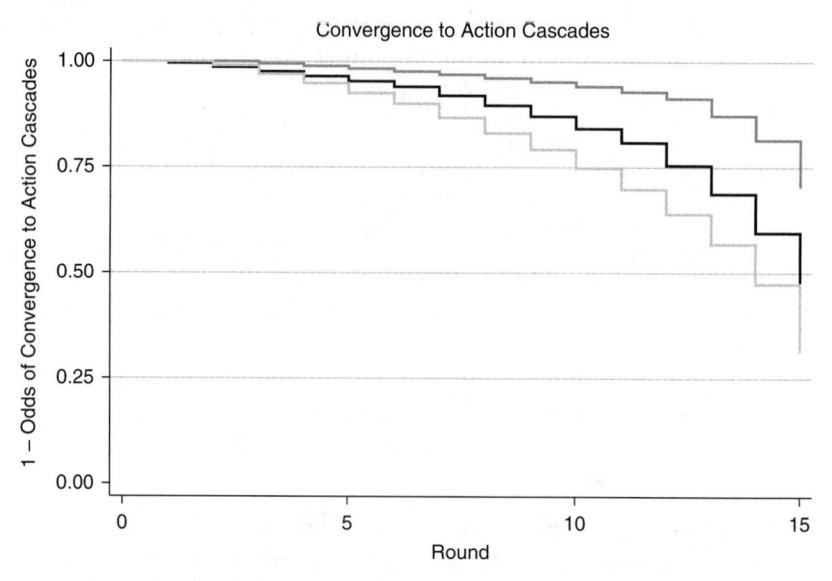

FIGURE 5.5. Kaplan–Meier survival analysis; success event = convergence to action cascade, for each of the three network treatments, cascade thresholds (0.75, 0.25). From top to bottom, *random*, *central* and *peripheral* assignment of the risk takers. *Peripheral* assignment yields the fastest average entry to cascades in session-rounds. Log-rank tests of pairwise differences are statistically significant.

divergence between the peripheral assignment compared to the other two network treatments. Log-rank tests of pairwise differences between the three treatments are all significant ($Pr > \chi^2 = 0.000$); see Figure (5.5). Similar results hold for action cascade thresholds between 70 and 90 percent. The latency results are also robust under the other class of cascade definitions.

To summarize, the peripheral assignment of the risk seeking vanguard in the network experiments of collective action generated more frequent cascades of collective action, compared to the random assignment baseline, as well as the central allocation of most seeking individuals. When the cascades happened, the peripheral assignment of the vanguard yielded the fastest convergence to cascades of collective action and apathy. Interestingly, peripheral assignment resulted in a bipolar pattern of cascades both of action and apathy: compared to the central assignment of the risk seeking vanguard and the baseline, the extremes were more frequent in both directions of action and apathy, and were quicker to converge to their final steady state. The central assignment of the risk seeking did not induce as many extremes, the results of the limited information collective lottery tended to be closer to the safe average levels of risk taking in the network status quo.

EVOLUTION OF CENTRALITY OF ACTION WITH TIME

In addition to detecting disparate correlations between starting and ending arrangement of action in distinct experimental treatments, the temporal dynamics of action propagation are of interest. In particular, if in *peripheral* assignment the underlying reason for risk-taking cascades is the activation of central nodes *before* influencing the intermediate ones, then a two-tier theory of information flow[34] (and collective action) still applies. If that is not the case, then the process of social propagation here is distinct from those of a two-tier nature with a clear distinction between central opinion leaders and the rest. I wondered if the propagation of action in the peripheral assignment, from the periphery to the center, was uniform in centrality and time. There can be two distinct processes at work: during a cascade, the peripheral instigators could have activated a number of central nodes in the initial rounds of the experiments, and the action could have then proliferated from the center to the rest of the network; or, alternatively, the flow of action from the periphery to the center could have happened more uniformly. The former explanation does not negate the two-tier distinction between "central opinion leaders" and the rest, while the latter does.[35]

To examine the evolution of the *centrality* of risk taking, I divided the nodes in each network realization to three groups of low, medium and high centrality, and visualized the progression of the rates of risk taking in these three regions in five temporal periods in Figure (5.6). The results show that, in sessions resulting in action cascade in the *peripheral* assignment, the most central of the three groups, on average, adopts risk taking after the other two less central groups. In other words, the action cascades are *not* the result of an activation of central nodes at the beginning of the experimental session. On average, the central nodes are the final group to adopt collective risk taking in the sessions resulting in action cascades.

---

[34] Zaller (1992).
[35] Aral et al. (2009).

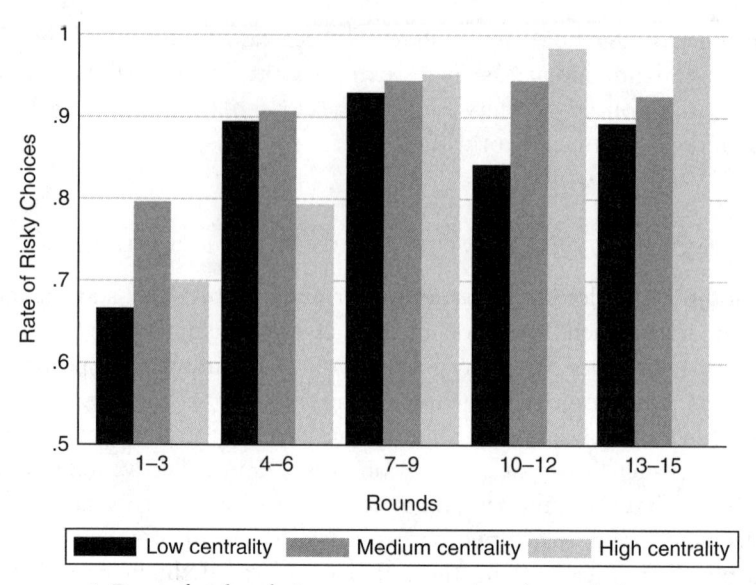

FIGURE 5.6. Rate of risky choices over categories of rounds by categories of centrality for peripheral action cascades.

A depiction of the rate of risk taking in each of these regions across five temporal segments in Figure (5.6) shows that the rates of risk taking rose in mid-range centralities after a surge in the periphery, and in central positions after an increase in mid-range centralities. Hence, the uniform propagation of action is the most likely explanation, not a transfer of risk taking from the periphery to the center, then to the rest.[36]

SUBJECT LEVEL COMPONENTS OF CASCADE STATUS

Session level analysis in the above shows a link between initial centrality of action and cascade status that operates differently in *peripheral* assignment compared to the *random* assignment baseline. To further explore the mircodynamics of cascade generation on the level of the individual subject, I examined the subject level components of risk taking in interaction with each of the three network treatments while controlling for the session level cascade status and experimental round.

[36] Note that the functionality of marginal instigators extends beyond mere *bridges* between subgroups Weimann (1982). The cascade of contagion can start from peripheral instigators and flow in the direction of the center, through intermediate network actors, to the most central ones.

The model for the logistic regression is included in equation (5.2); individual components of the interactions, other than treatment and cascade status are omitted for the sake of brevity. Standard errors were clustered on the session level. X is a vector of individual level controls.

$$\text{Act}_{kt} = \alpha_1 \text{Treatment}_{kt} + \alpha_2 \text{Cascade}_{kt} + \alpha_3 \text{Treatment} \times \text{Cascade}_{kt}$$
$$+ \alpha_4 \text{Treatment} \times \text{Centrality}_{kt}$$
$$+ \alpha_5 \text{Treatment} \times \text{Degree}_{kt}$$
$$+ \alpha_5 \text{Treatment} \times \text{Lagged average action of neighbors}_{kt} \quad (5.2)$$
$$+ \alpha_6 \text{Treatment} \times \text{Average risk rank of neighbors}_{kt}$$
$$+ \alpha_7 \text{Treatment} \times \text{Round}_{kt} + \beta X + \epsilon_{kt}$$

The results are included in Table (5.3), the treatment–cascade status interaction terms are as expected and are omitted. In line with the nature of treatments, in centrality-based assignments, subject centrality exerts a positive effect on risk taking in central assignment, and a negative effect in peripheral assignment.[37] Interestingly enough in none of the three treatment sessions, the network degree of a subject per se was as a significant component of risk taking.

The average rate of risk taking in one's neighborhood in the previous round is also highly correlated with one's decision to take risk.[38] Activity in the ego network in the previous round, i.e. action in the past in the immediate neighborhood, incited risk taking in the present.

The most interesting finding in Table (5.3) is on the correlation between one's network neighbors' risk propensity and one's own action, and the variation of this correlation term among the three network treatments. Figure (5.4) shows that the nature of diffusion of action from the instigators to the rest of the network in *peripheral* assignment is different from the same propagation in *central* assignment. In Table (5.3) that effect is reflected in the nature of neighborhood influence, and gives a clue to the reason for such a divergence between the two network treatments. *Only* for *central* assignment, most of action happens in the neighborhood of low *risk propensity* (higher risk ranks are associated with more risk aversion). Risk-takers in *central* assignments are surrounded by risk averse subjects. This is expected, because the instigators are positioned in the most central positions, and are in touch with the majority of the

---

[37] $p = 0.02$ central assignment, $p = 0.02$ peripheral assignment.
[38] $p < 0.001$ for all three treatments.

TABLE 5.3. *Estimation results: logistic regression of subject level action on cascade status, centrality, degree, lagged average action of neighbors, average rank of neighbors, round interacting with treatment. Number of subjects = 720. Standard errors adjusted for 45 session clusters.*

Variable	Coefficient	(Std. Err.)
Peripheral × Centrality	−0.037*	(0.016)
Random × Centrality	−0.023	(0.021)
Central × Centrality	0.042*	(0.018)
Peripheral × Degree	0.008	(0.058)
Random × Degree	−0.062	(0.043)
Central × Degree	−0.040	(0.054)
Peripheral × Lagged average action of neighbors	6.358**	(0.546)
Random × Lagged average action of neighbors	5.258**	(0.435)
Central × Lagged average action of neighbors	4.375**	(0.581)
Peripheral × Average rank of neighbors	0.301	(0.211)
Random × Average rank of neighbors	−0.248	(0.151)
Central × Average rank of neighbors	0.560**	(0.187)
Peripheral × Round	−0.228**	(0.027)
Random × Round	−0.207**	(0.025)
Central × Round	−0.159**	(0.016)
Intercept	−4.317**	(1.376)
N	10,800	
Log-likelihood	−5190.698	

Significance level: 10%: † 5% : * 1% : **

subject pool, who by definition are risk averse. *Peripheral* assignment, in contrast, does not show a similar correlation.

Risk averse neighbors in the vicinity of the most risk seeking individuals dampen the proliferation of action from the central instigators to the rest of the network. In contrast, in *peripheral* assignment, the correlation is not significant. In *peripheral* assignment, the lack of correlation between the risk-taking propensities of the ego's social neighborhood and the ego's risk-taking behavior itself ensures that the prevalence of risk taking in the periphery is not blocked from reaching intermediate and central locations in the network.[39]

---

[39] Note that this also means higher rates of action cascades in *peripheral* assignment are not because the risk-takers are clustered together, Aral et al. (2009); *peripheral* assignment

To summarize, the disadvantage of seeding at the center, was that most of the risk taking in this scheme was happening in the neighborhood of risk averse individuals, and they could adversely, and significantly, hamper the actions of the instigators positioned at the center.

Finally, the rates of risk taking decrease as the game of collective risk taking progresses to later rounds, and this relation is significant for all three treatments.

To summarize the discussion on the spatial evolution of risk taking in the experimental networks, compared to the peripheral assignment, the risk-takers in the central assignment treatment are more influenced by the majority's risk aversion; their propensity for risk is counterbalanced by the preference of the majority in favor of the status quo. In contrast, risk taking in the peripheral assignment does *not* arise solely because of the risk-takers' and abstaining individuals' polarization into separate groups; instead, peripheral risk-takers are able to effectively instigate and transmit rebellion from the periphery to the intermediate network neighborhoods, and from there to the center.

LEADING FROM THE PERIPHERY AND SOCIOPOLITICAL MECHANISM DESIGN

In the experiments convergence to cascades of global action happens most frequently when the radical vanguard, i.e. the risk-taking individuals, are in the periphery. Furthermore, when cascades do happen in a setting of peripheral provocateurs, they happen the fastest among the three network treatments, reaching global majority in earlier rounds of play. Unlike the network treatment with the risk-taking subjects at central positions, the sessions with the risk seeking individuals at the periphery depict a bipolar pattern: cascades of collective action or of apathy are both more frequent in the peripheral assignment and, on average, they start in earlier rounds during the sessions. The gap between success and failure cascades is wider in peripheral assignment compared to central positioning where intermediate rates of action are more frequent.

During the experiment the subjects were given local knowledge of risk taking in the social network and were rewarded based on global levels of risk taking. The same research strategy can be extended further to include network types other than the random Erdös-Rényi networks

does not show a significant influence of the risk propensity in the social neighborhood upon the ego.

implemented in the study in this chapter. The level of information available to subjects in relation to their risk propensity was altered based on three network treatments. Note that rumors can be modeled as noisy network interventions in the context of the research platform introduced here.

The results in this chapter are in line with the findings of the Cairo survey in Chapter (2) where the vanguard were found to be more geographically dispersed vis a vis the typical protester in the early phases of the 2011 Egyptian Revolution, and during information blackouts in Egypt and Syria. The experimental results also confirm the importance of decentralized peripheral contention in engendering rapid and far reaching cascades of collective risk taking. A potential resolution to the paradox of *leaderless revolution* emerged from the results.

In terms of mechanism design, the results invite more attention to dispersed campaigns for generating cascades of opinion reversal, voting and marketing campaigns on online and offline platforms alike. In the network experiments I outlined in this chapter, I altered the arrangement of potential instigators in three treatments and identified an influence process from the margins which is distinct from influencing from the center,[40] as well as the influence of many non-influentials.[41] It originates from risk-takers who reside at the margins of the social network, and act upon limited local information. It is customary to induce influence and promote social innovation via central figures on social media outlets. The findings of the experiment encourage exploring processes that, on the contrary, employ peripheral instigators of change. I will elaborate on this theme a bit more in the following chapter.

---

[40] See Katz and Lazarsfeld (2006) for a theory of influence based on central opinion leaders.
[41] Bakshy et al. (2011).

6

Decentralization and Power
Novel Modes of Social Organization

In the course of this inquiry I argued that social mobilization from the margins induces dynamics that are different from those of mobilization from the center. Luminaries are not the only ones who lead in social revolutions. The inquiry started from a curiosity, an anomalous escalation of decentralized conflict during two recent total blackouts in Egypt and Syria. I employed the events as massive social experiments of collective action in order to explore the reasons behind the spontaneity and apparent lack of leadership in mass social movements. The picture which has emerged from the cases as well as from a series of controlled network experiments is that of a decentralized one – dense on the local and sparse on the global levels, fast moving contagious processes that stand in contrast, and often in opposition, to the oft studied centralized and hierarchical structures of sociopolitical power. As such, the findings also provide a thought-provoking glimpse into the dynamics of social processes we have not yet mined in terms of their utility for political organization.[1]

POWER AND VISIBILITY

Modern political power necessitated clear distinctions between political categories and administrative bodies. Each division asked for predictable

---

[1] The availability of fine-grained empirics Pentland (2014) motivates and enables the analysis. New data obviate the need for economizing narratives; information on the structure of *social graphs* enables differentiating network locations, a novel pathway to induce influence. The implications of utilizing such new sources of social power are unknown. We may damage the possibility of it by merely trying to (intentionally) influence it via new modes of data.

adherence.[2] Allegiance to the uniting axes of society in the form of ideologies, either nationalistic or spiritual, reinforced a system of stratified governable groups. The forefathers of the modern polity, including Montesquieu, stressed the importance of rationalization. Chance had to be discarded and doubts were to be a matter of the past. Contingency was a matter of contempt.[3] It is no surprise that Weber's shrewd declaration on the origins of capitalism[4] was tied to the Calvinist predestination. Modernism at its roots enjoys inseparable intimations with exactitude, hierarchy and predictability. Its triumph lay in the employment of genus, classification to the limit and constructing predictability.[5] Predestination spoke to this desire for precision. However, in contrast to the perceived yearning for exactitude, what constituted the roots of modernity at its inception, was not the certain existence of predestination, but the unsettling reality of doubt. A doubt that had to be confirmed and put to rest, and the individual in doing so, not only needed oneself, but also required the affirmation of the others. At the center of this story of preordained certitude as the initiator of industrial capitalism lies a contradiction. Although the faithful are destined either for salvation or for damnation, they do not know if they are saved or not. Even the priest is of no help. One is left to doubt, a personal anxiety that needs to be tamed. John Calvin[6] himself opines on the anxiety and confusion that such a liberation may cause, and shortly after dismisses it as an *error*:

> There is hardly anyone who does not think sometimes, "If my salvation comes only from God's election, what proof have I of that election?" When this thought dominates an individual, he will be permanently miserable, in terrible torment or mental confusion. The fact that these thoughts deprive a man of peace and rest in God is proof of their error.

In Calvin's own words, the anxiety is so unbearable that there can be no verity to it. In these sentences, rationalization of the sentiment mirrors the project of scientific inquiry set into motion by similar and simultaneous historical movements. However, I would like to argue that the same erroneous thoughts, banished by trivializing force of rationality, raised rational individualist society to prominence as a mode of being. The anxiety of doubt motivates action, the "terrible torment of mental confusion" that John Calvin had acutely observed, but had decided to

[2] See Hirschman (1977).
[3] Montesquieu [1748] (1989), Montesquieu [1721] (2008).
[4] Weber [1905] (1958*b*).
[5] Foucault (1970).
[6] In Calvin [1536] (1995: 12.24.4).

dismiss, drives decisions that are aimed at resolution. I argued that the anxiety in a communication vacuum motivates similar psychological responses: the constituents are compelled to act in order to put their doubts to rest. During the calm of the status quo, a reliable and streamlined flow of information prevents such destabilizing moments.

Predestination facilitated modernist society through doubt as much as conviction. Everybody coveted absolution. Each had to prove the preordained verdict to oneself and the others using the means of material life. Those who gained in the mundane practices of commerce and citizenship would be proven to be saved, others were doomed. In other words, in the Weberian scheme what drove the individual was not conviction, but lack of information. Not knowing of one's absolution put each individual in a pressing bind to act upon that ignorance, so they had to prove their worth to themselves and the others. Anxiety produced by an absence of certitude motivated the economic commotion, and the contradiction between faith and doubt set the Calvinist parish into movement.

Against such an epistemological background, a break in the social routine could not be rational. In other words, the language of rebellion could not be a part of the *public transcript*. Rebellions from the subaltern always came as surprises, labeled unscientific and irrational. Crowd behavior was labeled as base and primitive.[7] Theoreticians of social mobilization overlooked the psychology of minutiae in favor of undercurrent formulae and elite leadership. Mobilization became synonymous with organization in groups, in practiced, tried and tired methods of group leadership and indoctrination. However, *the deviant, irrational and counterintuitive* language of rebellion cannot be the product of the public transcript, which is the logic and language of dominant organizations. Instead it is made and practiced away from the normalizing sight of the status quo. The division between hidden and public nomenclature reflects the divide between the sources of cultural hegemony on one side and the local language of the ruled on the other – a division that became more distinct as modernity moved to separate the public from the private, regulating the public as the political arena.[8] The public was the site of political power and public terminology, the private was left to the individual, but the individual was held responsible to the surveillance of the public.

---

[7] Le Bon [1895] (1960) finds crowds to be representations of a primitive state of human mind.
[8] Habermas (1991).

The public in that sense had to be predictable and reified. Bureaucratic geometry had to dissect the realm of the social to analytic reductions.

Visibility in the eyes of an omniscient power is a recurrent theme in the traditional narratives of power both in religion and politics. Modernity honed and promoted the same ideas to the extreme: with individuation came the possibility of identification, with hierarchies came efficient mechanisms of control. The need for visibility and maintaining order also privileged strong social links in the hierarchy, not only *to see*,[9] but also for the centers of political power *to be seen*.[10] Emblems and national monuments were erected. After the advent of the printed press, the post-Enlightenment media reinforced a mechanism similar to the surveillance routine: while the latter kept the individual visible to the hierarchy of power, the former kept power everpresent for the society to see.

Taking stock, the language of disruptive mobilization cannot be the public discourse, instead it is more likely to constitute aberrations from the editorial, not in the mainstream and closely edited narrative of *the public transcript*. At times it propagates below the surface of normality as pamphlets and audio cassettes, sometimes as a tweet or two.

LOGIC OF ANONYMITY

During the Romanian Revolution of 1989, one of the most visible signs of the rebellion was the ubiquitous old Communist flag with its emblematic coat of arms cut out (see Figure (6.1)). The flags with their absent message at the center, with the ostensible hole, became the symbol of the revolution. The void turned into a uniting force.

In the same vein, what is common among the Romanian revolutionary flag, the Occupy encampments and Anonymous web-based cults is the lack of a central emblem, the sign of authority and appropriation. The suppressed identity of the subterranean can identify with these performative acts of expression, everybody can claim the void and assume leadership and voice. Anonymity expands the circle of possible contributors. Not only does it escape surveillance, it also draws a unison in force that would have been impossible if only one entity could claim the credit. During the disruptions of the *public transcript* such anonymizing processes, instead of impeding action, facilitate collective participation.

---

[9] Scott (1998).
[10] Chwe (2001).

Lack of communication derails preplanned mobilization, but unintended contagion is relieved of the stilts of supervision, and implicates in rebellion those with no formal capacity of contention. The fastest rates of the diffusion of collective action happen when the leaders and followers are influencing each other outside the bounds of persuasion and manipulation processes; anonymity facilitates the contagion by leveling the playing field.

The prevalence of contagion mechanisms in the new media regime upsets the preexisting patterns of mobilization. Traditional modernism strove to give each individual a face and a distinct voice to diffuse the archaic obscurity that afflicted the downtrodden, but with it came the possibility of ready identification, surveillance and tracking. All were given a face, but with a price. In a culture of taxonomy, where anyone is given a name and a place, acquiring anonymity became a protest by itself. In a history of analytic processes, being anonymous has become an act of protest. Instead of *the voice of revolution*, an amorphous multitude has emerged.

The network dynamics of politics on the large scale becomes significant when small entities grow in importance and cascade effects and collective behavior are taken out of the closet of irrational, contingent and epiphenomenal. What was disparaged as base, primitive and uncouth is now scrutable, giving political voice to elements outside the realm of the self-aggrandizing manipulating elite.

NAIVE DATA AND THE STRATEGY OF CONTROL

> The censors shall draw up a list of the population, recording ages, children, households and possessions; they shall watch over the city's temples, streets, and aqueducts, and also the treasury and taxes; they shall divide the citizens and assign them to tribes; then they shall divide them according to possessions, age, and rank; they shall distinguish the sons of the cavalry and the infantry; they shall not allow men to remain bachelors; they shall regulate the behavior of the citizens and not permit a disreputable person to remain in the Senate; they shall be two in number and shall hold office for five years; the other officers shall be annual; the post of censor shall always have occupants.
>
> Cicero, The Laws, Book III[11]

---

[11] Cicero (1998).

FIGURE 6.1. Romanian Revolution and the denial of emblem, December 1989.

Past the beginning of the Enlightenment, modernism established itself in precision in the outside world and conviction in the inside realm.[12] Nation-state trumpeted mobilization based on national conviction; ethnic identification was used for the sake of nationalism, faith for rebellion. The economy of inference imposed easy-to-identify symbols, names for cultural genus, brands for political leanings and signifiers for internal malaise. The existence of this added layer of representation assisted the flow of information, which is nothing but *the inference of a fact from the existence of another*. The more surprising the finding, the higher the information content of the relation. The standardization of social symbols also brought tools for social control; it generated a predictability needed for the existence of a rational life.

[12] See Federalist No. 10 Madison [1787] (2003) for an early argument for political centralization.

The possibility of effective control is conditioned on the nature of available information in two ways: first, how the story of political life is cast, which finds its manifestation in the common idea of history; and second, in the modes of social mobilization relying on the personal perception of the political situation.[13] Crude means of censorship and social identification work on both levels, one destructive, the other constructive. There are opportunities for manipulating the narrative, but they rely on the need for simplification. Censorship, in its traditional meaning, is best done when the disallowed keywords are well known and are common knowledge. Identity building is the most efficient when there exist clear borderlines, with distinctive features for each pole, ready to be adopted.[14] Instead of theory building, stratification either in the language of the Enlightenment or in the Marxian nomenclature assisted mobilization.[15] The taxonomies necessary for control, were also employed to mobilize: ideologies assisted identification with the state; simultaneously self-awareness of one's social category economized mobilization.

In the course of the manuscript, I explored ways in which political mobilization is tied to informational classifications. Banishing vagueness and multiplicity in science, either natural or human, goes hand in hand

---

[13] The perception itself being a partial derivative of the idea of history.
[14] Modernist simplifications were accompanied with trivializing power of ideology and science. History indeed was a simplification, a modernist creature, which matched the centralizing forces of the eighteenth and nineteenth centuries. While natural history morphed into natural sciences, physics, chemistry and biology; human history did not shape up to become a similar practice. Stratification of political forms, introduced by Montesquieu and Hobbes, did not manage to produce a geometry of politics similar to the projects of their contemporaries. Newton's daring and meticulous theory-making transformed natural history to a natural science. The same was not true of Hobbes' biological similes, or Montesquieu's political classifications. Instead, the political connotations of the classifications influenced the historical course of monarchy in Europe. *Despotisme* became a target for passionate resistance when Montesquieu, among other Enlightenment thinkers, delineated it as an archaic (and often oriental) taxonomy of ruling power, opposed to progress. The utility of classification was not the same as in natural sciences.
[15] Hobbes and Montesquieu did for politics what Linnaeus did for biology. Montesquieu's differentiations gave the founders on both sides of the Atlantic an ideal to aspire to, and an antidote to fight. Linnaean categorization assisted biology becoming a science. The taxonomic era of the eighteenth century gave rise to the precision needed for the advances of capitalism in the following years. Without predictability science could not exist, and without control the nation-state could not sustain itself. Taxonomy in human sciences played a role slightly different from natural sciences. It channeled efficient mobilization, it helped reinforcing clear-cut identities that could be a part of the shaping nation-state system as a towering structure of the modernist order, and gave way to surveillance, a necessary component of post-Enlightenment normalization process. The individual was given a first and a last name, and was assigned a racial and cultural identity.

with ways in which social mobilization works. Of special interest to this project were alternative ways of mobilization that do not necessarily rely on such social stratifications.

Here the argument followed the traces of systemic demarcation between vagueness and exactitude on three distinct and interrelated grounds: first, the application of taxonomy organized "natural history" into "natural sciences", but in the realm of human sciences did not play the same role, instead it facilitated political mobilization. Second, on the level of social mobilization: that certitude, allegiance and visibility became tools of modern mobilization, hiding the less explored dimensions of mobilization which employ the mirror image of these chartered concepts, the realm of non-rationalizable and contingent that the Enlightenment had discarded for being out of the scope of determination. The second item is the pathway to the third component: that the taxonomy of identities went hand in hand with the imposition of the modernist state, and was accentuated by its need for effective mobilization, a trivializing science of human identity that matched the control mechanism devised after the advent of the Enlightenment. The modern social apparatus was pressured by an indispensable requirement of predictability, the human component of which found its manifestation in elaborate schemes of political control.

With the emergence and recognition of microlevel data on the massive scale, from the type often dubbed "Big Data", the necessity for a simplified, linear and unitary narrative of inference is alleviated. The part of the past that is more relational and contingent and nondescript comes to the fore. Collective behavior cannot be merely dismissed as primitive, just because the modern science, in its lack of efficient tools and data, was unable to analyze its dynamics. Similarly the concept of social mobilization is transforming. Leaders become more and more a part of the context – their importance partly is a result of their location in the network of relations as well as their innate characteristics. More attention is paid to the viral nature of mobilization, the network dynamics of collective action and the emergent nature of political message. It is more difficult to postulate that the message is separate and prior to the dynamics of action. The same can be said for the apparatus of control. Novel forms of control tend to be systemic, as a part of a decentralized force of conformity, they are less likely to be the result of a directed process of external suppression which is often predicated on identification.

7

Appendix

CH. 2: MAJOR EVENTS AND MEDIA ANNOUNCEMENTS, EGYPTIAN REVOLUTION 2011

Included here are the details of the 18 days of confrontation between Egyptian protesters and Mubarak's regime, and a list of major political announcements by the Egyptian and American leaders used in coding.

Dynamics of the Egyptian Unrest: Four important cycles of unrest are evident during the 18 days of the Egyptian uprising, each of which starts with a significant media event. There are four: January 25–27; January 28–February 1; February 2–7; and February 8–11. Source: The *New York Times*' Lede blog and Al Jazeera's website.

1. **January 25–27**: Initial mobilization on January 25, the social media campaign.
2. **January 28–February 1**: Disruption of the media on January 28 and the proliferation of the protests, the military steps in and acts as a game changer during the following clashes between pro- and anti-Mubarak crowds.
3. **February 2–7**: Provocative national address by Mubarak late at night on February 1 (stating he will stay in power till September and will die in Egypt), ensuing clashes on the 2nd and 3rd, the military's inaction emboldens prevailing opposition crowds, relative calm afterwards till the 8th.
4. **February 8–11**: Emotional appeal by Wael Ghonim on a late night television show on the 7th and his follow up speech in

Tahrir square in the morning of February 8 initiates the final phase of protests in Tahrir, eventual announcement of Mubarak's resignation by Suleiman on the 11th.

Political Announcements: A list of major announcements during the Egyptian protests is included below. "Announcements" are major addresses to the nation, broadcast from the state television or private TV channels with a national audience. Source: The *New York Times'* Lede blog and Al Jazeera's website. All times are Egyptian local time (EST+7 in January and February 2011).

1. **January 29**: at around 12:30 a.m., Mubarak's late night address (coded in the analysis as an announcement on the 29th): he gives concessions, dismisses the government, appoints a Vice President. Obama talks to the press immediately after Mubarak's speech.
2. **February 1**: at around 10 p.m. (earlier that day the largest protest to date in Tahrir), Mubarak gives another speech on the state television. He announces he intends to remain in office until the end of his current term. Obama again speaks after Mubarak's speech. Worst clashes start on February 2 and last for two days (February 2 and 3), by the 5th the situation has almost returned to normal.
3. **February 4**: Suleiman makes TV appearances – total of two television appearances before Friday the 4th.
4. **February 8**: Wael Ghonim gives an emotional interview on Monday night (7th) on a cable TV channel and appears in Tahrir the next morning (8th) to give a speech addressing the massive crowd in the square.
5. **February 10**: around 7 p.m. Egyptian state TV announces an address by Mubarak to be broadcast soon – Obama gives a speech around 8:30 p.m.: "Egyptians are making history." Around 10 p.m., Mubarak gives a speech on the state television, asserting that he is not stepping down and will remain in office till September.
6. **February 11**: Around 6 p.m. Suleiman gives an address on the state TV announcing that "President Hosni Mubarak has resigned and handed over power to the country's military." Obama gives a speech at 10 p.m.

CH. 2: MOBILIZATION EMAILS FROM APRIL 6'S YOUTH MOVEMENT

ومن المفترض أن ينضم المتظاهرون من الشرقية والقليوبية والمنوفية إلي المتظاهرين في القاهرة وكذلك سينضم المتظاهرين في قنا وسوهاج والمنيا إلي المتظاهرين في أسيوط

. ومن المفترض أن يكون هناك تحرك واسع من أهالي سيناء للمشاركة في يوم 25 يناير بشكل واسع

المطالبة والشعارات الخاصة بيوم 25 يناير:
1- حد أدني للأجور 1200 جنية
2- ربط الأجور بالأسعار
3- إلغاء حالة الطوارئ
4- إقالة حبيب العادلي ومحاكمة الظباط الذين إرتكبوا جرائم ضد الشعب المصري

وتم التنسيق مع تجمعات للمصريين في الخارج للتضامن معنا ومع مطالبنا والتظاهر أمام السفارات المصريه في تونس وبريطانيا وبيروت وأمريكا

FIGURE 7.1. Demands of the protesters in the announcement sent on January 22.

---------- Forwarded message ----------
From: April 6 Youth <media@6april.org>
Date: 2011/1/25
Subject: بخصوص المتابعة للأحداث اليوم 25 يناير علي مستوي الجمهورية
To:

،،الزملاء الأعزاء

بخصوص المتابعة اليومية للأحداث علي مستوي الجمهورية
ستكون غرفة العمليات جاهزة للرد عليكم اليوم

سيكون هاتفي   وهاتف الزميل   هي الأرقام المستعدة للرد علي إستفسارات الصحفيين والإعلاميين وتوجيهم

* التوزيع الجغرافي للفعاليات في القاهرة :

جامعة الدول العربية : (6 أبريل - حملة البرادعي - العدالة والحرية - الغد - الكرامة - الجبهه ... آخرون) نقطة التجمع والإلتقاء كافة المجموعات عند ميدان مصطفي محمود
بخصوص الكميرات ياريت تتقسموا عند بدايتي شارع جامعة الدول العربية في تمام الساعة 2 ظهرا هتلاقوا الشباب ظهرت قدامك بأعداد*

* دوران شبرا: التمركز في الدوران في تمام الساعة 2 ظهرا (حشد وكفاية *

(دار القضاء العالي (البرلمان الشعبي

(نقابة المحامين (المحامون

"نقابة الأطباء "دار الحكمة

جامعة القاهرة

==================
هناك تحركات من عدد من العمال سيكونون في وسط القاهرة في تمام الساعه 2ظهرا غير مسموح الإفصاح عن أسمائهم يمكنكم متابعتنا لاحقا لمعرفة أسمائهم
==================

: المحافظات
(المنصورة : شارع مشعل / تقاطع شارع الجلاء مع شارع بورسعيد
الإسكندرية : محطة مصر - ميدان المنشية - القائد إبراهيم
أسيوط : شارع الجيش
الغربية : طنطا : أمام مبني المحافظة
الغربية : المحلة الكبري: ميدان الشون
الإسماعيلية : شارع الثلاثيني وشارع السكة الحديد بجوار حمزاوي
الفيوم : ميدان الحواتم ببندر الفيوم

وبقية المناطق سوف أوفيكم بها تباعا

--

FIGURE 7.2. Groups' assignment to each six locations, the point of congregation of all of these groups is announced to be Mustafa Mahmoud Square (in Dokki east of Zamalek, not Tahrir), the time of congregation: 2 p.m. 1. Gameat Al Dewal Al Arabiya: April 6, El-Baradei Front and Supporters, Justice and Freedom, Al-Ghad, Al-Kerama, The Front, etc. 2. Shubra Square: Hashad and Kefaya movement. 3. Supreme Court (People's congress). 4. Bar association (lawyers). 5. Dar el Hekma (Doctors). 6. University of Cairo – as well as a number of workers "who will be in Cairo, but the names of their associations are not disclosed". In several Governorates including Al-Mansura, Alexandria, Assyut, Tantaa, Al-Mahalla, El Esmailia and Al Fayyum demonstrations were planned and "one" protest location was assigned; Alexandria was assigned three locations.

---------- Forwarded message ----------
From: **April 6 Youth** <media@6april.org>
Date: 2011/1/21
Subject: قام شباب 6 ابريل بتوزيع مايقرب من 20000 الف منشور بالقاهرة والمحافظات دعوه للمشاركة 25 يناير
To:

شباب 6 ابريل يوزعون مايقرب من 20000 الف منشور بالقاهره والمحافظات دعوه للمشاركه 25 يناي

قام شباب 6 ابريل في خلال 48 ساعه بتوزيع مايقرب من 20000(عشرون الفا) منشور دعوه ليوم 25 يناير, فلم تغفل اعين شباب 6 ابريل في الدعوه ليوم الانتفاضه المصريه 25 يناير ,والتي دعت لها حركه 6 ابريل هذا العام مثلما فعلنا العام الماضي وكان تحت شعار "لا للطوارئ ، ففى اكثر من 5 محافظات انتشر شباب 6 ابريل ببيانات الدعوه ليوم الانتفاضه المصريه وتعريف المصريين فى الشوارع باليوم 25 يناير وما سيتم.

ففي القاهره حيث طُبع اكثر من 10000 الاف منشور تم توزيعهم بالمناطق الشعبيه والإلقاء بهم من فوق الكبارى الرئيسيه وفى وسائل الموصلات ,وأمام الجامعات وفى إشارات المرور داخل السيارات وفى الأماكن الرئيسيه ، حيث دعا البيان الجميع لأهميه المشاركه فى يوم الغضب المصرى وألا نعود لبيوتنا دون ان نسترد حقوقنا.

وفى الأسكندريه قام شباب الحركه بتوزيع حوالى 500 منشور فى ميدان الساعه وفى محطة مصر ، ومن الأسكندريه إلى دمياط حيث قام اعضاء الحركة هناك بتوزيع 3000 منشور دعوه المواطنين للمشاركة يوم 25 يناير بالميكروباصات والمارة والملاقى قبول شديد مع المواطنين وتم الإجابة على جميع إستفسارات الناس فى الشوارع.

وفى محافظة الغربيه قام اعضاء الحركه هناك بدعوة الجميع لليوم في الشوارع ، واليوم الجمعه 21/ يناير تنظم الحركه والقوى السياسيه بالغربيه وقفه تضامنيه مع ثورة تونس بمدينة المحلة الكبرى يشارك فيها رموز نضاليه وسياسيه وعمال المحلة العظام وفيها ستحث المواطنين على اهميه المشاركه فى يوم 25 يناير لإسترداد حقوقنا ، الوقفه امام حزب الجبهه بمدينة المحلة الكبرى الثالثة عصراً.

ومايزيد عن 3الاف منشور تم توزيعهم بمدينة القليوبيه حيث قام شباب 6 أبريل بالقليوبيه بالانتشار بين المواطنين ونشر الدعوه للماشركه يوم 25 يناير من اجل المطالبه بحقوقنا

ومن الدلتا إلى الصعيد ، حيث مدينة سوهاج قام اعضاء الحركه هناك بتوزيع مايقرب من 2000 منشور على المواطنين وحثهم على اهميه المشاركه فى يوم 25 يناير ،
وقام شباب 6 ابريل بتوزيع 1000 منشور بمحافظه اكتوبر

وتستمر الحركه وبطاقة كل أعضائها تعمل على الدعوة لمشاركة جميع المصريين يوم 25 يناير بجميع محافظات

FIGURE 7.3. Preparations: Distribution of pamphlets before January 25.

ومع بدء العد التنازلي قام شباب 6 ابريل بمحافظة القاهره بتوزيع مايزيد عن 15 الف منشور (ببولاق والهرم وشبرا والمعادي و امبابه والسيده زينب والسيده نفيسه و ميدان رمسيس والسيده عيشه ومنطقة مجاوري وغيرها من المناطق وفالمواصلات العامه واشارات المرور وسط حالة من التفاعل الإيجابي من المواطنين على أختلاف أعمارهم حيث أكد العديد على مشاركتهم في يوم 25 يناير

قام شباب 6 أبريل القليوبيه بتوزيع 2000 نسخه من المنشور بكل من مدن بنها وشبرا وطوخ والقناطر لدعوة المواطنين للمشاركة يوم 25 يناير

ففي المنصوره قام شباب 6أبريل بالتعاون مع حملة البرادعي يتوزيع 8 الاف منشور

قام شباب 6 أبريل بمحافظة الغربيه بتوزيع 500 منشور للمشاركه يوم 25 يناير في الفعاليات التي ستتم بالمحافظه في هذا اليوم

وأيضا طلاب 6 أبريل شاركو في نشر الدعوه وتوزيع المنشورات الخاصه للمشاركه يوم 25 يناير حيث قاموا بتوزيع 3الاف منشور بكل من جامعة القاهره وجامعه عين شمس وجامعة الأزهر

والي أسيوط قام شباب 6 أبريل بمحافظة أسيوط بتوزيع 3 الأاف منشور بالتعاون مع الجمعيه الوطنيه للتغير وحملة البرادعي للمشاركه يوم 25 يناير

هذا و قد تلقى نشطاء الحركة العديد من المكالمات الهاتفيه من المحافظات و التى بينت ان الحملة الدعائيه ليوم 25 قد لاقت صدى كبير عند جموع المواطنيين اكثر من المتوقع
و ظهر ذلك فى العديد من مكالمات التليفونيه,الرسائل القصيرة

FIGURE 7.4. Preparations: 15,000 pamphlets were distributed before January 25 in Cairo, 15,000 more in other cities.

---------- Forwarded message ----------
From: April 6 Youth <media@6april.org>
Date: 2011/1/24
Subject: خبر صحفي هام \ يعلن شباب 6 ابريل عن غرفه عمليات مركزيه يوم الثلاثاء
To:

6 أبريل تعلن الطوارئ

تعلن حركة 6 ابريل عن غرفة عمليات مركزية ليوم غد الثلاثاء 25 يناير 2011

الارقام خاصه بيوم 25 يناير للتواصل والمتابعه مع المتظاهرين والاتصال علي هذه الارقام فى حالات الاعتقال او الاعتداء ولتوجيه الشباب الي اماكن التجمع من اجل حشد و توجيه المتظاهرين فى هذا اليوم لاماكن التظاهرات و إبلاغهم بأى تغيير فى هذة الاماكن ومتابعتهم وايضا تقديم المساعدة القانونية التى ستقدمها شباب 6 ابريل فى هذا اليوم لكل من يحتاجها
ارقام غرفه العمليات بالقاهره والمحافظات الاخرى

FIGURE 7.5. Distributing mobile numbers of the "operations room" members and the guiding committee on the 25th.

---------- Forwarded message ----------
From: April 6 Youth <media@6april.org>
Date: 2011/1/25
Subject: إعتذار شديد لعدم القدره علي التواصل الأمن أوقف موبيلاتنا
To:

أعتذار شديد لكل الشباب لعدم قدرتنا علي التواصل معكم
الأمن منع الإرسال أو الإستقبال لموبيل محمد عادل مدير المكتب الإعلامي وأحمد ماهر المنسق العام العام

إعتذار شديد ونتواصل عبر الإيميل

FIGURE 7.6. Update around 4 p.m., the authorities have disrupted transmission and reception via two of the leaders' mobile phones, promise to reconnect through alternate means.

---------- Forwarded message ----------
From: April 6 Youth <media@6april.org>
Date: 2011/1/25
Subject: للتواصل مع المكتب الإعلامي لحركة شباب 6 ابريل نرجوا منكم التواصل معنا علي الخط التالي
To:

للتواصل مع المكتب الإعلامي الرجاء الإتصال ب :   - للزميل

FIGURE 7.7. Around 6 p.m. new phone numbers announced, by now protesters have flooded Tahrir.

Ch. 2: April 6 Youth Movement

---------- Forwarded message ----------
From: **April 6 Youth** <media@6april.org>
Date: 2011/1/27
Subject: خبر صحفي\ شباب 6 ابريل يوزع 20 الف منشور دعوه للمشاركه بجمعه الغضب
To:

خبر صحفي\ شباب 6 ابريل يوزع 20 الف منشور دعوه للمشاركه بجمعه الغضب

--
قام شباب 6 ابريل بتصوير وتوزيع مايقرب من 20 الف منشور دعوه لجمعه الغضب التي سبق ودعا اليها شباب 6 ابريل بالمشاركه مع باقي الحركات والاحزاب
ونعلنها مستمرين مهما هددنا الأمن ومهما أعتقلوا منا؛ ولن يوقفنا أحد ولن نترك المنات الذين اعتقلوا من الشباب, حيث تم اعتقال المنات من نشطاء الحركه
لدينا 25 اسم معتقل من النشطاء بالحركه يتم عرضهم الان علي نيابة زينهم والباقي في مكان غير معلن حتي الان

لن نهدا و سنستمر حتي نتحرر و نحرر مصر من استعمار نظام مبارك
ونعلن عن جمعه الغضب بالقاهره والاسكندريه والاسماعليه ودمياط والشرقيه والمنصوره و الغربيه (المحلة - طنطا) - الاسماعيلية - كفر الشيخ - بنها - اسيوط
توضيح هام: دعوتنا ل يوم الجمعة ليس معناه انتهاء المظاهرات اليوم ... لكن معناه إن يوم الجمعة بإذن الله هيكون يوم الحسم.. اليوم حرب الشوارع مستمرة .. هنخرج من كل حاره وشارع وميدان ومن كل محافظه نطالب بحقوقنا

نظرا لاعتقال   (مدير المكتب الاعلامي)
ونظرا للتشويش علي ارفامنا
سيتم التواصل علي هذه الارقام

FIGURE 7.8. Call to protests on January 28, 2011, "Friday of Rage", in all major Egyptian cities.

CH 2: HOURLY EMAIL UPDATES FROM OPERATIONS ROOM

3:29 الأمن يعتدي على المتظاهرين بالعصي والهروات أمام مجلس الشعب مجموعة من المتظاهرين بدأو عند مجلس الشعب

3:26 آلاف المواطنين في شبرا بينهم نشطاء أجانب ونوارة نجم.. وانضمام الأهالي لهم... وسط هتافات "واحد اتنين الشعب المصري فين" و"ارحل ارحل يا مبارك".See More

3:45 آلاف في التحرير متجهون ناحية مجلس الشعب
3:40 تحركات جديدة في إمبابة في شارع البصراوي مايقرب من 1000 متظاهر
3:40 نساء السويس بالألاف في الشارع

3:40 مايقرب من 500 متظاهر متجهون من شارع طلعت حرب إلي ميدان التحرير وهتافات شديدة ضد مبارك

3:30 معتقلين من بورسعيد : شادي سليم ... محمد السويركي ... أحمد مراد .. إسلام ناجي .. محمد أبو النصر .. طارق مبروك :

3:30 معتقلين حاليا من أمام مجلس الوزراء في القاهرة : أحمد الرفاعي ... جمال الطوخي .. أحمد عبد الناصر ، محمد سعيد عبد الحميد :

3:00 وصل عدد المتظاهرين في المنصوره الى 10000 متظاهر في شارع توريل وهم لان متجهين الى شارع قناة السويس

3:55 متظاهرون من جاردن سيتي يتجهون نحو ميدان التحرير

3:55 الأمن يعتدي علي السيدات المتظاهرات في السويس

4:00 قنابل مسيلة للدموع في ميدان التحرير وهناك إصابات وسط المتظاهرين

FIGURE 7.9. 4 p.m. update, 12 entries, some are only 3 minutes apart.

---------- Forwarded message ----------
From: **April 6 Youth** <media@6april.org>
Date: 2011/1/25
Subject: تحديثات حتي الساعة 5 عصرا من الشارع ومن كل مكان
To:

4:00 الأمن يعتدي علي المتظاهرين في التحرير وفي شارع القصر العيني

4:09 - محمد جمال عبد العاطي - من ميدان التحرير

4:13 الأمن يكسر سيارات المدنين في ميدان التحرير

4:14 حوالي 1000 متظاهر في الزقازيق يقومون بمسيرة الان

4:16 الإسكندرية 1500 متظاهر والأمن يحاول تفريقهم وإعتداءات شديدة عليهم :

4:16 إعتقال العشرات في المنصورة، ووقوع إصابات عديدة في صفوف المتظاهرين، وعسكري يهدد بإطلاق النار علي المتظاهرين بإستخدام سلاحة الميري

4:17 مسيرة من الدقي من كوبري 15 مايو فيها ما يقرب من 5000 متظاهر
4:17 المتظاهرين يحتجزون مدير أمن السويس في كشك

4:18 مايقرب من 10 ألاف مواطن يكسرون الحاجز الأمني في الإسكندرية من ميدان المنشية متجهين إلي محطة مصر

4:19 ظهور فرق من الكراتية عند مستشفي أحمد ماهر في عابدين

4:23 المتظاهرون في التحرير يكسرون الكردون وهم متجهون ناحية مجلس الشعب

4:23 إبراهيم عيسي يصل إلي المظاهرة في ميدان التحرير

4:30 الأهالي في المنصورة يضربون الأمن ويفكون الحصار علي المتظاهرين

4:35 الأمن يغلق موبيلات محمد عادل مدير المكتب الإعلامي وأحمد ماهر منسق عام الحركة وموبيلات جبهه الدفاع عن متظاهري مصر
4:46 حصار 150 متظاهر في مقر الحزب الوطني في بور سعيد...وإطلاق الكلاب البوليسية عليهم
4:47 اعتقال 40 متظاهر من ميدان التحرير من ضمنهم "كريم الشاعر" ناشط حزب الغد
4:55 المتظاهرين في المحلة مايقرب من 15 ألف في ميدان الشون

5:00 عبد الرحمن يوسف - بلال فضل - إبراهيم عيسي في مظاهرة التحرير

--

FIGURE 7.10. 5 p.m. updates.

---------- Forwarded message ----------
From: **April 6 Youth** <media@6april.org>
Date: 2011/1/25
Subject: تحديثات حتي 6 مساءا بخصوص يوم الإنتفاضة
To:

5:00 الأمن يقطع شبكة الموبيل في التحرير ويحجب موقع تويتر
5:10 المتظاهرون ينظمون ثلاث مسيرات في الإسكندرية : 15 ألف في مسيرة وأخري 10 ألاف في مسيرة أخري ، والثالثة مايقرب من 10 ألاف متجهون جميعا إلي مكان واحد
5:14 أول جريح : علاء عبد الهادي كلية الطب البشري، مصاب ومتجهون به نحو معهد ناصر
5:17 المتظاهرون في المنصورة يتجهون نحو ديوان المحافظة
5:19 الاعتداء علي مجموعة المتظاهرين القادمة من امام بنك فيصل الاسلامي ومنعهم من مواصلة الطريق الي التحرير
5:22 أربعين يعبرون الشاطبي في الاسكندرية
5:23 مايقرب من 30 ألف في المحلة
5:34 مايقرب من 40 ألف متظاهر أمام مبني الحزب الوطني في الإسكندرية ، والأمن يعد حشد أمني كبير عند نادي سبورتنج
5:35 إصابة 4 عساكر وملازم شرطة ونقيب شرطة ، وهم الأن متجهون للعلاج في معهد ناصر
5:36 إصابات في صفوف المتظاهرين عند مجموعة من المتظاهرين في الدقي علي كوبري 15 مايو ، والأمن يحاول منعهم من التحرك ناحية ميدان التحرير
5:38 إصابة 3 عساكر من بينهم عسكري في حالة خطر
5:39 المتظاهرون يقررون قضاء ليلتهم في ميدان التحرير
5:41 إصابة إثنان من المتظاهرين بحالات إختناق من جراء إطلاق القنابل المسيلة للدموع في ميدان التحرير
5:42 القبض علي محمد جمال الدين وزميل أخر يدعي "نضال" في ميدان التحرير
5:45 المتظاهرون يستولون علي مقر الحزب الوطني في المحلة الكبري
5:50 أخبار عن تحركات للأهالي بالقرب من القصر الجمهوري بكوبري القبة
5:50 مايقرب من 10 أوتوبيسات تقل مئات من عساكر الامن المركزي ، ومايقرب من 300 عسكري أمن مركزي بالقرب من دار القضاء العالي
5:57 الافراج عن 15 تم القبض عليهم في المطرية
5:58 الأمن يقطع النور في الشارع المتواجد به المتظاهرين في الزقازيق
5:59 الأمن يفقد السيطرة علي المتظاهرين في كفر الشيخ حيث مايقرب من 20 ألف متظاهر في كفر الشيخ

FIGURE 7.11. 6 p.m. updates.

---------- Forwarded message ----------
From: **April 6 Youth** <media@6april.org>
Date: 2011/1/25
Subject: تحديثات حتي الساعة 7 مساءا
To:

6:05 الأمن يحاصر المتظاهرون في الإسكندرية في كليوباترا
6:06 مسيرة مكونة من 20 ألف يتجهون نحو مبني المحافظة
6:07 النشطاء في التحرير يتوجهون نحو مبني مجلس الشوري
6:08 الأمن يعتدي بشدة علي المتظاهرين في الإسكندرية
6:10 الأهالي في سيناء يقطعون الطريق الدولي في رفح، وهذا يعني فصل رفح والشيخ زويد عن باقي الجمهورية
6:11 الأمن يطلق الرصاص الحي علي المتظاهرين في سيدي جابر وفي نهاية شارع بورسعيد
6:15 المتظاهرين يقتحمون مقر قسم الأربعين في السويس
6:16 وصول 6 مدنين مصابين "متوسطة" بينهم طفله عندها 9 سنين في مستشفي ناصر
6:27 الأمن يقطع الكهرباء في طنطا علي المتظاهرين ويعتدي عليهم بقوة
6:30 اللواء عبد الرؤوف عادل ورئيس مباحث قسم شرطة مدينة السويس عاصمة المحافظة الرائد محمد عادل أصيبا بحجارة رشقها محتجون
6:40 مايقرب من 1000 متظاهر عند مسرح السلام في الإسكندرية، بالقرب من كيلوباترا
6:42 الإسماعيلية : المتظاهرون في الإسماعيلية يغلقون شارع الإستاد وشبين وشارع البحري، وعددهم يقترب من 5000 متظاهر
6:56 المتظاهرون في الدقي يقررون الإعتصام وإغلاق ميدان الدقي

FIGURE 7.12. 7 p.m. updates.

CH. 2: APRIL 6 YOUTH MOVEMENT, EMAIL ANNOUNCEMENTS, ENGLISH TRANSCRIPTION FROM ARABIC

Before 2 p.m.:

> More than 1000 protesters in front of the Supreme Court set off in a demonstration in Ramses Street in the Tahrir Square area
>
> Security forces arrested nearly nine activists in Assiut in addition to a number of journalists in the city likely including five members of the April 6 Youth Movement
>
> Sources close to Dr. A. Nour said that there were demonstration led by Dr. Ayman Nour
>
> There are demonstrations in all of Dar es Salaam, as well as in *Old Egypt* area involving thousands of demonstrators
>
> In Alexandria, correspondents say that mosques in Alexandria are overcrowded and the population is intent to march
>
> In another area, 15 of the Muslim Brotherhood were arrested at Cafe Cilantro on the Arab League Street

2 p.m.:

> Promptly at 2 p.m. more April 6 protesters from Bulaq, Meyt Agaba and Arz el Lava marched in the Arab League Street to meet with other groups in the same street
>
> Many participated in the march, which included activist Abu Fajr and singer Hamza Numeira, et al. and began marches starting from all areas in the direction of the Arab League Street. The demonstrations were attended by many locals, many joined in the process
>
> The protesters in Nahia were able to break the security cordon imposed on them in the area by the security forces and entered the Arab League Street, chanting the national anthem and the chant "Ya Mubarak, see righteousness"
>
> Now at 2:25 p.m. approximately 20,000 demonstrators arrived at the rally and are on their way to Tahrir. Currently they are in Batal Ahmed Abdel Aziz Street
>
> Now nearly 200 protesters in front of the Supreme Court, as well as the bar association

In Mansoura governorate there are nearly 4000 demonstrators in Mashaal Square

In Mahalla, there are approximately 2000 demonstrators who began promptly at 2:20, and now they are moving along the street

3 p.m.-A:

Here in the Tayyar Fekri street in Imbaba there are 2000 demonstrators, the locals broke the cordon imposed on the protesters

There are nearly 20,000 demonstrators in the Arab League Street

In Mahalla Kubra numbers at 2:45 are approximately 5000

Aswan, nearly 5000 protesters

Tanta, nearly 1000 demonstrators

More than 3000 people in Araba'in Square in Suez governorate, they have been chanting against Mubarak since 12 o'clock

In As'aaf there are nearly 1000 demonstrators in the July 26 Street

3 p.m.-B:

There are demonstrators on Ibrahim bridge

In Zakki Matar Street in Imbaba there are nearly 1000 demonstrators

In front of the People's Assembly there are nearly 4000 demonstrators

Occupation of Dar es Salaam (Police) Department by protesters

The protesters besieging Dokki (Police) Department

4 p.m.-A:

3:00 The number of demonstrators in Mansoura reaches 10,000, demonstrators in Toril and heading toward Suez Canal Street

3:26 Thousands of locals as well as nonresident activists in Shubra. Among their slogans: "one two, people of Egypt [sic]" and "'go go Mubarak"

3:29 Security forces assault demonstrators with sticks. These are protesters who started at the Parliament

3:30 Detainees in Port Said: Shadi Salim ... Muhammad Swairki ... Ahmad Murad ... Islam Naji ... Mohammed Abu Nasr ... Tariq Mabruk

3:30 Detained now in front of the Council of Ministers in Cairo: Ahmed Al-Rifai, Jamal El-toukhy. Ahmed Abdel Naser, Mohamed Saeed Abdul Hamid

3:40 New movements in Imbaba in Al Basrawi Street, nearly 1000 protesters

3:40 Thousands of women in streets in Suez

3:40 Approximately 500 demonstrators are headed toward Tahrir from Talaat Harb vehemently chanting against Mubarak

3:45 Thousands in Tahrir are headed to the People's Assembly region

3:55 Demonstrators from Garden City heading toward Tahrir

3:55 Security forces assault female protesters in Suez

4:00 Tear gas in Tahrir Square, and injuries among protesters

4 p.m.-B:

Sincerely apologize to the youth for our inability to communicate with you. Security forces prevent transmission or reception from Mohamed Adel's (Information Office Director) mobile phone as well as Ahmed Maher the General Coordinator

Sincere apologies, and we will communicate via email

5 p.m.:

4:00 Security forces' assault on demonstrators in Tahrir and in the Qasr al-Aini Street

4:09 Mohamed Gamal Abdel Ati in Tahrir Square

4:13 Security forces break civilian cars in Tahrir Square

4:14 About 1000 protesters marching in Zagazig now

4:16 Alexandria 1500 demonstrators and security forces are trying to disperse them, severe attacks

4:16 Dozens arrested in Mansoura, and the occurrence of many casualties among the demonstrators, and the military is threatening to shoot at demonstrators, using weapons

Ch. 2: April 6 Youth Movement

4:17 March from Dokki via bridge of May 15 contains nearly 5000 protesters

4:17 Demonstrators holding Suez security director in a booth

4:18 Nearly 10,000 people break the security barrier in Alexandria's Manshiya square heading to Egypt station

4:19 Presence of security teams at the Ahmed Maher hospital in Abdeen

4:23 Demonstrators in Tahrir break the security cordon and they are headed to NDP headquarters (People's Assembly)

4:23 Ibrahim Issa joins the demonstration in Tahrir Square

4:30 People in Mansoura beat the security and break the siege on demonstrators

4:35 Security disrupts mobile phones of Mohamed Adel, Director of Information Office and Ahmed Maher, general coordinator of the movement, and all mobile phones of Egypt Demonstrator Defenders Front

4:46 Siege of 150 protesters in the National Party headquarters in Port Said ... and the launch of sniffer dogs on them

4:47 Arrest of 40 protesters in Tahrir Square, including Karim Sha'er, a Ghad Party activist

4:55 Demonstrators in Mahalla, approximately 15,000 in the field

5:00 Abdel-Rahman Youssef – Belal Fadl – Ibrahim Issa in the demonstration in Tahrir

6 p.m.-A:

5:00 Security disrupts the mobile network in Tahrir and limits Twitter service in the square

5:10 Protesters organized three marches in Alexandria: 15,000 in the first and another 10,000 in the second march, the third nearly 10,000. All three headed to one place

5:14 The first wounded: Alaa Abdul Hadi College of Human Medicine, injured and heading toward the Nasser Institute

5:17 Demonstrators in Mansoura governorate heading toward [security] office

5:19 Assault on a group of protesters coming from the front of the Faisal Islamic Bank, preventing them from continuing their way toward Tahrir

5:22 40 crossing the El Shatby, Alexandria

5:23 Approximately 30,000 in Mahalla

5:34 Nearly 40,000 demonstrators in front of the building of the National Democratic Party in Alexandria, security forces are running a major security mobilization at the sporting club

5:35 Four policemen and a police lieutenant and a police captain injured, and now they are headed to Nasser Institute for treatment

5:36 Casualties among protesters from Dokki on the 15 May bridge, and security forces are trying to prevent them from moving on to Tahrir

5:38 Three troops injured, including military personnel

5:39 Protesters decide to spend the night in Tahrir

5:41 Two protesters injured and suffocated by tear gas in Tahrir Square

5:42 Mohammed Jamal al-Din arrested, and another person code-named "struggle" in Tahrir

5:45 Protesters seizing the NDP headquarters in Mahalla al-Kubra

5:50 News about the movements of residents towards the Presidential Palace close to Qobba bridge

5:50 Approximately 10 buses carrying hundreds of central security troops, about 300 military security forces near the High Court

5:57 Release of 15 captured in Matarriya

5:58 Security forces turn off lights on the street around protesters in Zagazig

5:59 Security forces lose control of the demonstrators in Kafr El-Sheikh, where there are nearly 20,000 demonstrators

6 p.m.-B:

To communicate with the media office, please contact: [] - with colleague []

7 p.m.:

6:05 Security forces besiege protesters in Alexandria in Kleopatra

6:06 March of 20,000 heading toward Security Department

6:07 Activists in Tahrir going toward the Shura Council building

6:08 Security forcefully assaults demonstrators in Alexandria

6:10 People in Sinai close the crossing road in Rafah, this means the Rafah and Sheikh Zuweid separated from the rest of the Republic

6:11 Security charges live bullets on protesters in Sidi Gaber, at the end of the Port Said Street

6:15 Demonstrators burst into the headquarters of the 40th Division in Suez

6:16 Arrival of six injured civilians, including a minor, 9 years old, in hospital

6:27 Security cuts electricity in Tanta and forcefully attacks demonstrators

6:30 Protesters throw stones at General Abdul Rauf Adel and Chairman of Suez City Police Department, Major Mohamed Adel

6:40 Nearly 1000 protesters at the theater Salam in Alexandria, near Kleopatra

6:42 Protesters in Ismailia block the Weshbin Road and Bahri Street, about 5000 demonstrators

6:56 Protesters in Dokki decide to strike and close Dokki

186   Appendix

CH 2: SURVEY LOCATIONS IN CAIRO

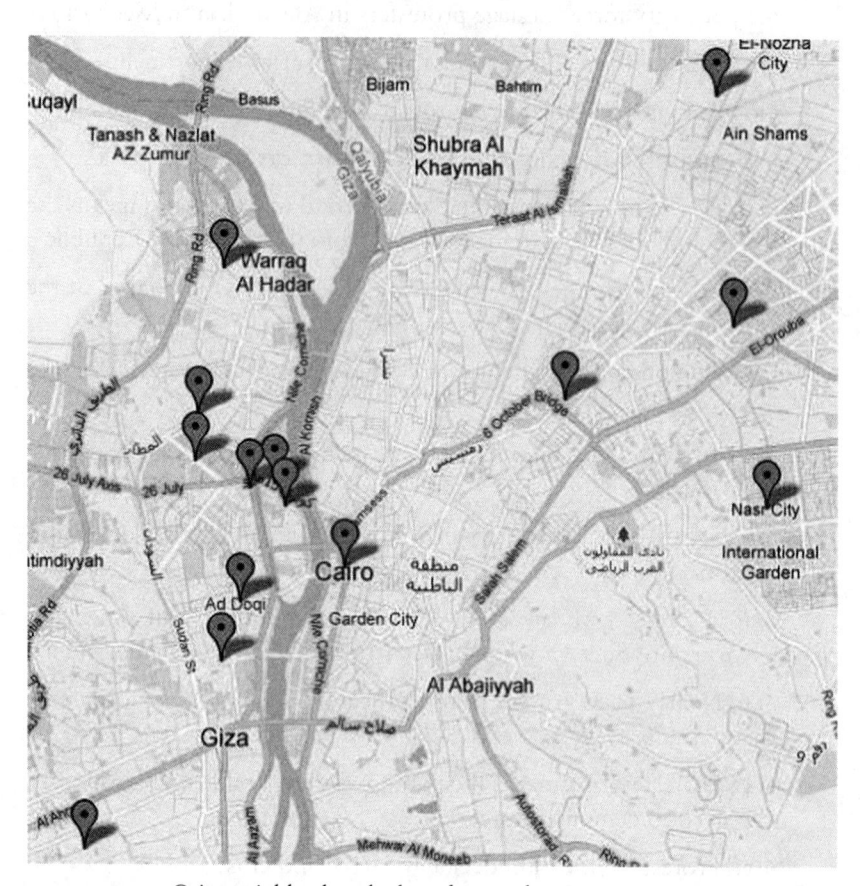

FIGURE 7.13. Cairo neighborhood where face-to-face interviews were conducted. The AUC campus is not included in this map. An online representation can be found at http://goo.gl/maps/rsGox.

CH 2: CAIRO PROTEST PARTICIPATION SURVEY

1. *General*

    1.1. Did you participate in protests at all? (January 25 to February 11) *Yes/No, General Remarks*
    1.2. Did you go to Tahrir Square during the 18 days? (January 25 to February 11) *Yes/No, General Remarks*

2. *January 25–27*

    2.1 Did you participate in protests on January 25, 26, and/or 27 before the communications blackout (of mobile phones and the Internet)? *Yes/No, General Remarks*
    2.2 Did you go to Tahrir Square on January 25, 26, and/or 27 before the communications blackout (of mobile phones and the Internet)? *Yes/No, General Remarks*
    2.3 How did you hear about the protests for the very first time? You can choose more than one answer.
    State Radio/TV, Satellite/Private TV (Al Jazeera, Ontv, etc.), Newspapers (Ahram, Al Masry Al Youm, etc.), Internet (Facebook, Twitter, Blogs, etc.), from friends and acquaintances, Other: please specify below in the General Remarks text box

3. *January 28*

    3.1. What was your first reaction on January 28, when you noticed your cell phone/Internet connection was not functioning?
    3.2. Did you go out to the protests on January 28, 2011, the first day of the communications blackout (of mobile phones and the Internet)? *Yes/No, General Remarks*
    3.3. Did you go to Tahrir on January 28, 2011? *Yes/No, General Remarks*
    3.4. How did you hear about the developments on the 28th during the communications blackout (of mobile phones and the Internet)? You can choose more than one answer.
    State Radio/TV, Satellite/Private TV (Al Jazeera, Ontv, etc.), Newspapers (Ahram, Al Masry Al Youm, etc.), from friends and acquaintances, Other, please specify below in the General Remarks text box

3.5. If you heard about the unrest from friends and acquaintances, how did you contact/meet them during the communications blackout (of mobile phones and the Internet)?

4. *January 29–February 1*

   4.1. Did you go to protests on January 29, 30, 31, and/or February 1, 2011 (after the mobile phone service was restored but before the return of the Internet connection)? *Yes/No, General Remarks*
   4.2. Did you go to Tahrir Square on January 29, 30, 31, and/or February 1, 2011 (after the mobile phone service was restored but before the return of the Internet connection)? *Yes/No, General Remarks*
   4.3. How did you hear about the developments during the period between January 29, 30, 31, and February 1, 2011 (after the mobile phone service was restored but before the return of the Internet connection)? You can choose more than one answer.
   State Radio/TV, Satellite/Private TV (Al Jazeera, Ontv, etc.), Newspapers (Ahram, Al Masry Al Youm, etc.), from friends and acquaintances, Other: please specify below in the General Remarks text box
   4.4. What type of television did you rely on to learn about the developments during the period between January 29 and February 1, 2011 (after the mobile phone service was restored but before the return of the Internet connection)?
   State TV, Satellite/Private TV
   4.5. If you heard news about the unrest from friends and acquaintances, how did you contact/meet them during this period (after mobile phone service was restored but before the return of the Internet connection)?

5. *February 3–February 11*

   5.1. Did you participate in the protests during the last week of the demonstrations, February 3 to February 11, 2011 (when the mobile phone service and the Internet connection were restored)? *Yes/No*
   5.2. Did you go to Tahrir during the period between February 3 and February 11, 2011 (when the mobile phone service

and the Internet connection were restored)? *Yes/No, General Remarks*
- 5.3. Did you revert to the Internet and cell phone for communicating news after the connections were restored (mobile phones and the Internet)? *Yes/No, General Remarks*
- 5.4. Did you continue to communicate with people who provided you with news during the blackout period after the restoration of communications (mobile phones and the Internet)? *Yes/No, General Remarks*

6. *General*

- 6.1. Was shutting down the Internet/cell networks helpful to the movement? *Yes/No, General Remarks*

A screen shot of the first two pages of a sample survey response is included in Figure (7.14). There are about 500 of these filled questionnaires at the author's disposal. Scans are available in the book's online appendix.

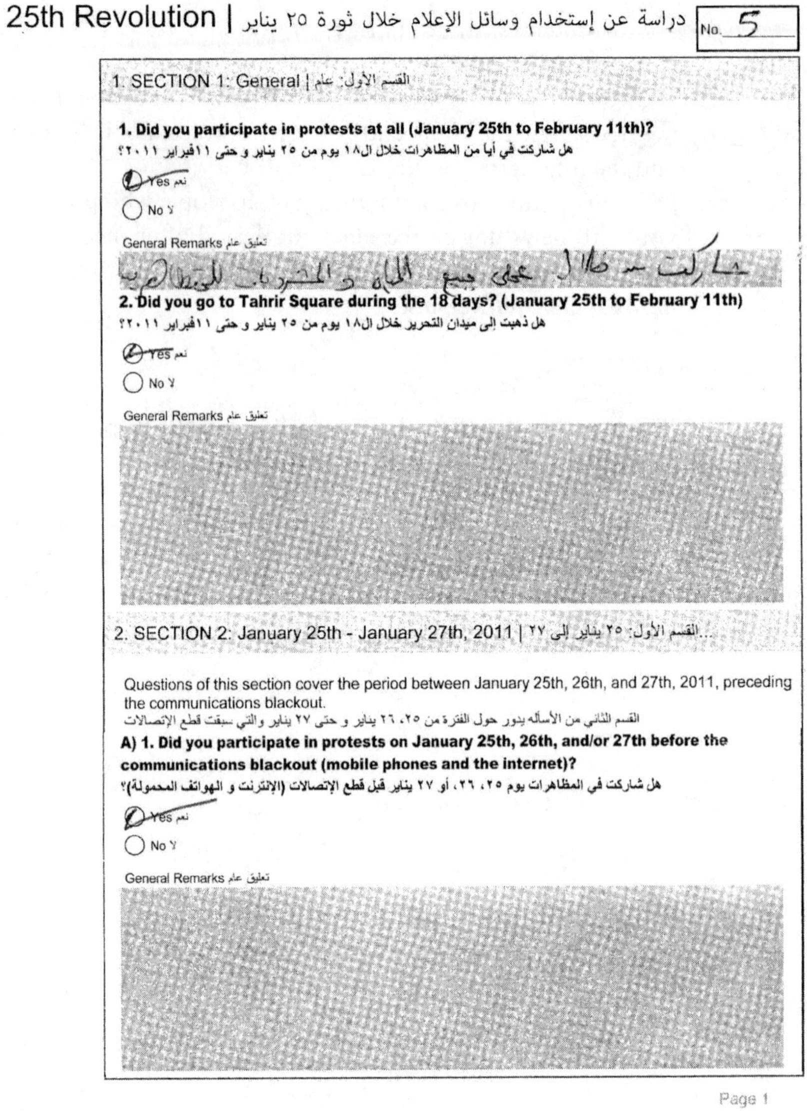

25th Revolution | دراسة عن إستخدام وسائل الإعلام خلال ثورة ٢٥ يناير

No. 5

1. SECTION 1: General | القسم الأول: عام

1. Did you participate in protests at all (January 25th to February 11th)?

هل شاركت في أيا من المظاهرات خلال ال١٨ يوم من ٢٥ يناير و حتى ١١فبراير ٢٠١١؟

Yes نعم

No لا

General Remarks تعليق عام

2. Did you go to Tahrir Square during the 18 days? (January 25th to February 11th)

هل ذهبت إلى ميدان التحرير خلال ال١٨ يوم من ٢٥ يناير و حتى ١١فبراير ٢٠١١؟

Yes نعم

No لا

General Remarks تعليق عام

2. SECTION 2: January 25th - January 27th, 2011 | القسم الأول: ٢٥ يناير إلى ٢٧...

Questions of this section cover the period between January 25th, 26th, and 27th, 2011, preceding the communications blackout.

القسم الثاني من الأسئله يدور حول الفترة من ٢٥، ٢٦ يناير و حتى ٢٧ يناير والتي سبقت قطع الإتصالات

A) 1. Did you participate in protests on January 25th, 26th, and/or 27th before the communications blackout (mobile phones and the internet)?

هل شاركت في المظاهرات يوم ٢٥، ٢٦، أو ٢٧ يناير قبل قطع الإتصالات (الإنترنت و الهواتف المحمولة)؟

Yes نعم

No لا

General Remarks تعليق عام

Page 1

FIGURE 7.14. A scan of a sample filled survey questionnaire. Approximately 500 of these forms were distributed among Cairo residents, the scans of all the multiple hundred filled forms are available in the online appendix at https://goo.gl/MPtSkB.

CH 2: PATTERNS OF PROTEST PARTICIPATION AND MEDIA USAGE

TABLE 7.1. *The distribution of participation in the four phases of the uprising: 25–27, 28, 29–1, 3–11, e.g. 0010 represents those who did not protest during the first, second and fourth phase, but protested during the third period. Total number of survey respondents = 740*

Participation Pattern	25–27	28	29–1	3–11	Total Count
0	0	0	0	0	278
1	0	0	0	1	61
2	0	0	1	0	7
3	0	0	1	1	49
4	0	1	0	0	27
5	0	1	0	1	29
6	0	1	1	0	9
7	0	1	1	1	62
8	1	0	0	0	8
9	1	0	0	1	15
10	1	0	1	0	3
11	1	0	1	1	19
12	1	1	0	0	10
13	1	1	0	1	21
14	1	1	1	0	13
15	1	1	1	1	129
Total	218	300	291	385	

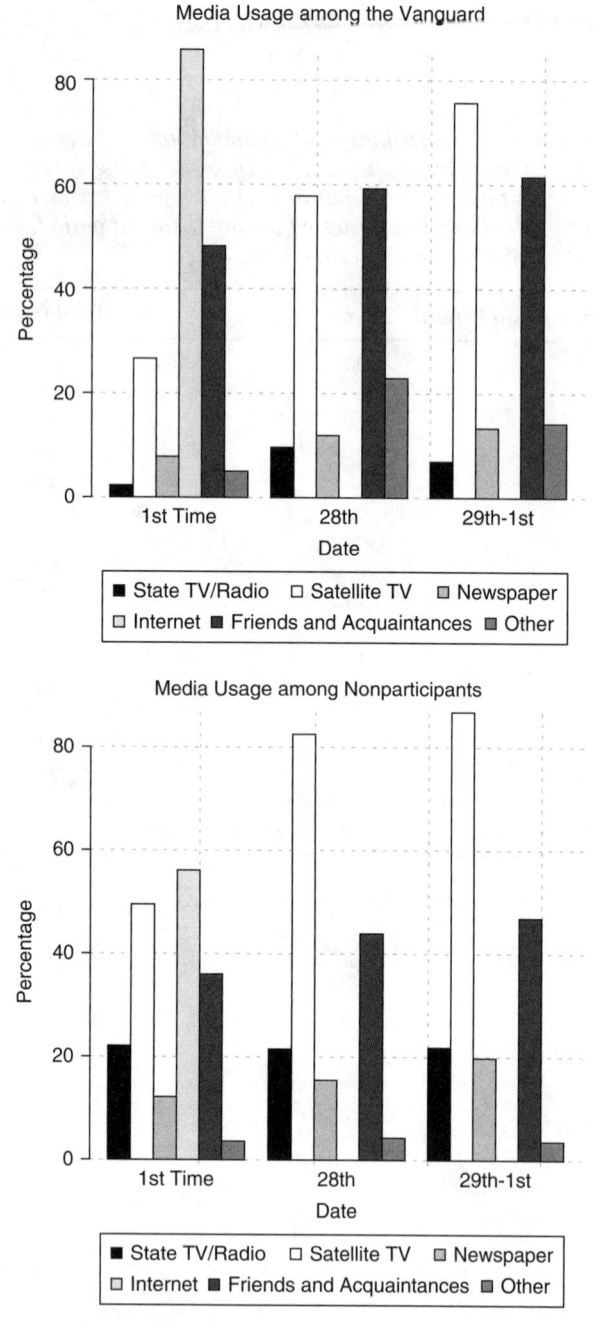

FIGURE 7.15. Media usage levels. Top: the vanguard – defined as those who took part in the protests on January 25 to 27th. Bottom: nonparticipants – defined as those who never took part in the protests.

CH 4: THE TEMPORAL DISTRIBUTION OF "FIRST INCIDENTS"

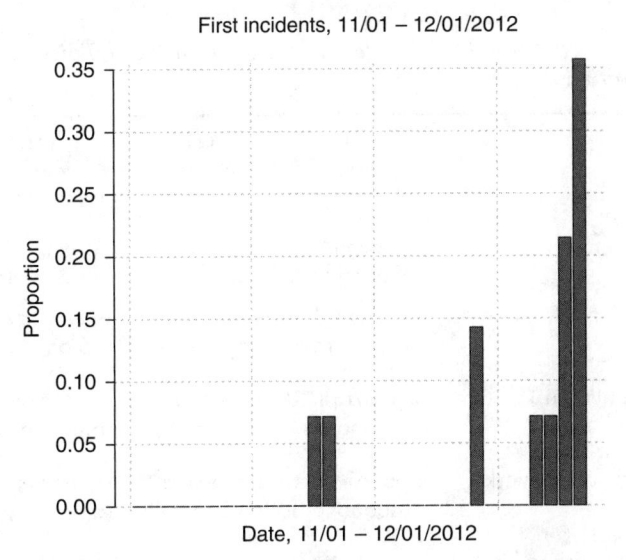

FIGURE 7.16. Distribution of *first incidents* at a particular location during the month of November and December 1. The blackout persisted from November 29 to December 1. November 30 and December 1, the last two days in the plot, show an unprecedented number of such occurrences, and are the only two data points at least 2σ away from the mean.

CH 4: ABSENCE OF SPATIAL SPILLOVER IN TEMPORAL AVERAGES

TABLE 7.2. *Number of violent incidents in each cell, Poisson count regression*

	(1) count_	(2) count_	(3) count_
count_			
cell index	0.00431***	0.00426***	0.00439***
	(0.000785)	(0.000789)	(0.000780)
average elevation	−0.00327***	−0.00312***	−0.00372***
	(0.000613)	(0.000636)	(0.000635)
population	0.0000148***	0.0000146***	0.0000146***
	(0.00000241)	(0.00000241)	(0.00000242)
sum street length	0.0000169***	0.0000162***	0.0000192***
	(0.00000376)	(0.00000383)	(0.00000391)
neighborhood index	0.0186***	0.0184***	0.0183***
	(0.00491)	(0.00492)	(0.00482)
ethnicity	0.0968	0.105	0.130
	(0.131)	(0.131)	(0.131)
income	1.632***	1.612***	1.764***
	(0.128)	(0.130)	(0.136)
spatial_lag_d		0.142	
		(0.151)	
spatial_lag_count			−0.00469**
			(0.00163)
_cons	1.494***	1.299**	1.860***
	(0.433)	(0.482)	(0.451)
N	252	252	252
Log-likelihood	−848.1	−847.6	−843.8
χ^2	1021.6	1022.5	1030.1

Standard errors in parentheses
* $p < 0.05$, ** $p < 0.01$, *** $p < 0.001$

CH 5: SUBJECT INSTRUCTIONS, PHASE TWO OF NETWORK EXPERIMENTS

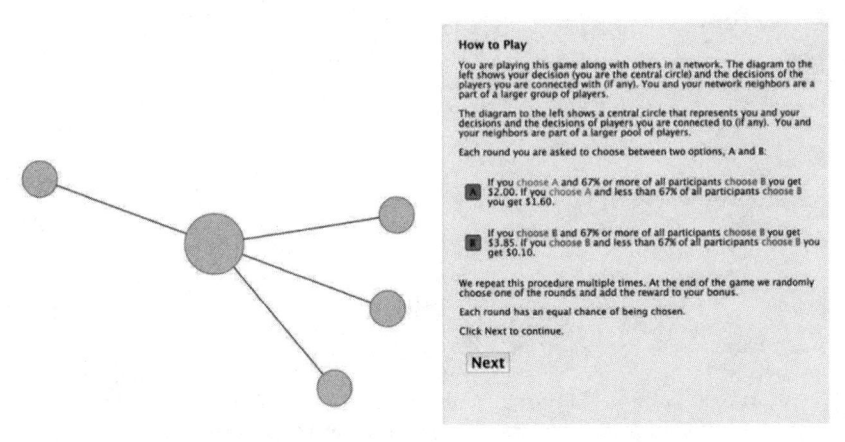

FIGURE 7.17. A snapshot of subject instructions for the second phase of the network experiments.

Bibliography

Adorno, T. W. [1963] (1991), "Culture industry reconsidered" in Bernstein, J. (Ed.), *The Culture Industry*, Routledge, New York, NY.

Afary, J. and Anderson, K. B. (2005), *Foucault and the Iranian Revolution*, The University of Chicago Press, Chicago, IL.

Alexander, J. (2011), *Performative Revolution in Egypt: An Essay in Cultural Power*, Bloomsbury Academic, New York, NY.

Alexander, K. (2013), "National security agency data collection programs", *C-SPAN*. www.c-span.org/video/?313429-1/nsa-chief-testifies-damage-surveillance-leaks.

Al-Masry Al-Youm (2011), *Al-Masry Al-Youm* Archives. http://bit.ly/u1P5aG.

Angeletos, G.-M. and Pavan, A. (2007), "Efficient use of information and social value of information", *Econometrica* 75(4), 1103–1142.

April 6 Youth Movement, Email Collection (2012).

Aral, S., Muchnik, L. and Sundararajan, A. (2009), "Distinguishing influence-based contagion from homophily-driven diffusion in dynamic networks", *Proceedings of the National Academy of Sciences (PNAS)* 106(51), 21544–21549.

Aral, S. and Walker, D. (2012), "Identifying influential and susceptible members of social networks", *Science* 337(6092), 337–341.

Axelrod, R. (1997), "The dissemination of culture: A model with local convergence and global polarization", *Journal of Conflict Resolution* 41(2), 203–226.

Bakshy, E., Hofman, J., Mason, W. and Watts, D. (2011), "Everyone's an influencer: Quantifying influence on Twitter", *Proc. WSDM11* pp. 65–74.

Bamford, J. (2014), "The most wanted man in the world", *Wired*. www.wired.com/2014/08/edward-snowden.

Banerjee, A., Chandraekhar, A., Duflo, E. and Jackson, M. (2015), "Gossip and identifying central individuals in a social network", *Proceedings of American Economic Association Annual Meeting*.

Barabási, A.-L. and Albert, R. (1999), "Emergence of scaling in random networks", *Science* 286(5439), 509–512.

Becker, M. (1970), "Sociometric location and innovativeness: Reformulation and extension of the diffusion model", *American Sociological Review* 35(2), 267–282.

Beinin, J. (2011), "Egypt at the tipping point?", *Foreign Policy*. http://bit.ly/PwpFOq.

Beissinger, M. R. (2002), *National Mobilization and the Collapse of the Soviet State*, Cambridge University Press, New York, NY.

Beissinger, M. R. (2013), "The semblance of democratic revolution: Coalitions in Ukraine's orange revolution", *American Political Science Review* 107(3), 574–592.

Beissinger, M. R., Jamal, A. and Mazur, K. (2012), "Who participated in the Arab Spring? A comparison of Egyptian and Tunisian revolutions", *Proceedings of APSA 2012 Annual Meeting*.

Bennett, W. L. (1990), "Toward a theory of press–state relations in the United States", *Journal of Communication* 40(2), 103–125.

Bennett, W. L. and Segerberg, A. (2013), *The Logic of Connective Action: Digital Media and the Personalization of Contentious Politics*, Cambridge University Press, New York, NY.

Berelson, B. (1949), "What "missing the newspaper" means", *Communication Research*, 111–129.

Bergemann, D. and Morris, S. (2013), "Robust predictions in games with incomplete information", *Econometrica* 81, 1251–1308.

Berinsky, A. J., Huber, G. A. and Lenz, G. S. (2012), "Evaluating online labor markets for experimental research: Amazon.com's Mechanical Turk", *Political Analysis* 20(3), 351–368.

Bilefski, D. (2009), "Celebrating revolution with roots in a rumor", *Historical New York Times* p. A16. http://nyti.ms/2tioTq.

Bloch, M., Carter, S., Schoenfield, A., He, E., E., Peçanha, S., Tse, A. and Xaquin, G. V. (2011), "Mapping the protests in Cairo, day by day", *Historical New York Times*. Retrieved from http://goo.gl/aogbS.

Bond, R., Fariss, C., Jones, J., Kramer, A., Marlow, C., Settle, J. and Fowler, J. (2012), "A 61-million-person experiment in social influence and political mobilization", *Nature* 489(7415), 295–298.

Boorman, S. and Levitt, P. (1980), *The Genetics of Altruism*, Academic Press, New York, NY.

Brym, R., Godbout, M., Hoffbauer, A., Menard, G. and Zhang, T. H. (2014), "Social media in the 2011 Egyptian uprising", *British Journal of Sociology* 65(2), 266–292.

Cairo Protest Dataset (2012), http://goo.gl/7fo7W8.

Calvin, J. [1536] (1995), *Institutes of the Christian Religion*, Wm. B. Eerdmans Publishing Company, New York, NY.

Castells, M. (2009a), *Communication Power*, Oxford University Press, Oxford, UK.

Castells, M. (2009b), *The Rise of the Network Society*, Wiley-Blackwell, New York, NY.

Cederman, L.-E., Weidmann, N. B. and Gleditsch, K. S. (2011), "Horizontal inequalities and ethnonationalist civil war: A global comparison", *American Political Science Review* 105(3), 478–495.

Centola, D. (2010), "The spread of behavior in an online social network experiment", *Science* 329(5996), 1194–1197.

Centola, D. and Macy, M. W. (2007), "Complex contagions and the weakness of long ties", *American Journal of Sociology* 113(3), 702–734.

Chozick, A. (2012), "For Syria's rebel movement, skype is a useful and increasingly dangerous tool", *The New York Times* p. A12. http://goo.gl/J8yZuR.

Christia, F. (2013), What can civil war scholars tell us about the Syrian conflict?, *in* M. Lynch, ed., "The Political Science of Syria's War, POMEPS Briefings 22", Washington, DC.

Chung, F. R. K. (1997), *Spectral Graph Theory*, AMS Publications. CBMS Lecture Notes Providence, RI.

Chwe, M. S. (2001), *Rational Ritual: Culture, Coordination, and Common Knowledge*, Princeton University Press, Princeton, NJ.

Cicero (1998), *The Republic and The Laws*, Oxford University Press, New York, NY.

Clark, P. J. and Evans, F. C. (1954), "Distance to nearest neighbor as a measure of spatial relationships in population", *Ecology* 35(4), 445–453.

Collier, P. and Hoeffler, A. (2004), "Greed and grievance in civil war", *Oxford Economic Papers* 56(4), 563–595.

Coppock, A., Guess, A. and Ternovski, J. (2015), "When treatments are tweets: A network mobilization experiment over twitter", *Political Behavior* 37, 1–24.

Cowie, J. (2011), "Egypt leaves the internet", *Renesys Blog*. www.renesys.com/2011/01/egypt-leaves-the-internet/.

Della Porta, D. (2013), *Clandestine Political Violence*, Cambridge University Press, New York, NY.

Diggle, P. J. (2013), *Statistical Analysis of Spatial and Spatio-Temporal Point Patterns*, Chapman and Hall, New York, NY.

Dobson, J., Coleman, P., Durfee, R. and Worley, B. (2000), "Landscan: A global population database for estimating populations at risk", *Photogrammetric Engineering and Remote Sensing* 66(7), 849–857.

Doyle, J. (2002), *The Oxford History of the French Revolution*, Oxford University Press, New York, NY.

Dunn, A. (2011), "Unplugging a nation: State media strategy during Egypt's January 25 uprising", *The Fletcher Forum of World Affairs* 35(2), 15–24.

El-Ghobashy, M. (2011), "The praxis of the Egyptian revolution", *Middle East Research and Information Project* 41. http://bit.ly/fpoIJL.

Enemark, D., McCubbins, M. D. and Weller, N. (2014), "Knowledge and networks: An experimental test of how network knowledge affects coordination", *Social Networks* 36, 122–133.

Entman, R. (2004), *Projections of Power*, The University of Chicago Press, Chicago, IL.

Fearon, J. D. and Laitin, D. D. (2003), "Ethnicity, insurgency, and civil war", *American Political Science Review* 97(1), 75–90.
Foucault, M. (1970), *The Order of Things*, Vintage, New York, NY.
Foucault, M. (1984), *The Foucault Reader*, Vintage, New York, NY.
Gleditsch, K. S. and Weidmann, N. B. (2012), "Richardson in the information age: Geographic information systems and spatial data in international studies", *Annual Review of Political Science* 15, 461–481.
Gohdes, A. R. (2015), "Pulling the plug: Network disruptions and violence in civil conflict", *Journal of Peace Research* 52(3), 352–367.
Golub, B. and Jackson, M. O. (2010), "Naive learning in social networks and the wisdom of crowds", *American Economic Journal: Microeconomics* 2(1), 112–149.
Gould, R. V. (1991), "Multiple networks and mobilization in the Paris Commune, 1871", *American Sociological Review* 56(6), 716–729.
Gould, R. V. (1993), "Collective action and network structure", *American Sociological Review* 58(2), 182–196.
Gould, R. V. (1995), *Insurgent Identities: Class, Community, and Protest in Paris from 1848 to the Commune*, Chicago University Press, Chicago, IL.
Gramsci, A. [1926] (1971), *Prison Notebooks*, International Publishers, New York, NY.
Granovetter, M. S. (1973), "The strength of weak ties", *The American Journal of Sociology* 78(6), 1360–1380.
Granovetter, M. S. (1978), "Threshold models of collective behavior", *The American Journal of Sociology* 83(6), 1420–1443.
Granovetter, M. and Soong, R. (1983), "Threshold models of diffusion and collective behavior", *Journal of Mathematical Sociology* 9, 165–179.
Granovetter, M. and Soong, R. (1986), "Threshold models of interpersonal effects in consumer demands", *Journal of Economic Behavior and Organization* 7, 83–99.
Habermas, J. (1976), *Communication and the Evolution of Society*, Heinemann, London.
Habermas, J. (1991), *The Structural Transformation of the Public Sphere: An Inquiry into a Category of Bourgeois Society*, The MIT Press, Boston, MA.
Hardin, R. (1995), *One for All: The Logic of Group Conflict*, Princeton University Press, Princeton, NJ.
Hasegawa, T. (1981), *The February Revolution: Petrograd, 1917*, The University of Washington Press, Seattle, WA.
Hassanpour, N. (2014), "Media disruption and revolutionary unrest: Evidence from Mubarak's quasi-experiment", *Political Communication* 31(1), 1–24.
Hibbs, D. A., Jr (1974), "Problems of statistical estimation and causal inference in time-series regression models", *Sociological Methodology* 5, 252–308.
Hill, A., Rand, D., Nowak, M. and Christakis, N. (2010), "Emotions as infectious diseases in a large social network: The SISa model", *Proc. Royal Society B: Biological Sciences* 277(1701), 3827–3835.
Hirschman, A. O. (1977), *The Passions and the Interests: Political Arguments for Capitalism before Its Triumph*, Princeton University Press, Princeton, NJ.

Holliday, J. (2012), *Syrian Civil War's Location Dataset*, Institute for the Study of War, Washington, DC.

Holliday, J. (2013), *The Assad Regime: From Counterinsurgency to Civil War*, Institute for the Study of War, Washington, DC.

Holliday, J. and Lynch, M. (2012), *The Battle for Damascus: The Current State of Play in Syria*, Institute for the Study of War, Washington, DC.

Holt, C. and Laury, S. (2002), "Risk aversion and incentive effects", *American Economic Review* 92(5), 1644-1955.

Horowitz, D. L. (2000), *Ethnic Groups in Conflict*, 2nd edn, University of California Press, Berkeley, CA.

Howard, P. N., Agarwal, S. D. and Hussain, M. M. (2011), "When do states disconnect their digital networks? Regime responses to the political uses of social media", *The Communication Review* 14(3), 216-232.

Izady, M. (2013), "The gulf/2000 project". http://gulf2000.columbia.edu/maps.shtml.

Jackson, M. O. (2008), *Social and Economic Networks*, Princeton University Press, Princeton, NJ.

Jadbabaie, A., Lin, J. and Morse, A. S. (2003), "Coordination of groups of mobile autonomous agents using nearest neighbor rules", *IEEE Transactions on Automatic Control* 48(6), 988-1001.

Judd, S., Kearns, M. and Vorobeychik, Y. (2010), "Behavioral dynamics and influence in networked coloring and consensus", *Proceedings of the National Academy of Sciences (PNAS)*, 14978-14982.

Kalyvas, S. N. and Kocher, M. A. (2007), "How "free" is free riding in civil wars? Violence, insurgency, and the collective action problem", *World Politics* 59(2), 177-216.

Kam, C. D. and Franzese, R. J. (2007), *Modeling and Interpreting Interactive Hypotheses in Regression Analysis*, University of Michigan Press, Ann Arbor, MI.

Karpf, D. (2012), *The MoveOn Effect: The Unexpected Transformation of American Political Advocacy*, Oxford University Press, New York, NY.

Katz, E. and Lazarsfeld, P. (2006), *Personal Influence: The Part Played by People in the Flow of Mass Communication*, Free Press, Glencoe, IL.

Kayhan (1978-1979), *Kayhan Archives*, January 6, 1979.

Kearns, M., Suri, S. and Montfort, N. (2006), "An experimental study of the coloring problem on human subject networks", *Science* 313(824), 824-827.

Kempe, D., Kleinberg, J. and Tardos, E. (2003), "Maximizing the spread of influence through a social network", *Proc. KDD03* pp. 137-146.

Kern, H. L. and Hainmueller, J. (2009), "Opium for the masses: How foreign media can stabilize authoritarian regimes", *Political Analysis* 17(4), 377-399.

Keynes, J. M. (1936), *The General Theory of Employment and Money*, Macmillan, London.

Khaddour, K. and Mazur, K. (2013), "The struggle for Syria's regions", *POMEPS Briefings* 20 43(269), 2-11.

Kuran, T. (1989), "Sparks and prairie fires: A theory of unanticipated political revolution", *Public Choice* 61(1), 41-74.

Kuran, T. (1991), "Now out of never: The elements of surprise in the East European revolution of 1989", *World Politics* 44(1), 7–48.

Kuran, T. (1995), *Private Truth, Public Lies*, Harvard University Press, Cambridge, MA.

Kurzman, C. (2004), *The Unthinkable Revolution in Iran*, Harvard University Press, Cambridge, MA.

LandScan (2013), "Landscan global web applications". http://goo.gl/bfwQND.

Le Bon, G. [1895](1960), *The Crowd*, Penguin Books, New York, NY.

Lenin, V. [1902] (1975), "What is to be done?" in Tucker, R. (Ed.), *The Lenin Anthology*, W. W. Norton and Company, New York, NY.

Lewis, D. (2002), *Convention: A Philosophical Study*, Blackwell, New York, NY.

Lichbach, M. I. (1995), *The Rebel's Dilemma*, University of Michigan Press, Ann Arbor, MI.

Liu, Y.-Y., Slotine, J.-J. and Barabási, A.-L. (2011), "Controllability of complex networks", *Nature* 473(7346), 167–173.

Locke, J. [1689] (1980), *Second Treatise of Government*, Hackett Publishing Company, New York, NY.

Lohmann, S. (1994), "The dynamics of informational cascades: The Monday demonstrations in Leipzig, East Germany, 1989–91", *World Politics* 47(1), 42–101.

Lyall, J. (2010), "Are coethnics more effective counterinsurgents? Evidence from the second Chechen war", *American Political Science Review* 104(1), 1–20.

Lynch, M., Freelon, D. and Aday, S. (2014), '*Blogs and Bullets 3: Syria's Socially Mediated Civil War*, United States Institute of Peace, Washington, DC.

Mackey, R. (2011), "Updates on Friday's protests in Egypt", *The New York Times' Lede blog*. http://goo.gl/wphS4D.

Madison, J. [1787] (2003), "The federalist papers no. 10: The same subject continued: The union as a safeguard against domestic faction and insurrection". Federalist No. 10 in Hamilton, A., Madison, J. and Jay, J. [1787] (2003), *The Federalist Papers*, Signet, New York, NY.

Marwell, G. and Oliver, P. (1993), *The Critical Mass in Collective Action: A Micro-social Theory*, Cambridge University Press, New York, NY.

Marwell, G., Oliver, P. E. and Prahl, R. (1988), "Social networks and collective action: A theory of the critical mass. III", *American Journal of Sociology* 94(3), 502–534.

Marx, K. and Engels F. [1848] (1978), "Manifesto of the Communist Party" in Tucker, R. (Ed.), *The Marx-Engels Reader*, W. W. Norton and Company, New York, NY.

Masoud, T. (2011), "The road to (and from) liberation square", *Journal of Democracy* 22(3), 20–34.

McAdam, D. (1982), *Political Process and the Development of Black Insurgency 1930–1970*, University of Chicago Press, Chicago, IL.

McAdam, D. (1986), "Recruitment to high-risk activism: The case of Freedom Summer", *The American Journal of Sociology* 92(1), 64–90.

Metternich, N. W., Dorff, C., Gallop, M., Weschle, S. and Ward, M. D. (2013), "Antigovernment networks in civil conflicts: How network structures affect conflictual behavior", *American Journal of Political Science* 57(4), 892–911.

Mironov, B. N. (1991), "The development of literacy in Russia and the USSR from the tenth to the twentieth centuries", *History of Education Quarterly* 31(2), 229–252.

Mondak, J. J. (1995), *Nothing to Read*, University of Michigan Press, Ann Arbor, MI.

Montesquieu [1748] (1989), *The Spirit of the Laws*, Cambridge University Press, New York, NY.

Montesquieu [1735] (1999), *Considerations on the Causes of the Greatness of the Romans and Their Decline*, Hackett, Cambridge, MA.

Montesquieu [1721] (2008), *Persian Letters*, Oxford University Press, New York, NY.

Morris, S. (2000), "Contagion", *Review of Economic Studies* 67, 57–78.

Morris, S. and Shin, H. S. (2002), "Social value of public information", *American Economic Review* 92, 1521–1534.

Mourtada, R. and Salem, F. (2011), "Arab social media report, civil movements: The impact of facebook and twitter", *Dubai School of Government* 1(2). www.arabsocialmediareport.com/.

Muller, E. N. and Opp, K.-D. (1986), "Rational choice and rebellious collective action", *The American Political Science Review* 80(2), 471–488.

Nordhaus, W. (2006), "Geography and macroeconomics: New data and new findings", *Proceedings of the National Academy of Sciences* 103(10), 3510–3517.

Nordhaus, W., Azam, Q., Corderi, D., Hood, K., Victor, N. M., Mohammed, M., Miltner, A. and Weiss, J. (2006), "Detailed description of derivation of g-econ data", *Yale University, Typescript*.

Olson, M. (1971), *The Logic of Collective Action*, Schocken Press, New York, NY.

Opp, K.-D., Voss, P. and Gern, C. (1995), *Origins of a Spontaneous Revolution: East Germany, 1989*, The University of Michigan Press, Ann Arbor, MI.

Park, R. E. (1950), *Race and Culture*, Free Press, New York, NY.

Parkinson, S. E. (2013), "Organizing rebellion: Rethinking high-risk mobilization and social networks in war", *American Political Science Review* 107(3), 418–432.

Pascal, B. [1670] (1995), *The Pensées and Other Writings*, Oxford University Press, New York, NY.

Pentland, A. (2014), *Social Physics: How Good Ideas Spread: The Lessons from a New Science*, The MIT Press, Cambridge, MA.

Petersen, R. (2013), Roles and mechanisms of insurgency and the conflict in Syria, *in* M. Lynch, ed., "The Political Science of Syria's War POMEPS Briefings 22", Washington, DC.

Pierskalla, J. H. and Hollenbach, F. M. (2013), "Technology and collective action: The effect of cell phone coverage on political violence in Africa", *American Political Science Review* 107(2), 207–224.

Popkin, J. D. (1990), *Revolutionary News: The Press in France 1789–1799*, Duke University Press, Durham, NC.

Popkin, J. D. (1995), *Media and Revolution: Comparative Perspectives*, The University Press of Kentucky, Lexington, KY.

Rand, D. G., Arbesman, S. and Christakis, N. A. (2011), "Dynamic social networks promote cooperation in experiments with humans", *Proceedings of the National Academy of Sciences (PNAS)* 108, 19193–19198.

Raoof, R. (2011), "Egypt: Sequence of communication shutdown during 2011 uprising", *Global Voices Advocacy* 9. http://goo.gl/DxoFe.

Reynolds, J. (2012), "Syria conflict: "Fierce clashes" near Damascus airport", *BBC News*. www.bbc.com/news/world-middle-east-20547799.

Rogers, E. M. (2003), *Diffusion of Innovations*, Free Press, New York, NY.

Rohozinski, R. (2013), "Communication disruption in Syria", *personal correspondence*.

Sarotte, M. E. (2009), "How an accident caused the Berlin wall to come down", *Historical Washington Post*. http://wapo.st/4wXDkC.

Schelling, T. C. (1960), The Strategy of Conflict, Harvard University Press, Cambridge, MA.

Schelling, T. C. (1978), *Micromotives and Macrobehavior*, W. W. Norton, New York, NY.

Schumpeter, J. A. (1950), *Capitalism, Socialism and Democracy*, Harper Prennial, New York, NY.

Scott, J. C. (1990), *Domination and the Arts of Resistance: Hidden Transcripts*, Yale University Press, New Haven, CT.

Scott, J. C. (1998), *Seeing Like a State: How Certain Schemes to Improve the Human Condition Have Failed*, Yale University Press, New Haven, CT.

Seale, P. (1988), *Asad of Syria: The Struggle for the Middle East*, I. B. Tauris, New York, NY.

SecDev (2012), "Syria goes offline". https://secdev-foundation.org/syria-goes-offline/.

Shapiro, J. N. and Weidmann, N. B. (2015), "Is the phone mightier than the sword? Cell phones and insurgent violence in Iraq", *International Organization* 69(2), 247–274.

Shehata, D., El-Hamalawy, H. and Lynch, M. (2011), "Youth movements and social media: Their role and impact", *Proceedings of 'From Tahrir: Revolution or Democratic Transition'*. Videorecordings http://bit.ly/pOy1QJ.

Siegel, D. A. (2009), "Social networks and collective action", *American Journal of Political Science* 53(1), 122–138.

Siegel, D. A. (2011), "When does repression work? Collective action in social networks", *American Journal of Political Science* 73(4), 993–1010.

Stonequist, E. V. (1937), *The Marginal Man: A Study in Personality and Culture Conflict*, Charles Scribner's Sons, New York, NY.

Strang, D. and Tuma, N. B. (1993), "Spatial and temporal heterogeneity in diffusion", *American Journal of Sociology* 99(3), 614–639.

Suri, S. and Watts, D. J. (2011), "Cooperation and contagion in web-based, networked public goods experiments", *PLoS ONE* 6(3).

Syrian Observatory of Human Rights (2012), "Syrian Observatory of Human Rights". www.facebook.com/syriaohr.

Tilly, C. (1978), *From Mobilization to Revolution*, Addison-Wesley Publishing Company, Reading, MA.

Trotsky, L. (1937), *The History of the Russian Revolution*, Simon and Schuster, New York, NY.

Tufekci, Z. and Wilson, C. (2012), "Social media and the decision to participate in political protest: Observations from Tahrir Square", *Journal of Communication* 62(2), 363–379.

Valente, T. (2012), "Network interventions", *Science* 337(6090), 49–53.

Van Dam, N. (2011), *The Struggle for Power in Syria: Politics and Society under Asad and the Ba'th Party*, I. B. Tauris, New York, NY.

Wade, R. A. (2005), *The Russian Revolution, 1917*, Cambridge University Press, New York, NY.

Wang, J., Suri, S. and Watts, D. J. (2012), "Cooperation and assortativity with dynamic partner updating", *Proceedings of the National Academy of Sciences (PNAS)* 109, 14363–14368.

Ward, M. D. and Gleditsch, K. S. (2002), "Location, location, location: An MCMC approach to modeling the spatial context of war", *Political Analysis* 10(3), 244–260.

Ward, M. D. and Gleditsch, K. S. (2008), *Spatial Regression Models*, Sage, Thousand Oaks, CA.

Wasserman, S. and Faust, K. (1994), *Social Network Analysis: Methods and Applications*, Cambridge University Press, New York, NY.

Watts, D. J. (2002), "A simple model of global cascades on random networks", *Proceedings of the National Academy of Sciences* 99(9), 5766–5771.

Watts, D. J. (2003), *Small Worlds: The Dynamics of Networks between Order and Randomness*, Princeton University Press, Princeton, NJ.

Watts, D. J. (2004), *Six Degrees: The Science of a Connected Age*, W. W. Norton and Company, New York, NY.

Watts, D. J. and Dodds, P. S. (2007), "Influentials, networks, and public opinion formation", *Journal of Consumer Research* 34(4), 441–458.

Watts, D. J. and Strogatz, S. (1998), "Collective dynamics of "small-world" networks", *Nature* 393(6684), 440–442.

Weber, M. [1919] (1958a), "Politics as a vocation" in Gerth, H. and Mills, C. (Eds), *From Max Weber: Essays in Sociology*, Oxford University Press, New York, NY.

Weber, M. [1905] (1958b), *The Protestant Ethic and the Spirit of Capitalism*, Scribner's, New York, NY.

Wedeen, L. (1999), *Ambiguities of Domination*, University of Chicago Press, Chicago, IL.

Weimann, G. (1982), "On the importance of marginality: One more step into the two-step flow of communication", *American Sociological Review* 47(6), 764–773.

Weinstein, J. M. (2007), *Inside Rebellion: The Politics of Insurgent Violence*, Cambridge University Press, New York, NY.

Wilkinson, S. (2009), "Riots", *Annual Review of Political Science* 12, 329–343.

Wood, E. J. (2003), *Insurgent Collective Action and Civil War in El Salvador*, Cambridge University Press, New York, NY.

Wood, E. J. (2008), "The social processes of civil war: The wartime transformation of social networks", *Annual Review of Political Science* 11, 539–561.

Wurtzel, A. H. and Turner, C. (1977), "What missing the telephone means", *Journal of Communication* 27(2), 48–57.

Zaller, J. R. (1992), *The Nature and Origins of Mass Opinion*, Cambridge University Press, New York, NY.

Index

1848 revolutions 13
2011 Egyptian Revolution 5, 11, 10, 19, 20, 28, 34, 40, 54, 117, 161, 171; center and periphery 36; demands of protesters 173; four phases 58, 171; national announcements 46; protest convergence mechanisms 53; protesters outside Tahrir 58–59

Abbé Sieyès 35
action cascades 150, 151, 154; rate and speed of convergence 150–152
Adorno, T. 75
advertising 5
Africa 106
Aleppo 111
Alexandria 36, 50, 52, 67
Algeria 29
Amazon Mechanical Turk (AMT) 145
anonymity: as protest 167; logic of 166–167
Anonymous 166
anti-regime incidents: more dispersed 129
anxiety of doubt: motivating action 164
appendix 53
April 6 Youth Movement 19, 20, 37, 39, 50, 173; operations room 51; emails from control room 52; emails on January 25 and 28 53; mass emails 44. *See also* 2011 Egyptian Revolution
Arab Spring 31, 111
al-Assad, Hafez 111

audio cassette 28, 29, 36
authoritarianism 34
average elevation 133
average rates of collective action: versus instances of cascades 144
Axelrod, R. 69, 110

bank runs 8
Bashar Assad 111
behavioral experiments 7, 140
Bennett, L. 5, 32, 55
Berlin Wall 33
betweenness centrality 145, 147; initial average in experimental session 154
Big Data 170
blackout 40, 101, 105, 107, 120, 139, 117, 120; in Syria 163; 2011 Egyptian Revolution 56, 58, 61, 67; 2011 Egyptian Revolution, first reaction 62; role in escalation 64; subjective reaction and sources of news 66. *See also* media disruption
Bouckaert, P. 27, 68
building identity 169

Cairo 10, 12, 19, 27, 36, 40, 52, 53, 117, 27; in 2011 141
Cairo protest participation survey 20, 185
Calvinist predestination 164
capitalism 164
cascade sessions, definition 150
cascade status, latency to 155

cascades of collective action 25, 140, 155; centrally induced 155; intermediate dynamics of action 156
cascades: of apathy 24, 155; of contention 31; of risk taking 24, 140. *See also* minimal core
Castells, E. 113, 30, 32
cell networks 112
censors 167
censorship 169
central emblem: lack of 166
Central Intelligence Agency (CIA) 103
central leadership 143
centrality 15; in social network 19, 142; myth 153; of action, temporal evolution 156
centralization 9, 11
centralized campaigns 1
centralized media 35, 62, 67, 75
centralizing, media 28
Chwe, M. 2, 32, 74
Cicero 167
civil conflict 6; in urban areas 110, 115; contagion activated by disruption 122; coordination and clustering 121; in sparsely populated areas 110; network processes in urban settings 111; preplanned attacks 132; relation between orientation and coordination 131; role of communication technology 106; socioeconomic patterns 119; structural components 133; urban v. rural 94–95, 110. *See also* collective action; network collective action; protest
Civil Rights Movement 4
civil violence 106
Civil war 103
Cleopatra 17
close-knit communities 98
clustered contention: and small world networks 71
clustering 71, 121, 126, 130
collective action 31, 40, 72, 141, 142; based on coordination 30; bipolar distribution of cascades 144; cascades 15, 34; centralized 104; clandestine 73; conventional wisdom on centrality of leaders 74; coordinated 95; coordination v. contagion 106; decentralized 16, 84; dispersed 7; dynamics of 27, 71; from the center 4; from the margins 4; global cascade 69; global prospects of success 55, 144; group size 110; in small world networks 99; in the margins 30; in urban environments 28; inspired by doubt not conviction 6; itinerant 74; local 8; locally dense and globally dispersed 105; local influence 53; logic of 27; minimal cores 84; more information not helpful 6; network formulation 3; network logic 73; network models 6, 69; other regarding models 78; peripheral processes 30; resource mobilization theories 111; role of information 6; spontaneity and speed puzzle 1,4; spontaneous 8; spread of 105; subversive 16; surprise factor 8, 23; threshold dynamics 22; threshold models 69, 72, 75; time 8; *See also* civil conflict; network collective action; protest
collective action cascades 6, 144; latency and frequency 149; subject level components 158
collective action diffusion processes 157
collective action extremes, frequency and intensity 152
collective action models: based on public–private signals 95; inward and outward looking 73; signaling 73
collective action problem 1; existing solutions 1–3
collective action theory: central organization 8,14; coordination 9; focal points 8, 9, 11; networked version 14–15; peripheral organization 7; selective incentives 9; vanguardist 4
collective action thresholds, for action 79
collective behavior 167, 170; network patterns 115; spatiotemporal patterns 115
collective civil conflict, surprise factor 139
collective game of risk taking 147
collective lottery 141; with limited information 147
collective risk taking: coordination or contagion 40; decentralized 69; dynamics 30; from the margins 139; games 24
collective violence 120

communication: face to face 12; intermediaries 31; local 12, 30; of news 55; personal tools 55; personalized 55; with friends and family 62; with local social network 63. *See also* contagion; information
communication conflict nexus 112
communication disruption 29, 38, 74, 100, 133, 135; government intentions 48; nationwide 115; Syria 119
communication media, alternative modes 101
communication shutdown 106
communication technology, catalyst for rebellion or not 110
communication vacuum 165
communications, mobile 34
communications, seditious 33
communicative dynamics, threshold model 78, 81, 82, 91
conflict dispersion 117
conflict in Damascus, contagion in spatial neighborhood 108
conflict locations: daily account 10; daily locations 120; geolocated 100; two main results from nearest incident analysis 108
conflict, spatiotemporal dynamics 106
conflictual event's orientation, coordinated or not 129
conflictual incidents: coordinated 129; orientation and coordination 129
confounding factors 34, 132
connection, informational 79
connective action 5, 55
connectivity, average levels in each square mile of Damascus 113
conservatism of majority 6, 7
contagion 7, 10, 14, 16, 19, 22, 70, 104, 105, 110, 121, 132, 135, 120, 139; in small world networks, activated by media disruption 137; mechanisms of 167; processes of 137, 163, 123; and dispersion of rebel activity 108; complex 84, 103, 109; definition 107; easier in larger groups 110; geometry of 109; interacting with communication disruption 109; on the battlefield (Montesquieu) 69; simple kind 109; spatial 131; spatiotemporal 10, 122; and spread of violence 6;

with multiple reinforcements 109. *See also* coordination; communication; information
contention: local clusters 77; marginal cells 69; peripheral 104
contentious social network 61
control 26
controlled experiments 7
conventions 11
convergence: to global focal point 63; mechanisms of 11, 50, 62
conviction 168
coordinated collective action 107; orientation of 130
coordinated collective violence, list 129
coordinated conflictual incident 129
coordination 6, 7, 8, 10, 16, 19, 107, 109, 110; in conflict 129; and dispersion of conflict in Damascus 108; calculus of 109; centralized 104; harder in larger group 110; over public goods 2; pro-regime incidents 129. *See also* contagion
Corriere della Sera 29
counterinformation 29, 32, 33
critical mass 6, 70, 70, 74
crowd behavior 8, 19, 165
crowd psychology 8
crowds 2, 3
culture industry 32, 75
Czech Velvet Revolution 33

Damascus: 7, 10, 22, 34, 100, 107, 106, 108, 110, 111, 112, 113, 114, 115, 117, 119, 122, 123, 132, 133. 1-mile grid 122, 123–124; ethnic and economic composition 122; ethnic composition 124, 133; ethnicity and religion 125; income levels 125; neighborhood delineation 126; neighborhoods 120, 121, 126; poor neighborhoods 133; socioeconomic patterns 124. *See also* Syrian Civil War
Damascus conflict location dataset 22, 108
Damascus GIS dataset 122; variables 113, 123
Damascus International Airport 112, 120
Damascus neighborhoods 133; connectivity levels 113
Damascus violent incidents, criteria 113
Dar'a 111

Index

data, realization instances 18
De Gaulle, C. 29
decentralization 6, 12, 15, 16, 27, 100; of contention 116; processes of 11, 104; and political power 163; confounding factors 47, 117; reinforcing and escalating cycles 23; See also dispersion of conflict
decentralized communication 31, 35
decentralized conflict 163
decentralized contention 28
deescalation, and communication 107
Della Porta, D. 73
democracy 32
demonstration 2, 28, 32
dense networks, on the local level 71
dependent variable, lagged 133
Despotisme 169
diagonal urban grids 87
dictatorship 32
diffusion 19, 70
diffusion of collective action, and connectivity 89
diffusion of protest, local patterns 55
diffusion, complete 92
dispersion 130; and coordination in Syrian Civil War 129; measure 54
Dispersion Hypothesis 7, 27, 30, 43, 54, 105, 116
dispersion of conflict 6, 22, 24, 30, 107, 116, 117, 118, 152, 132; based on pairwise distances 116–117; locally concentrated and globally dispersed 6, 14. See also decentralization
dispersion of protests 41, 55, 58; dynamic profile 54
disruption of communication: local 113; selective 115. See also blackout
disruption of public information 94; and rates of collective action 95
disruption of public signal in small world networks 97–99
dissent 31
distance from nearest conflictual incident 127, 131; as a proxy for clustering 127; temporal averages 128; temporal profile 127
Domain Name System (DNS) 104
Duma 29, 35
dynamic models of collective action 79

dynamic threshold models of collective action: communicative and observational 78; example 76–78
dynamics of contagion v. coordination 129
dynamics of contention, originating from the periphery 101

early adopters 14
East Germany 31, 33
Eastern Bloc 31
economic meltdowns 1
Egypt 27, 31, 34, 68
Egypt, state of emergency 50
electoral opinion 32
elevation 123; and civil conflict 133; role in urban v. rural conflicts 123
emails, mobilizational 27, 49
Enlightenment 166, 168
Entman, R. 32
Erdös-Rényi (ER) random networks 145
escalation 27, 64, 71; decentralized 101; during blackout 105; self-reinforcing 67, 71; through decentralization 28
ethnic composition of Damascus 126
ethnic identification 168
experimental network 140
experimental network session, initial action centrality 153
experiments in collective risk taking 140
experiments on cooperation 143

face to face communication 28, 31, 53, 55, 61
face to face interaction 138
Facebook, mobilization campaign 40
February 1917 Russian Revolution 4, 29, 35, 140
Federalist Papers 168
first conflictual incidents 119; temporal distribution 191
fixed effect results 138
flow of information, reliable and streamlined 165
focal point 2, 8, 10, 38; global 63; ideational 11; local 38, 40, 47
focal point explanation, alternative 10
followers 2, 157; peripheral 19
Foucault, M. 8, 18, 28, 29, 164
free-riding 9, 110
Freedom Summer 143

French Revolution xv, 32, 35
Friday of Rage 36
Friday prayers 43, 46

gaining news, from friends 56
geocoded tweets 115
geographical dispersion 106
geolocated dataset of violent conflict locations in Damascus 113
Get Out The Vote (GOTV) campaigns 15
GIS (Geographic Information System) 22
GIS analysis of Syrian Civil War: three components 121–122
global dispersion 121; of conflict 138
global focal point 64
global games: "beauty contest" model 73; and network structure 96
Google Transparency Report 43, 106, 116
Gould, R. 15, 73, 87, 103, 110
Gramsci, A. 32
Grand Central Terminal 10
Granovetter, M. 15, 69, 74, 75, 141
grids, two-dimensional 23

Habermas, J. 2, 35, 165
Hama 111
Hardin, R. 2, 11
Haussmann 13
Heinmueller, J. 31
heterogeneous networks 142
hidden transcript 16, 30, 165
hierarchy 16, 26; and control 166
high risk collective action 143
Hirschman, A. 164
historical aberrations 18
history 169; common idea of 169; grand narratives 18; human 169
Hobbes, T. 17, 169
Homs 111
hourly email updates, January 28, 2011 183
Human Rights Watch 27, 68
human science and mobilization 170

identity 11, 169; mutual 8
ideology 1, 2, 4, 11, 164
incentives 1, 103
incumbent 32
individual risk preference 145, 147; measurement 146

individual risk rank 146
influence 15; local 61, 62, 67
influence maximization 5, 142, 143
influence process, from the margins 162
information blackout 28, 30 55
information levels, manipulation of 144
information propagation 5; two-stage model 2, 17, 19, 157
information sources, conventional 17
information vacuum 28, 30; and making of new links 102
information 143; accurate 12; authoritarian supervision of 143; available in social network 161; blackouts 13; definition 168; ephemeral 18; from friends and family 43; institutionalized 18; local 13, 43, 143, 144, 148; public 14, 22; public and private 94; social value of 139. *See also* contagion; communication
innovation adoption 70, 95; collective 1; from the periphery 5; social innovation 15
innovation, promotion 5
instigators: peripheral 84, 93, 143, 162; peripheral assignment 150, 152
institutional politics 3
interaction, contagion and disruption 137
Internet 34, 42, 104, 31; and cell networks 27
Internet Protocol (IP) layer 104, 112
Internet usage 62
Internet-based communications 112
Iran 28, 31
Iran, post-election protests of 2009 28, 48
Iranian Revolution xv, 35; media hiatus 35
Iraq 106
isoperimetric problem 21; in graphs 85, 86; pointwise 71

Jackson, M. 80, 83
James Scott xv, 30
January 25, 2011 11, 27, 37, 39, 49; initial protest locations 39, 50, 51; protest dynamics from hourly emails 52–53. *See also* 2011 Egyptian Revolution
January 28, 2011 11, 27, 28, 36, 44, 47, 54, 58, 60, 61, 75, 117, 178; dispersion of protesters 60; mechanisms of escalation 38, 40. *See also* 2011 Egyptian Revolution

Index

Kaplan–Meier estimators 155
Katz, E. 17, 162
Keynes, J. 73, 95
Khaled Said 49
Kuran, T. 1, 3, 12, 32, 69, 141
Kurzman, C. 28

lack of information 165
lag, spatiotemporal 133
landline phones 53
language of rebellion, deviant, irrational 165
latency to cascade status 155
Lazarsfeld, P. 17, 162
Le Bon, G. 2, 165
leaderless and spontaneous revolutions: paradox 141, 162
leadership: central 8, 24, 105; peripheral 15, 16, 24, 30, 72, 105; local 6, 14, 29
leading from the periphery 70, 72, 93, 104, 105, 108, 109, 140, 143, 144, 161; dynamics 90, 101, 107; empirics 34; five implications 5–6; four observations 12; network formulation 72; paradigm 1, xv, 3, 6, 8, 19, 20, 22, 25, 28, 30, 34, 55, 61, 69, 70, 71, 72, 73, 102, 129, 139, 144; research agenda 30; as a strategy 73; three features 105; and two-stage logic 73. *See also* network collective action; vanguard
learning, dynamics 22
Leipzig 12, 32
Lenin, V. 2
levels of connectivity 113
Libya 49
Lichbach, M. 2
limited information regimes 143
limited information, not precluding collective risk taking 144
linguistic shifts 1
local clusters 102, 121
local escalation, global dispersion in Syrian conflict 130
local interaction 55
localization: and proliferation 30; of protests 61; processes 62, 100
localization effect 71
locally dense, globally sparse collective action 163
Locke, J. 8

logic of collective action, minimal cores versus critical mass 70
logistic regression 62, 158
Lohmann, S. 12, 32
longitude and latitude 113
Louis XVI 35

Madison, J. 168
marginal leaders 1
marginals, inciting risky behavior 70
Marx, K. 3, 2
mass mobilization 3, 5; aberrant empirics of 166
mass opinion reversals 150
mass religious conversions 1
mass self-communication 30
mass social movements, lack of leadership 163
mass uprising 31
McAdam, D. 5
mechanism design 19, 142, 161, 162
media 31, 33
media coverage, change in 34
media disruption 6, 22, 27, 30, 34, 58, 67, 71, 72, 98, 138; catalyst for collective action 28, 67; effect on protest dispersion 44; Egypt 2011 36, 37, 48, 67; escalation of civil conflict 143; exacerbating revolutionary unrest 40; phone network in Manhattan 54; psychological effects 53, 54; two processes of escalation 34. *See also* blackout; network collective action
media outlets 33
media usage, among the vanguard 61
media: alternative and local 61; contradictory roles in revolutions 33; inducing normalcy 33; personalized 3; role in social unrest 31; traditional 31; transition from centralized to local venues 94. *See also* communication; information
messaging, cellphones 41
microlevel economic data 124
Middle East 30
military 27, 36
military action, threat of 67
minimal core 22, 23, 70, 72, 74, 78, 84, 85, 120, 121, 126, 131, 138, 144; definition 84–86; in a given graph 85; in canonical graphs 86; in grid 87; size

increasing with connectivity 88; versus critical mass 70. *See also* cascades of collective action; leading from the periphery; network collective action; radius of diffusion
minimal cores, of collective action 70
Mirabeau 35
misinformation 8
mobile communications 42, 112
mobile phones 45
mobilization: from the center 163; from the margins 3, 5, 142, 163; local 63; party-based 2; viral nature 170. *See also* protest
mobilizational emails 173
mobilizing from the periphery, employing the network structure 142
modernism, and precision 168
Moldova 31
Montesquieu 8, 17, 69, 164, 169
Moore neighborhoods 135
Morris, S. 80, 87
Mubarak, H. 10, 27, 28, 36, 171
mutual information 11

naive data, and strategy of control 167
narrative: supervised 31; unified 30
National Security Agency (NSA) 103
nationalism 168
natural history, into natural science 169
nearest incident 121, 126
nearest neighbor analysis 122
neighborhood 138
neighbors' thresholds, estimating 83
network bridges 109; diametrical 91, 99; local 90
network collective action 8, 19, 20, 30, 34, 67, 69, 75, 94, 102, 105, 116, 121, 139, 140, 142, 143, 149; cascades 150; decentralized 40; dense locales 99; and diffusion from dispersed minimal cores 131; escalating in the absence of public signal 97,98; escalating in the absence of public signal, example 99; logic of 140; three components 34. *See also* leading from the periphery; minimal core
network collective action experiments: random assignment of the vanguard 152

network collective action treatments: frequency of cascade status 152
network degree, of experimental subjects 159
network dynamics 78; of collective action 170
network edges, directed and undirected 79
network effects 70; of majority's risk aversion 161; peripheral 18
network experiments 5, 24, 141, 152, 140; of collective action 145
network experiments of collective action: first phase 146; second phase 147–148; subject instructions 193; synchronous 141
network game: asymmetric equilibria 80; equilibria 79, 80; non-trivial pure strategy equilibria 80; static 79
network heterogeneity in risk preference 148
network neighbors 81; acting 85; reversion to 61; risk aversion of 159; risk propensity of 159
network structure 73, 75, 148; and collective action 94; and collective risk taking in limited information regimes 143–144; in threshold models of collective action 141
network thresholds, Markov dynamics 83
network treatment 156; central assignment 159; in collective risk taking experiments 141
network: adding links 87; heterogeneity 80; homogeneous 80; levels of connectivity 86
networks: hierarchical 3; local 81
New York 4, 10, 53
New York Times 29
news communication 55
news consumption 58; local 64
news production, local 31
news, from alternative sources 62–64
news, from friends 61, 62, 67
news, methods of communication 56
Nile 48
non-coordinated incidents, more clustered 129
nonparticipants 56, 61; subjective views of media disruption 56

Obama, B. 172
observational dynamics: logic of usage 85; threshold model 78, 81, 83, 85
Occupy movement 166
OLS regression 117, 154, 129
Olson, M. 2, 9, 110
online appendix 20, 23, 26, 50, 58, 62, 108, 122, 132, 148, 149, 152, 188, 189
online communications, 63; alternatives 37, 63–64
operations room, April 6 Youth Movement 37, 49, 51, 52, 75, 176
opinion leaders 2, 19; central 157; visible 84
opinion reversal 142
opportunity structure 49
organization, hierarchical 17

pamphlets 28, 32, 35, 36, 51, 175, 176; distribution in the 2011 Egypt Revolution 51
Paris 5
Paris Commune 13, 110
Paris, summer 1789 141
participation, frequency profile 59
Party 4, 140
Pascal, B. 17
perception 13, 35
peripheral agents of change 142; inducing more extreme outcomes compared to central vanguard 152
peripheral influence 140
peripheral minimal cores 89
personal network 61
personal threshold 85, 141
personalized communication, role in mobilization 55
Petrograd 4, 5, 29, 140; February 1917 141
phase transition 69
Poisson count regression 124, 133
police 27, 36
political centralization 168
political communication 2
political control 170; novel forms 170
political mobilization, via classification 169
political power 26, 163
political revolutions 1
politics: modernist 17; predictability 16, 26; reified 17
population, of Damascus 122
Port Said 50

positive externalities 8, 142
power: and visibility 163; of numbers 3
predestination 164
predictability 164, 168, 169, 170
prediction of conflictual incidents 117, 135
Princeton xvi
printed press 35, 166
Prisoners' Dilemma 9
private information 75. *See also* public information
progression of risk taking from periphery to center 157
proliferation: dynamics 85; of conflict 123
protest 10, 31, 103; decentralization of 62; dispersion of 40, 43; dispersion measure in Cairo survey 54; participation levels 62; relation with local news consumption 55. *See also* civil conflict; collective action
protest activity 58; and local news consumption 56
protest dispersion; in Cairo 2011 43, 46; not related to size 48
protest location: in Cairo 2011 42, 45; dynamic profile 41
protest participation and media usage, temporal patterns 189
protest wave: of 1989 5; of 2011 1, 5
protesters 60; contrast between steadfasts and nonparticipants 56; profile 58; steadfast 56; typical 11
protests 27, 41, 79; decentralization 43, 67
public information 2, 72, 74, 93; and collective action 95; centers of social life 1, 10; dissuading from collective action 75; public landmarks 93; social value of 95. *See also* private information
public signal 75; absence 23; and media disruption 97; suppression of 98
public sphere 33
public transcript 16, 18, 30, 165, 166
public–private signaling 22

quasi-experiment 37

radio 36
radius of connectivity 23, 91, 92; in grid networks 87, 89

radius of diffusion 70, 72, 74, 85, 89, 132; and connectivity 89–90; and increasing connectivity 90; and network thresholds 90; decreasing with connectivity 93; definition 90. *See also* minimal core; network collective action
randomized experiments 106
rates of risk taking, based on initial centrality of risk propensity 154–155; progression in three network regions 157
rebel strongholds 120
rebellion 95; cycles of 36
rectangular grid 87; minimal core examples 89
regression, OLS 44
repeated collective lotteries 147; payoff structure 148
repertoires of action 1, 2, 8, 11
resource mobilization 107
revolutionary surprise 17
revolutionary unrest 27
revolutionary vanguard 141; distribution in the social network 141
revolutions 8, 32; distinct from riots 32
ring networks 90, 92; connectivity radius 92
riots 32
risk aversion 22; of majority 67, 110
risk awareness 31; independent of the state 32
risk propensity 72; in the network neighborhood 84
risk taking; central 7; in social networks, with local knowledge 161; in the margins 22; of vanguard 140; propensity to 143; thresholds of 74
risk-takers: in central assignment, influenced by neighbors' risk aversion 159; in the periphery 142, 162
rituals 11
Rogers, E. 15
Roman Empire 17
Romanian Revolution of 1989 166
rumors 12, 29, 29, 31, 33, 36, 161
Russian provisional government 29
Russian Revolution xv, 4

Schelling, T. 2, 8, 10, 75
Schumpeter, J. 32

science of history, lack of empirics 5
science of society 17
Scott, J. 87, 166
sedition 33
selective incentives 2, 6, 9, 70, 107, 141, 120
Shah 28, 29
signaling model of collective action,: conformity utility 96; correlations 96; distance between private signals 98; network proxy 96; utility structure 96. *See also* private signal; public signal
signaling, public v. private 74
signals, correlated 75
sit in 2
sleeper cells 73
small world networks 7, 13, 22, 23, 30, 67, 71, 93, 97, 99, 109; and escalation in the absence of public signal 100; from grid networks 101; rewiring to 101. *See also* network collective action
Snowden, E. 103, 112, 115
social control 168
social experiments of collective action 163
social graphs 163
social information 3, 103
social media 31, 142; and civil unrest 27; discouraging unrest 31; incomplete blockage of 41; role in fostering unrest 67
social mobilization 165
social network 5, 10, 24, 57, 70, 75, 84, 140, 144; connections, local 53; structure of 111, 139; largest component 70; localization processes 46; periphery of 7; rewiring of 94
social organization 143, 163; alternative modes 26
social revolutions 150
spatial correlation 105
spatial spillover 139; of violence in Damascus, absence in average data 192
spatiotemporal localization 126
spatiotemporal patterns of conflict in Damascus 121
speed of diffusion 139
spillover of violence 135
spillovers 10; of contention 72
spontaneity 16
spontaneous revolution 140

state control, via structural elements 87
state cultural hegemony 33
state media 66
state, hierarchical 13
strike 2, 11
strong ties 8, 17, 143
subject centrality and rates of action 159
Suez 36, 52
sum length of throughways 122, 133
surveillance 74, 111
survey 11
survey locations in Cairo 185
survey, protest participation in Cairo 40, 53, 54, 56, 57–58, 101; sampling strategy 57; two main findings 54–55; summary of results 67
Syria 49, 103, 125; blackout November 2012 120; countrywide blackout 112, 115; countrywide communication network 104; decentralization of civil conflict 117; ethnic and religious allegiances 111; National Security headquarters 112; rebel groups 112. *See also* Damascus
Syrian Arab News Agency (SANA) 113
Syrian Civil War 5, 14, 22, 40, 106, 111, 112; airstrikes 113; anti-regime incident 121; assassinations 113; bombing 113; framed locally 133; indirect fire 113; pro-regime incident 121; urban setting 110
Syrian conflict location dataset, GIS analysis 132
Syrian conflict, orientation and dispersion 132; removal of public signal 109
Syrian Observatory of Human Rights 112, 113

Tahrir Square 10, 11, 10, 20, 27, 36, 38, 40, 39, 50, 58, 63, 67, 172, 174, 177; global convergence to 38. *See also* 2011 Egyptian Revolution
taxonomy 167
Tehran 28, 29, 32
television 31
temporal average; for rejecting confounding parameters 135; not showing contagion 135
Thailand 31
The Pensées 17

Third Estate 35
threshold dynamics: action and threshold 82; communicative model 82; observational model 83
threshold models of collective action 73, 75–76, 109; dynamic 76, 78, 81; static 79
threshold update mechanism 81; definitions 82
Tilly, C. 2, 8, 11, 16
tipping point 37
totalitarianism 33
treatment effects; average 17; ephemeral 17, 18
Trotsky, L. 4, 140
Tunisia 49
Tunisian uprising 2011 50

Ukraine 31
unrest: and the media 31; level of 34; proliferation 27
urban conflict 22, 94, 123
urban environment 13
urban neighborhood patterns 94
urban planning, as a tool for political control 110
urban uprising, Damascus 120

vanguard 2, 11, 20, 24, 34, 49, 53, 55, 60, 61, 67, 80, 84, 86, 144, 161; and increasing connectivity 89; central 2, 3, 5, 59; clustering of 84; detection based on risk preference 146; dispersed from the start 55; dispersion levels 55; high levels of initial dispersion 142; initial dispersion 59; local 102; localization 34; marginal 74, 84, 94, 116; network location 73; network modeling 80; of the Egyptian Revolution 61; of the Egyptian Revolution, definition 58; peripheral 3, 6, 7, 14, 16, 30, 58, 69, 81, 139, 140, 142. *See also* leading from the periphery; network collective action
violence: local concentration of 138; routine and coordinated 105
visibility 93, 166; logic of 10
void, as a uniting force 166

Watts, D. 71
weak ties 15, 55, 143
Weber, M. 32, 164; definition of the state 32; on origins of modernism 165
West Germany 31

Wilkinson, S. 32
World War II 4
Yale xvi

Zaller, J. 2, 17, 157